Studies in Comparative World History

D0217179

Lives in Between

LIVES IN BETWEEN:
Assimilation and Marginality in Austria, Brazil, West Africa, 1780–1945

LEO SPITZER
Dartmouth College

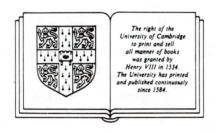

The right of the
University of Cambridge
to print and sell
all manner of books
was granted by
Henry VIII in 1534.
The University has printed
and published continuously
since 1584.

CAMBRIDGE UNIVERSITY PRESS
Cambridge
London   New York   New Rochelle
Melbourne   Sydney

Published by the Press Syndicate of the University of Cambridge
The Pitt Building, Trumpington Street, Cambridge CB2 1RP
40 West 20th Street, New York, NY 10011, USA
10 Stamford Road, Oakleigh, Melbourne 3166, Australia

First published 1989

Printed in Canada

Library of Congress Cataloging-in-Publication Data
Spitzer, Leo, 1939–
  Lives in between.
  (Studies in comparative world history)
  Includes bibliographical references.
  1. Jews – Austria – Cultural assimilation.   2. Zweig,
Stefan, 1881–1942.   3. Austria – Ethnic relations.
4. Blacks – Africa, West – Cultural assimilation.
5. May, Joseph, ca. 1817–1890.   6. May, Cornelius,
d. 1939.   7. Blacks – Brazil – Cultural assimilation.
8. Rebouças, André Pinto, 1838–1898.   9. Brazil –
Ethnic relations.   10. Marginality, Social.   I. Title.
II. Series.
DS135.A9S65   1990   303.48′2   89–24004

ISBN 0-521-37214-3 hard covers
ISBN 0-521-37827-3 paperback

British Library Cataloging in Publication available.

for
ROSE
and for
MARIANNE

Contents

Illustrations

Acknowledgments

This book, touching on so many aspects of a historical process of which I am a product and to which I am still profoundly connected, has been a difficult one to write. But it has provided me with the opportunity to engage in an immensely rewarding and enriching intellectual and multicultural journey. During the course of the decade involved in its creation, I have learned much about my own cultural heritage: about lives experiencing the enticements of assimilation, the pains of exclusion, and the predicaments of marginality. I have also learned to incorporate that heritage within the broader fabric of nineteenth- and twentieth-century world history. I have come to understand the necessity to draw connections, parallels, and differences between the modern Jewish historical experience in Europe and the histories of individuals and groups attempting to rise from subordination to challenge domination in other regions of the world.

In moving from my earlier professional focus on the history of Africa to include Brazil and Central Europe, I have been generously guided and helped by many persons, and supported by many institutions and grant-giving agencies. Although I am, of course, solely responsible for any mistakes or inadequacies the reader may find in this book, I wish to acknowledge their kindnesses and to thank them for their assistance and good faith.

No one deserves more credit for inspiring me to pursue a comparative historical approach than Philip D. Curtin, an imaginative and wide-ranging scholar and teacher of immense talent. It was he who convened the 1974 Summer Workshop in Comparative World History, in which I was invited to participate, and where the earliest formulation of this project developed. Michael Adas, Allen Isaacman, Joseph Miller, John Richards, the other members of the workshop, as well as Steven Feierman, Barbara Isaacman, and David Henige offered important critiques and good advice, and posed some of the key methodological questions that have informed my inquiry throughout.

My focus on the May family developed from my earlier work in Sierra Leone and Nigeria. But my knowledge of this family's history benefited tremendously from visits to Sierra Leone and England in 1976 and 1978 that were sponsored by the American Philosophical Society and the Dartmouth Research Committee. I received invaluable help in Freetown from Tungi Stuart and Isa Smith, granddaughters of Cornelius May; from E. W. Blyden III, grandson of Edward Wilmot Blyden; from Eldred Jones, principal of Fourah Bay College; and from Gladys Sheriff, director of the Sierra Leone National Archive. My search for May family materials was also greatly facilitated by the librarians of the Methodist Missionary Archive and the Royal Commonwealth Society in London.

My interest in the Rebouças family began to crystallize during my first, yearlong, research trip to Brazil in 1972, which was funded by a grant from the Social Science Research Council and by a Faculty Fellowship from Dartmouth College. This interest developed into a primary concern during my subsequent visits, in 1974, 1980 and 1983 – briefer research trips supported by awards from the Ford Foundation, by a Summer Stipend from the National Endowment for the Humanities, and by a Senior Faculty Fellowship from Dartmouth College. As a relative newcomer in the field of Brazilian studies, I have been the fortunate recipient of guidance, encouragement, and help from Thomas Skidmore, Richard Graham, Rebecca Baird Bergstresser, Anani Dzidzienyo, Dr. Carlos Souza Rebouças, Luiz Carlos Saroldi, Guido and Milena Araujo, and the late Peter Reichard and Kalman H. Silvert. I owe the greatest gratitude, however, to Dulce and Nelson Ramalho, who adopted me into their extended family in Rio de Janeiro, introduced me to their network of friends and relatives, and instilled in me a profound love for the vitality of Afro-Brazilian life and culture through its history, language, music, art, religion, and superb cuisine. They are truly my Brazilian mentors and best friends.

Another Senior Faculty Grant from Dartmouth College, as well as a Research Committee award and a grant-in-aid from the American Council of Learned Societies, permitted me to carry out research in 1978 and 1980 in Austria, Czechoslovakia, England, and the United States on the history of the Zweig and Brettauer families. Harry Zohn, who has vast knowledge about Stefan Zweig's life and writing, and Donald Prater, Zweig's biographer, were extremely generous in the amount of time they spent with me, and in the information and materials they made available to me. I have learned much from both of these men. I have also benefited from my conversations with Alberto Dines in Rio de Janeiro about Stefan Zweig's last years; and from the insights about Zweig offered by Leon Botstein, Klara Carmely, Editha S. Neumann, and Erdmute Wenzel

White at the International Stefan Zweig Symposium, in which I participated in 1981 at the State University College of New York, Fredonia. I am also extremely grateful to the librarians at the Leo Baeck Institute in New York, the Wiener Library in London, the Israelitische Kultusgemeinde in Vienna, and to the curators of the International Stefan Zweig Gesellschaft in Vienna and the Stefan Zweig Collection at Fredonia. All were indefatigable in tracking down many obscure documents illuminating the histories of the Jewish communities in Hohenems and Prossnitz as well as aspects of the life histories of the Zweigs and Brettauers.

Along the way, many people have read portions and drafts of this work and have permitted me to benefit from their comments, critiques, and specialized knowledge. Alice Brown, Michael Carter, Jane Coppock, James Duffy, Charlotte Hirsch, Daniel Neumann, Deborah Pellow, Susanne Zantop, and the late Thomas Hodgkin were especially kind in this regard. Allen Howard helped me with his particularly careful and insightful reading of the Sierra Leone sections of the book, and Jonathan Boyarin did likewise in parts concerning modern Jewish history. I also profited from questions and commentary offered by members of the Study Group on the Jew in the Modern World and the Study Group on Biography, at Harvard University's Center for European Studies.

My colleagues in the history department at Dartmouth have been extremely supportive of my interests throughout the years. I am greatly indebted to Marysa Navarro and Kathleen Higgins for their precise readings of the Brazilian sections of this book, and to Charles Wood and Jere Daniell for their editorial suggestions and for allowing me to benefit from the clarity of their thinking and directness of writing. Gail Vernazza, our administrative assistant, has been more than helpful in facilitating the preparation of this work at every phase in its development; she has also been an encouraging presence, essential to its creation. To Douglas Haynes and Michael Ermarth I owe a special debt of gratitude for the many discussions we have had concerning theoretical issues relevant to this book, and for their generosity in commenting so thoughtfully and extensively on its various chapters. It is friendship and goodwill like theirs that has made our department such a congenial and intellectually stimulating haven for me.

Manon Spitzer Ruben helped me to conceptualize this book in its early stages, provided me with editorial as well as invaluable factual assistance, and never faltered in her support for its completion. I am immensely grateful to her. My brother Carl has always been keenly interested in this project and has been an encouraging and nurturing friend during its evolution. He and my sons, Alex, Oliver, and Gabriel, have lived in a kind of sibling relationship to "Leo's book" for so many years that they will undoubtedly sigh relief that the rivalry can finally be terminated. Their patience has been extraordinary; their love and good humor essential.

Without Marianne Hirsch, whose life history and immigrant awareness complement my own in so many ways, I would not have been able to complete this book. Partner and best friend, her intelligence, creativity, and tenacious belief in this project and my abilities have been the invigorating qualities that have sustained, stimulated, and cheered me over the years. Despite her own demanding share in our familial life and her passionate academic involvement – while in the process of teaching and writing a book herself – she has read every page of this work on several occasions, and commented constructively and imaginatively on its development. Merely to thank her would be insufficient acknowledgment of the irreplaceable role she plays in every facet of my life.

Rose Spitzer, my mother, read a completed draft of this book, but died before its publication. It was she who introduced me to Stefan Zweig's writing (a Spanish translation of the biography of Joseph Fouché that I read as a child in Bolivia), she who accompanied me on my first trip to Austria, she who introduced me to the beauty but also the dark side of "her Vienna," where she was born, raised, and from which she fled a year after the *Anschluss*. Indirectly, this book has been my effort to understand facets of her experience, aspects of her life. I had hoped it would be hers to celebrate in joy. Instead I offer it as a token to her memory and mourn her absence.

Leo Spitzer

Norwich, Vermont
November 1988

Lives in Between

Introduction

The other day two Jewish merchants, partners in the same textile business, both decided to change their names. You must understand them – they were called Zoberman and Moscovi! And that combination didn't look at all well on the sign over the door!...

After much thought, Zoberman decided to call himself Smith. Yes, Smith! What could have been more unobtrusive?

Then Moscovi thought for a long time and had an equally marvelous inspiration: he would call himself Smith too!

"Smith and Smith!" What a happy coincidence! How could one be more socially acceptable? Find a sign more discreet?

Only here is how it worked out in the course of their daily routine: A client telephoned:

"Hello? I would like to speak to Mr. Smith!"

"Smith? Yes, he's here...but which one do you want? Zoberman or Moscovi?"

Albert Memmi, The Liberation of the Jew

Shame. Shame and self-contempt. Nausea. When people like me, they tell me it is in spite of my color. When they dislike me, they point out that it is not because of my color. Either way, I am locked into the infernal circle...I tell you, I [am] walled in: No exception [is] made for my refined manners, or my knowledge of literature, or my understanding of the quantum theory.

Frantz Fanon, Black Skin, White Masks

This book is a comparative study of the process and experience of assimilation and of movement within class-society. Employing a cross-cultural life-history approach, it focuses on members of several generations of families who were products of two or more social worlds: the Afro-Brazilian Rebouças family; the West African Creole May family, from Sierra Leone; and the Austrian-Jewish Zweig-Brettauer family. The volume examines the assimilationist journey of previously subordinated individuals into the world of the dominant – a journey at once self-motivated and officially encouraged. It compares long-term historical experiences that have previously not received close comparative scrutiny: the social ascent of individual blacks, mulattoes, and Jews "up from slavery" and "out of

3

the ghetto" into bourgeois society during the era initiated around the time of the French Revolution that has become known as the Century of Emancipation. And the book makes an effort to understand how assimilating individuals viewed themselves privately and represented themselves publicly: how they identified and oriented themselves over time.

This work also explores the "predicament of marginality" – that liminal situation, "between two worlds," in which assimilating individuals often find themselves as a consequence of "barriers" that are raised, both to impede their social integration into the world of the dominant, and to block their share in dominant privileges and powers. The book studies the connections between individual consciousness of this predicament, and the variety of individual responses to exclusion and subordination – responses ranging from collaboration to revolt, from adaptation to exile, from resignation to "passing," to suicide.

On one level, by probing the nexus between individual action and individual perceptions of self and social reality, this work seeks to illuminate the complexity of a relationship that Erik Erikson has succinctly identified as that between "life history and the historical moment."[1] On a broader level, by analyzing notions of individual identity and varieties of individual responses within a comparative framework – cross-culturally, over time and space – this book attempts to refine our theoretical understanding both of the concept and of the function of marginality in the nineteenth and twentieth centuries, and to draw some general conclusions about identity formation in contexts of subordination and dominance in colonial and emergent capitalist societies.

• • •

On initial consideration, it would seem that no self-evident comparative linkage exists between the disparate geographical and cultural settings for this volume's inquiry, and between the three families on which it focuses. All seem worlds apart, so exotic to each other, as well as to us today, as to exclude common terms. The Mays of Sierra Leone were black Africans whose male founding member, Ifacayeh, was born in Yoruba in 1817, captured and sold into slavery during the era of civil wars that led to the disintegration of the Old Oyo Empire in what is now western Nigeria, and liberated in Freetown after a British patrol of the Anti-Slavery Squadron intercepted the ship carrying him and more than three hundred other slaves to labor in Brazil. The Brazilian Rebouças, by the early nineteenth century, were persons of mixed racial background: *pardos* whose eighteenth-century forebears in Bahia had included both native-born Portuguese and African slaves. The Zweig and Brettauers were Jews, with roots in the Central European ghettos of Moravia, Bohemia, and the Vorarlberg.

During the century and a half in which this study is set, moreover, these three families were normally removed from each other by considerable cultural and geographical distances, inhabiting places with fundamentally distinctive political and social characteristics, as well as with dissimilar historical backgrounds. Sierra Leone, in which Ifacayeh (who was renamed Joseph Boston May by British missionaries) married Ann Wilberforce, and where, together, they raised their nine children, had been a British Crown colony since 1808. This colony had begun in the late eighteenth century as a settlement for Africans and people of African descent from Europe and the Americas liberated from slavery. Throughout the nineteenth century, it was a culturally and ethnically diverse locale, periodically wracked by tensions among the British-sponsored black settlers and their colony-born offspring, their European mentors and colonial masters, and the African peoples indigenous to the neighboring areas. The colony was also a place that remained nearly homogeneous racially, with many of its ruling whites dying off from tropical diseases, and few other Europeans risking long-term residence in what was feared as the "White Man's Grave."[2]

In contrast, Brazil, from the sixteenth until the mid-nineteenth century, had imported millions of Africans as slaves to labor on the sugar, tobacco, and coffee plantations and in the mines. Its population of European ancestry had also grown and continued to grow – through natural increase and a steady inflow of new immigrants, predominantly from Portugal but also from other areas of Southern Europe. It had early become a multiracial society, with miscegenation widespread among blacks, whites, and Amerindians. Brazil became independent from Portugal in 1822, when Antônio Pereira Rebouças, the son of the family's Brazilian founders, was in his mid-twenties. Although individual and group manumission of slaves occurred with increasing frequency throughout the nineteenth century, the country remained a slaveholding society until 1888, dominated by the interests and outlooks of a powerful rural aristocracy.

Sierra Leone's colonial system and Brazil's "plantocracy" differed immensely from the Central European Hapsburg dominions inhabited by the Jewish Zweig and Brettauer families. Color-based racial differentiation played no significant role in these "Hapsburg lands," but their ethnic and cultural diversity became the subject of growing emotional debate and the cause of political tension throughout the nineteenth century. Moreover, by 1850, a considerable increase in immigration into Lower Austria had begun, particularly into Vienna, from countries comprising the Hapsburg Empire and its immediate neighbors. The newcomers included Jews recently emancipated from communities (*shtetlekh*) and ghettos in the empire, the Zweigs and Brettauers among them, who were attracted by the emerging cosmopolitanism and sophistication of Vienna. They also included many Eastern European Jews fleeing oppression. Although Jews had officially been recognized as a tolerated religious minority in Austria since the time of the reforms initiated by Emperor Joseph II in the late eighteenth century, the increasing size of this "alien" group stimulated the rise of new forms of anti-Semitism and breathed new life into the specter of Jewish *Ueberschwemmung* (inundation).[3]

But, despite the obvious societal, cultural, and physical differences among the May, Rebouças and Zweig-Brettauer families, they all shared important experiences and characteristics as heirs of lengthy historical contact between peoples of unequal power. In the case of the Mays and Rebouças, this contact resulted from the circumstances of European imperial expansion and the enslavement of Africans for American service; and, in the case of the Zweigs and Brettauers, from the relationship between a dominant Gentile majority and a subordinate Jewish minority.

By the mid-nineteenth century, individuals in all these families had become engaged in the process of assimilation: they were traveling on a road opened up and, in part, cleared for them by the beginnings of commercial and industrial modernization, and by the legal, social, and economic changes associated with the emancipation of slaves, minorities, and various other subordinated groups. As such, these individuals were personally involved in a process of social change taking place on several scales at once, from the family to the global political economy. For them, as for so many others, this process seemed to offer the possibility of mobility into, and identification with, a class-based social order. The cultural values and standards of this order were in large part defined and set by the most energetic and economically powerful group in the industrializing world: the bourgeoisie.

The extent to which members of these families were able to identify with the dominant society and to gain access to its institutions differed from person to person, from situation to situation. Certainly neither the fact of emancipation, nor the willingness to assimilate, guaranteed Mays, Rebouças, or Zweigs and Brettauers unimpeded integration into the dominant culture. Their paths to full belonging were often blocked by barriers based on the racial, religious, ethnic, or gender-based "otherness" of the assimilating aspirants. These barriers manifested themselves in a variety of forms, with varying intensity, and they were perceived in equally various ways by the people against whom they were directed.

They seemed least formidable when expressed as prejudice – subtly, through jokes or some type of social aloofness that precluded intimacy, or arrogantly, through insult and petty abuse. They appeared more obstructive when expressed as legal or extralegal institutionalized discrimination proscribing participation in spheres of social, economic, or political activity. And they were most destructive when they assumed the form of outright persecution condoned by the state. In every case, however, the responses to them varied – often significantly – *at the level of the individual*. That is why one of the goals of this book is to explore the nature of these barriers and the ways in which they were encountered and perceived, as well as to examine and analyze the range of responses they engendered.

• • •

That a particular historical situation and moment may be perceived differently by individuals sharing the same situational universe – that, as Jacques Barzun once explained it, "individuals and groups do not all see the same realities, and from those they see they take hopes and fears that are not the same" – is the primary justification for the comparative life-history approach employed in this book.[4] My contention is that by turning to the life histories of individuals, by engaging in the effort to approximate and understand the meaning of conditions and events as they perceived them over time, we are able to discover what Martin Duberman has called "that tangle of individual strivings which underlies behavior – the system of motivation at the sources of action."[5] Such discovery, embraced as a vital component within the overall structure of historical interpretation, then enables us to refine explanations for the genesis of action and response based on factors like ideology, economic interest, political principle, or class consciousness. We are permitted to gain a more profound sense of the connecting thread between the individual and collective society.

A history that places such great importance on the *qualitative* experience of individual lives is, of course, open to challenge. Proponents of a more positivistic analytical orientation, one based on aggregate and "statistically significant" measurement of collective experience, might question the representativeness of the individuals and families selected for exposition in this book. After all, my method appears to rely on incomplete or possibly inaccurate retrospective materials – on data that is "introspective" and "subjective" rather than "quantitative" and "objective." And critics could also question my generalization from the specific. A life-history perspective, with its concentration on an in-depth understanding of individual experience and mind over time, seems inherently tied to a singular, if not atomistic, conception of the social – to individual peculiarities that would make generalizations and the "testing of general causal theories" impossible. As W. M. Runyan expressed the position: "If you can't generalize from ... studies of individual lives, what's the point of doing them?"[6]

Two assumptions lie at the heart of this kind of criticism. The first, a methodological one, privileges group-level analysis as most appropriate for social scientific inquiry; and posits that generalizations derived from the study of collective experience will effectively "illuminate ... facets of individual lives" and "adequately explain and predict behavior [both] at the group and individual level."[7] The second, attitudinal in nature, subscribes to a scientific notion of objectivity in which the historian's effort to maintain a "neutral stance" vis-à-vis the object of study is best demonstrated in the pursuit of "maximally reliable" knowledge. This relegates the "subjectivity" inherent in studies of individual experience to a "less reliable" category, and conceives the goal of scholarly inquiry to be the dispassionate "domination" of the object of study: its "mastery" or "control," without the interference of emotionality or of "the intrusive self."[8]

To a degree, certainly, the first assumption is correct. As this volume illustrates, life paths are indeed molded, given direction, and frequently modified through the interaction between individuals and their collective social and historical environments. In the sense that individuals live by "internalizing the external," as Jean-Paul Sartre observed in his *Search for a Method* – inscribing on their personal history economic, political, social, as well as linguistic and belief structures that are "generalizable" from the collective environment in which they find themselves – important aspects of the "individual condition" can be illuminated and explained in the analysis of collective experience.[9]

But this book's comparative and cross-cultural life-history approach clearly allows matters to go the other way around as well. History, after all, is both a *social* and a *human* science. Through the multiple perspective of individuals, across cultures, and diachronically, this approach facilitates a richer and more nuanced understanding of the many meanings and implications of emancipation, assimilation, and the "new" racism: of the three social and ideological processes that constitute the core of this book. Indeed, a life-history approach permits the extraction of general typologies *as well as* the recognition of particular differences at the individual level. The comparison of generational responses of individuals *within* the May, Rebouças, and Zweig-Brettauer families, and *between* their members, warrants the conceptual linking of disparate lives, the identification of common elements in their individual experiences, and the discovery of similar patterns in their life-course and societal orientation. At the same time, the focus on individual lives within the context of a comparative perspective supports the effort to comprehend the uniqueness of experience. It enables us to evoke the shadow areas of historical motivation that we cannot know, but only sense empathetically.

Furthermore, historical knowledge exclusively based on the scientific ideal of "neutral objectivity" is potentially exclusionary of the insights offered by qualitative, subjective, experience. Tied to the attainment of mastery and domination over the object of study, this scientistic scholarship demands a relationship between scholar and topic in which, almost by definition, the less-easily "mastered" and less "maximally reliable" realm of individual experience finds little room. As a general rule, I have found, this type of valuation of objectivity to be constraining – too limited for the interpretive understanding of the variety of psychological, emotional, and social concerns examined in this book.

My own approach seeks to present what Elaine Showalter has called an "authority which inscribes its own uncertainty."[10] Given the nature of my sources – indeed, given my frequent lack of sources and the informational lacunae they engendered – this approach is less a reflection of humility than of reality. But it also reflects an effort to situate myself in a less "dominant," less autonomous, and more "other-directed" stance vis-à-vis the individuals in this study. As such, it clearly departs from any theory of knowledge based on the notion of objective neutrality. My goal, rather, has been to achieve a more embodied, dialogical, kind of analytical understanding – one that makes use both of subjective experience and of objective context, one which, in Evelyn Fox Keller's phrase, "draws explicitly on the commonality of feelings and experiences" between myself and the persons on whom I have chosen to focus.[11]

• • •

Given this stance, it may be relevant and of some explanatory interest to the reader to disclose aspects of my own life history. Certainly, my choice of the processes to analyze and the questions to pose in this work has been inextricably linked to the fact that both assimilationism and exclusion have been intimately a part of my own life experience, and of my family and friends. Marginality has been a presence as well as a predicament for as long as I can remember. Having been born in Bolivia to parents fleeing Nazi persecution in Austria, I was raised within a community of German-speaking, largely Jewish, immigrants who had been forced to abandon a land with which they, and generations of their forebears, had identified and into whose dominant culture they had attempted to assimilate. Although my parents' background was working-class, and their youthful political ideology was influenced by Labor-Zionism and Austro-Marxism, their world view, and that of many of their fellow immigrants, had been formed by the assimilationist values and ideals that accompanied the emancipation of Jews in Central Europe – values and ideals closely associated with those of the bourgeoisie. They never felt "at home" in Bolivia – that most non-European of Latin American countries – nor did its governments, which had provided them with a haven, encourage them to make that country their permanent abode. They remained outsiders in fact and in feeling. And I, despite my Bolivian citizenship through birth, was both an outsider and a child of outsiders.

In the United States, to which we emigrated when I was ten years old, I acquired a new language and, through it, experienced the cultural remolding and reshaping that schooling, contact with peers, and exposure to the majority way of life effects. Largely unconscious of what was happening to me, I was gradually "North Americanized" by an assimilationist process. I was socialized, politicized, and educated to become part of the dominant culture, and I was rewarded by its institutions. But, having already been profoundly inscribed in childhood with the history and culture of a people who had been defined as "other," and who had been persecuted and marginalized, I also never felt totally absorbed by this process.

My perspective in this book – the orientation from which I examine both the assimilationist response to emancipation and the nature of individual confrontations with racism and other forms of exclusion and domination – is, therefore, not neutral. Nor is the "place from which I speak" – the values, experiences, and historical consciousness that inform my outlook in the present as I write about the past – something that I wish to disguise or render invisible. But an important caveat surrounds this declaration. Although my background, my life history, has helped me to conceptualize this book, and though it has enabled me to sympathize with the hopes, aspirations, and frustrations of the persons on whom I have focused, it has not allowed me to achieve the impossible. I have not been able to "get inside the skins" of these individuals, nor to put myself in their places, nor to perceive the world *exactly* as they perceived it. No matter how thorough my exploration of the evidence they "left behind," no matter how deep my factual knowledge of the setting in which they found themselves, my account of their experiences is an *interpretation* that cannot be divorced from my personal locus in a time and place that is distant from their own. Nor can it be separated from my familiarity with the twentieth-century horrors that invest the individual efforts of the Mays, Rebouças, and Zweigs to assimilate into the dominant society with a particularly poignant, if not tragic, aura.

In pointing to the interpretive nature of this work, however, and to the impossibility of attaining an exact perception of the persons it studies, I emphatically do not wish to imply that one cannot *approximate* a view of experience from their perspective – that one cannot conduct research and frame an analysis in such a way as to *understand* how they confronted their world and how they responded within its constraints. Certainly a sympathetic stance, echoing one's own life history, is a distinct advantage in trying to achieve this type of understanding. But it also calls for a kind of synoptic approach, an examination of the individual and social context that requires what Clifford Geertz has described as "a continuous dialectical tacking between the most local of local detail and the most global of global structure in such a way as to bring them into simultaneous view."[12] This approach demands a reading that follows the trajectory of Wilhelm Dilthey's hermeneutic circle: one in which the historian, like the anthropologist, literary critic, or psychoanalyst, moves interpretatively back and forth between the general and the specific – between "the whole conceived through the parts that actualize it and the parts conceived through the whole that motivates them" – in order to ensure that each informs the other and that each discloses a *sense* of life experience, if not the actual experience itself.[13]

It is, of course, true that any historian attempting to penetrate and understand the arena of individual experience has to come to terms with practical difficulties that inhibit and complicate the task of interpretation. Unlike the sociologist or psychologist, who can normally fill in lacunae with follow-up interviews, the historian is limited by the realities of source materials, documents that are all too often frustratingly vague or nonexistent. The historian, studying a more distant past whose human participants are no longer alive, cannot clarify, supplement, or reconstruct biographical information or seek explanation for behavior through direct inquiry. But, insurmountable as some of these difficulties are, they must not be permitted to frighten the historian away from individual analysis. Evidence relating to individual life histories *can* be discovered, and significant conclusions *can* be extracted from it. Such was my experience.

My initial interest in Sierra Leone, Brazil, and Austria derived both from personal and historical familiarity with these three areas of the world and from my conviction that an examination of the postemancipation assimilationist experience of Liberated Africans and Creoles, mulattoes, and Jews would illuminate different aspects of the movement "up from slavery" and "out of the ghetto." Having decided to stress individual response as the basis for my study, however, I soon realized that I had to cast a net that would extend well beyond these three countries and include a broad range of source materials.

I searched not only through public archives and private family collections in Vienna, Freetown, and Rio de Janeiro, three cities central to my study, but also in Prague, Hohenems, London, Ponte de Lima, Salvador, São Paulo, New York, New Haven, and Boston. In all these places, I looked for "personal" evidence: for books, articles, newspapers, and manuscripts – for records, documents, letters, diaries, and journals – that might contain biographical and autobiographical information pertaining to persons whom I was studying. I supplemented these materials with oral accounts whenever possible: with oral traditions in the case of the Yoruba background of Ifacayeh May, but generally with interviews of descendants and relatives of principals.

I was eclectic in the use of these resources and also seized on any nugget of personal evidence that I could uncover. In Vienna, for example, my discovery of documents recording Alfred and Stefan Zweig's circumcision helped me to grasp the strength of their parents' religious identification with Judaism in the last decade of the nineteenth century. And even highly impersonal sources occasionally revealed aspects of personality. Often I encountered "silence": for instance, the general absence of autobiographical materials concerning the individual experiences of assimilating women. But I soon realized that such a consistent absence of personal evidence was also analytically significant. In my efforts to find sources and clues to the experience of assimilation and exclusion as it was viewed "from within," I freely acknowledge that I was not reluctant to give sway, occasionally, to "unscientific" auxiliaries like intuition and luck.

My decision to concentrate on the May, Rebouças, and Zweig-Brettauer families was certainly influenced by the quantity and quality of the evidence uncovered. At an early point in my project, for example, when I was focusing mainly on materials relating to the general societal adjustment of Afro-Brazilian freedmen, discovery of some of André Rebouças's diary books in the *Instituto Historico e Geografico Brasileiro* inspired me to search for surviving members of the Rebouças family in Rio de Janeiro, São Paulo, and Salvador. This search led to the proverbial researcher's treasure chest: a family archive containing diaries, letter books, genealogical charts, as well as biographical and autobiographical fragments relating to the life histories of individuals in the family since the end of the eighteenth century. In turn, this discovery, stimulated me to make a trip to Ponte de Lima, in Portugal, to search for materials illuminating the family's European roots.

My accidental discovery in Dan Rottenberg's *Finding Our Fathers* that Zweig and Spitzer family members frequently married each other in the eighteenth and nineteenth centuries personalized my effort to study postemancipation Jewish assimilation in Central Europe, and provided me with additional stimulus to get at the roots of this experience through the Zweig-Brettauer – and, by extension, my own – family history.[14] This led me to search in Europe and the Americas – to visit the towns and cities where Zweigs and Brettauers had been born and lived, and the cemeteries in which many of them were buried. Eventually, I was able to gather and piece together what amounted to a great deal of factual information about individual Zweig and Brettauer lives over several generations, and to detail the specific circumstances and mechanics of Jewish assimilation and social mobility within a family context.

For the Mays, the combined evidence contained in oral traditions, materials relating to slave captures and liberation at Sierra Leone, family Bibles and albums, missionary archives in England, and in numerous articles and editorials in the Sierra Leone newspapers with which members of the family came to be associated provided biographical details and insights into the complex texture of individual survival and adjustment within a colonial situation.

The richness of sources for these three particular families made the reconstruction of their life histories and perceptions easier than might otherwise have been the case. The comparative and cross-cultural perspective has convinced me, however, that the responses of the Mays, Rebouças, and Zweig-Brettauers are in no sense extraordinary. They are certainly not uncharacteristic or unrepresentative of responses to the experience of assimilation or of exclusion in general.[15] At the same time, to the extent that individual human behavior is determined in the relationship and interaction among the variables that define a person and those that characterize his or her situation, the comparative life-history focus on members of these three families also highlights the *unpredictability* of behavioral responses at the individual level.[16] For me, this finding has confirmed what Paul Thompson has called "the untidy reality" on which historical understanding rests: the complexity, depth, and existential intractability of the human experience.[17] We can compare, generalize, explain, but there remains the possibility of distinctive individuality: of a *sui generis* life narrative.

• • •

This book is divided into two parts. Part I, "The Way In, 1780–1870," consists of four chapters. The first of these, "The Journey Upward, the Journey Outward: Assimilation in the Century of Emancipation," presents the general characteristics and ideological contexts of the modern process of emancipation that began in the era of the French Revolution and through which, in varying degrees, legal, social, and political restrictions were lifted from a number of minority and subordinated groups in Europe, the Americas, and regions of Africa under European influence. The chapter also provides an overview of assimilation, both as process and as ideology closely associated with emancipation. It examines assimilation from the perspective of dominant groups who often controlled its implementation and set its limits, as well as from that of subordinate ones, who were its objects and, not infrequently, its agents.

Chapters 2, 3, and 4 then explore the process of assimilation and the assimilationist experience in the late-eighteenth and early-nineteenth centuries among "founding" members of the May, Zweig-Brettauer, and Rebouças families. These chapters analyze the variety of means employed by dominant groups in colonial Sierra Leone, Hapsburg Central Europe, and Brazil to mold and absorb individuals emerging from subordinate strata: through language and the imposition of a dominant mode of discourse; through authority over the availability and content of formal education; through definition of "acceptable" public behavior, outward appearance, and societal norms; and through control over legal, political, and economic institutions. These chapters also detail the other dimensions of assimilationism: the concrete as well as subjective attractions of the assimilationist journey for individuals emancipated from slavery or the restrictions of ghettoized subordination, and the deliberate as well as unwitting complicity of such individuals in sustaining the hegemony of dominant values and power.

Part II, "The Predicament of Marginality, 1870–1945," focuses on the reaction to emancipation during a period when a new, biologically based racism began to challenge the prevailing assimilationist ideology and its various "successful products." Within the dominant realm, this was a time when pseudoscientific ideas connecting "race" and "cultural potential" served as a basis for the resurgence of old exclusionary practices and new patterns of discrimination and persecution.

Part II contains three chapters. The first of these, Chapter 5, "The Marginal Situation, Individual Psychology, and Ideology," advances a theoretical argument connecting the marginality of assimilating persons to their perceptions of life-chances within a particular social context and historical moment. It places the assimilationist experience and individual constructions of future goals within a conceptual framework informed by Adlerian psychological and Gramscian/Althusserian ideological theories. Chapter 6, "I belong nowhere, and everywhere am a stranger," illuminates and expands upon this theoretical argument by comparing, over time, the variety of adjustments and responses to subordination and exclusion of Cornelius May, André Rebouças, and Stefan Zweig: three successful second- and third-generation products of the assimilationist dynamic who became "marginal men."

The book's concluding chapter, "The Way Out: From the 'Savage God' to 'Holy Violence,' " has the personal disenchantment with assimilationism as its underlying thread. Moving beyond the May, Rebouças, and Zweig-Brettauer family members, it expands on their various responses to this disenchantment by presenting examples of other possibilities. It sets *all these responses* – individual and collective, intellectual and political – within the framework of a typology ranging from suicide to revolution. In mapping and representing the possible routes of flight from continued subordination and exclusion, this chapter illuminates and accentuates a theme woven through the pages of this book. It highlights the intense anguish as well as energizing power that the predicament of marginality so frequently engendered.

PART I

THE WAY IN
1780–1870

Chapter 1

The Journey Upward, the Journey Outward:
Assimilation in the Century of Emancipation

What is the great concern of our times? It is emancipation. Not only the emancipation of the people of Ireland, of the Greeks, the Jews of Frankfurt, the blacks of the West Indies or similarly oppressed peoples, but of the entire world, especially of Europe... tearing itself loose from the iron bonds of a privileged aristocracy.

Heinrich Heine, *Reisebilder*

The bourgeoisie, by the rapid improvement of all instruments of production, by the immensely facilitated means of communication, draws all, even the most barbarian nations into civilization.... In one word, it creates a world after its own image.

Karl Marx and Friedrich Engels, *The Communist Manifesto*

Mr. von Bleichröder, who since his elevation to nobility almost bursts with pride and who publicly no longer entertains his former friends and associates, keeps himself apart from them even in his walks: on the promenades in the Sieges-Allee, he walks on the western side, instead of on the eastern side with the great majority of the promenaders, who are almost all Jews. Asked why he walked on the other side, he is said to have answered that the eastern side smelled too much of garlic.

Quoted by David Landes, "Bleichröders and Rothschilds,"
The Family in History, C. E. Rosenberg, ed.

I

In the span of one hundred years between the outbreak of the French Revolution and the republican coup that overthrew the empire in Brazil in 1889, the old European world with its corporate structures and absolutist governments was eclipsed by the rise of a new one. Based on the growth of technology and capitalist industry, and sustained by a belief in ever-growing human enlightenment and in

19

continuous material and moral progress, this new world was everywhere characterized by the loosening or elimination of restrictions
that had bound various groups in subordination.

Indeed, as Heinrich Heine and other contemporaries who reflected
on the changes correctly perceived, a process of emancipation became
a constituent element of this century of modernization – an essential
principle of its structure.[1] "Each era creates its particular expression
for the eternal interests of the Spirit," Karl Rosenkranz observed in
1838. "In our time it is the idea of freedom – of emancipation – which
has penetrated the Euro-American realm in most sweeping manner."[2] Not only did bourgeois classes in Europe and its colonial off-
shoots flourish and rise to ascendancy when constraints inhibiting
their opportunities for economic and social mobility were eased or
eliminated by the growth of factories and the expansion of industrial
production and trade, but other groups, more deeply submerged in
the strata of society, were also freed of confining legal and social
disabilities and "emancipated" into the modern world. The liberation
of slaves in Europe and the Americas, the emancipation of the Catholic minority in the United Kingdom, of Jews in Western and Central
Europe, and the elimination of the remnants of serfdom were among
the major milestones attesting to the emancipatory spirit of this
period of change.[3]

Emancipation, of course, was an ancient concomitant of human
slavery and other types of subordination, and was not "invented" in
that century. Throughout ancient and medieval times, however, and
until the French Revolution, emancipation was generally an act
involving *individuals*. In classical Roman law, it referred to the
release of adult sons from paternal control and to the public, voluntary manumission of slaves. Although such individual – "private"
– acts of manumission certainly continued to occur in the late eighteenth and throughout much of the nineteenth century, emancipation during this era of modernization was characteristically a
collective action, applied to legally, politically, and socially subordinated *groups* by a public governmental authority generally ex-
terior to the social situation involved.[4]

It was a process rooted in the rational ideas of the Enlightenment
and made possible by the economic developments of the age of industrialization. Its energies derived from the vigorous push for civil
and political liberties on the part of the increasingly powerful
bourgeois-liberal classes – from the articulation of a public opinion
that at times was passionately hostile to legal servitude and in
sympathy with the grievances of the oppressed. The process was
fortified by the rise of a new economic order to hegemony, one chal-

lenging antiquated and static social arrangements inimical to new notions of "growth" and "progress." And it was facilitated by the widespread expansion of industrial capitalism, the revolution in machine manufacturing, and the persuasive voices of economists who argued against mercantilist protectionism and for the superior productivity of free labor.[5]

The specific course of the emancipatory process in each society, as well as the speed and thoroughness with which it was carried out, depended on a number of variables. The level of control each state or imperial authority exerted over its implementation – a factor closely related to a combination of particular demographic, political, and economic considerations – played a crucial role in molding the structure and influencing the dynamic of the process. The extent to which the subordinated themselves worked actively and cooperatively toward their own emancipation, or struggled for it overtly or covertly (in slave rebellions or through passive resistance, for example) was also a determinant in the genesis, form, and evolution of the process. Conversely, the power retained by "old order" groups opposed both to fundamental changes in society as well as to competing modes of social organization often inhibited the spread of emancipatory movements, reversing, if not obliterating, their opportunities and benefits.[6]

Because the specific characteristics of the process of emancipation during that century differed from place to place and over time, and the goals of its advocates varied according to their own particular interests and to local changes in political and social environments, it is not surprising that no single approach emerged to address the manner in which newly emancipated peoples would fit and fare within the realm of the emancipators. Beyond the general agreement which evolved about the principle that slavery be abolished, servile tenures eliminated, and civil and political disabilities of excluded minorities modified, emancipating governments and their associated institutions differed about the extent of their *involvement* with, and *responsibility* for, the members of the subordinate groups whose legal status the acts of emancipation had so dramatically altered.

How far into society would the modification in civil and political disabilities reach? How complete would such modification be? How, if at all, would the integration of the emancipated into the culture of the dominant "mainstream" be brought about? Although perhaps all proponents of emancipation concurred that the legal status of the subordinated would be altered, and that the "energetic and enterprising," the "intelligent and meritorious," among them would abandon the restrictions of their previous lives to enter into – and *move up within* – social, economic, and political arenas from which they had previously been excluded, opinion was divided about the allowable limits of this mobility and the expected role of the state and dominant establishment in stimulating and helping it to take place at all. In general, however, two broad approaches to these questions can be distinguished.

In the first, in what might be termed the "laissez-faire" approach – for which the French Revolution's Declaration on the Rights of Man and of the Citizen, the granting of citizenship rights to Jews in France in 1791, and France's abolition of colonial slavery in 1794 can be viewed as paradigmatic – the responsibility of the state and its dominant institutions toward the newly emancipated remained in large part confined *only* to the legal realm. This approach was congruent with political ideas about the restricted functions of governments and the inherent aptitude of individuals for self-generated "improvement." It was also congruent with physiocratic ideas that associated freedom with "natural" rights rather than "cultural" attributes – that considered the culture and economic situation of any individual as irrelevant to his or her right to be free.[7]

The "laissez-faire" approach to emancipation thus involved minimal interference of the "social engineering" variety. Its practitioners – officials of the state and agencies of the dominant establishment – had no plans or programs for the newly emancipated groups beyond the legal change of status inherent in the act of emancipation. These officials had no agenda to "transform" or "reeducate" emancipated persons according to some preconceived sociocultural model, nor did they act to modify or ease economic "handicaps" impeding the potential material and social benefits of civil emancipation. In essence, as Reinhard Rürup has observed, they left the cultural and economic integration of the newly emancipated into the dominant "mainstream" "to the unfettered interplay of social forces."[8]

Such a "laissez-faire" approach, for example, characterized the predominant attitude toward various groups of blacks who were liberated from slavery in Brazil in the eighteenth and nineteenth century, and, especially, toward those affected by the May 1888 emancipatory decree that finally abolished slavery throughout the Brazilian Empire.[9] Without any concerted effort on the part of the liberating authorities to ease the ex-slaves' economic and social transition into "freedom" – without any plan to help them acquire an alternative livelihood or to inform and reorient them culturally and socially through education – abolition immediately contributed to the proletarianization and marginalization of the newly emancipated masses. The majority of ex-slaves, unprepared and untrained for their new role as independent wage earners, and at a competitive disadvantage with the large number of European immigrants who were flowing into the industrialized sections of the country, lived in conditions of degradation and squalor. Surviving as best they could in urban hovels, or returning – oftentimes demoralized – to seek rural employment, these Afro-Brazilian freedmen and women were abandoned to their own resources. In effect if not in law, they generally remained excluded from the potentially beneficial economic and societal opportunities of a modernizing Brazilian system.[10]

A number of extant oral accounts by Brazilians freed in 1888 describe the dire conditions and personal disillusionments during the decades following the final abolition of slavery; they attest to the potentially negative consequences of this particular example of "laissez-faire" emancipation. In one of these accounts, cited by the sociologist Florestan Fernandes in his classic study *The Negro in Brazilian Society*, an ex-slave complained that "the law of May 13 [which freed slaves throughout Brazil] had been premature and that before it was passed, 'the Negro should [have been]...taught how to live in freedom,' for he 'didn't know how to live in freedom, and wasn't even acquainted with money.' "[11] Similarly critical, another man who was emancipated in 1888 observed that "the Negro, for lack of the transitional period necessary to his complete adjustment to the condition of being a free man, was left in the most awkward situation...[and assumed] this new condition without plans, without objectives, without guidelines – without anything that might permit him to make a suitable adjustment."[12]

"Laissez-faire" also characterized the predominant attitude of metropolitan officials to the emancipation of slaves in the British colonial system. Thus, in the so-called Great Experiment of the 1830s that emancipated approximately three-quarter of a million slaves throughout the far-flung reaches of the British Caribbean Empire, the emancipating colonial authorities in London (like their counterparts in revolutionary France) did not take responsibility for guiding and directing the economic transition and social adjustment of the newly liberated peoples. Such a "hands-off" approach was especially paradoxical, given the fact that many members of the British public judged the progress and success of slave emancipation according to the extent to which the Christian religion and European cultural patterns penetrated the emancipated population.[13] In order for the standards in this judgment to have been even potentially realizable, officials would have needed to affect the values and outlooks both of the ex-slaves and their former masters by sponsoring and overseeing a radical transformation in colonial political, economic, and social relations. Ultimate authority – and responsibility – for the colonial system, after all, rested in London.[14]

In enacting the Emancipation Bill of 1834, however, British metropolitan officials were influenced by a liberal idea of government that was minimalist rather than paternalist: it restricted intervention by central governmental authorities largely to the legal realm and discouraged interference in other societal processes.[15] Therefore, these officials effectively abdicated their direct influence over the social and economic transformation of the West Indian emancipated masses. They bequeathed control over the postemancipation "apprenticeship" process, and over the well-being of the ex-slaves, to colonial legislatures that were dominated by a planter class committed to its own economic survival through the re-establishment of as much of the status quo ante as possible.[16] The so-called "failure of emancipation" in the British Caribbean – a perception that gained increasing prominence in British public opinion in the second half of the nineteenth century and that, by the 1860s, fueled racist sentiment throughout the United Kingdom and its colonies about the "inherent" deficiencies of blacks – was clearly attributable to this abdication.[17]

But the obverse of the "laissez-faire" approach to emancipation and to the emancipated had tremendously far-reaching consequences as well. This approach, more paternalistic and "statist," was reflected in the belief that the social redemption and elevation of submerged groups would not occur through the removal of legal disabilities alone: that the state or established religious, philanthropic, or educational institutions would be required actively to bring about the integration and social adjustment of the emancipated. At the heart of this approach lay a central principle of European Enlightenment rationalism, articulated by liberal thinkers such as John Toland in England and Gotthold Ephraim Lessing in Germany during the eighteenth century, that declared the essential oneness of all human nature.[18] This principle led to the conviction on the part of social reformers that members of subordinated groups were "endowed by nature with the same capacity of becoming happier and better human beings, more useful members of society."[19] It also led social reformers to their rejection of explanations for inferiority that were based on theological concepts like Original Sin, or on racist assumptions like inborn deficiency, and moved them to conclude that the causes for the "backwardness" of the subordinated could be found in history. In other words, "backwardness," in effect, was a product of past policies governing the treatment of subordinated peoples, and it therefore was amenable to change.[20] This convinced the reformers that the human condition, no matter how debased, could be rationally altered, and human progress shared by all.

A corollary to this belief, however, was the ideological assumption that individual as well as civic and social reform was not only *possible*, but that subordinated groups, to be truly emancipated, *had to be made to change*. Thus, although the state and various religious or educational institutions associated with the dominant establishment would play an ongoing role in bringing about the reform, it was expected – indeed, it was demanded – that the members of emancipated populations adapt and conform in some degree to the values, outlooks, and ways of the emancipators. In other words, whereas this rational and enlightened approach to emancipation rejected racist and biblically determined explanations for the inferior position of subordinated peoples, its ideology was unequivocally saturated with cultural chauvinism: an unquestioned faith in the superiority of the dominant culture. According to the emancipators, the emancipated, to be truly liberated from subordination, had to "become like us."

The theoretical underpinnings for this "conversionist" approach to the civic and social "elevation" of subordinated groups – for what one might call "acculturation induced from above" – are particularly well illustrated in Christian Wilhelm von Dohm's book *Ueber die bürgerliche Verbesserung der Juden*, which was published in Berlin in 1781. The appearance of this influential work, according to the noted scholar of Jewish emancipation, Jacob Katz, marked "the commencement of the social movement for the adoption of the Jews as citizens in European countries."[21]

The term *Verbesserung* (improvement) in Dohm's title carried a double meaning. It attested, on the one hand, to the liberal-humanistic conception of the Jews as a legally and politically disadvantaged group in need of improved civic rights and incorporation into society at large. This conception built on the proposition, which Dohm articulated and developed in the book, that "the Jew is a human being even more than he is a Jew" and, as such, was entitled to "civic betterment."[22] But Dohm also judged Jews in their unemancipated state to be *culturally backward* and *inferior*, morally deficient and socially degenerate. Before they could hope for civil acceptance in the dominant mainstream, their very character as a group needed to be modified and transformed – "uplifted" from what he and many of his contemporaries viewed as their degraded character and existence. In that regard, the meaning of *Verbesserung* carried within it the notion of "culture change for-the-better" – of

an externally stimulated "self-improvement" based on the values
and convictions of the dominant society.[23]

The instrument with which Dohm and other reformers hoped to
"recast an entire people" was education. Given the rationalist faith
in the "plasticity and perfectibility" of all human beings, the Jews
were to be exposed to the positive influence of the dominant culture
and induced to change through direct and indirect tuition that was
supervised and guided by the institutions of the state.[24] The reformers correctly perceived that the traditional Jewish culture – the
supporting pillar for the unemancipated, unmodern "Jewish type"
they disliked – was transmitted from generation to generation
through the institutions of traditional Jewish religious learning: the
religious elementary schools (hadarim) and the talmudic academies
(yeshivot). For young Jews, therefore, the "recasting" was to occur
institutionally through a new kind of schooling: by requiring that
childhood and adolescent instruction in secular subjects complement
or replace the exclusive educational concentration on religious
learning. For adult Jews, it was to come about through the enactment of legislation that would both permit them to enter into economic spheres from which they had previously been shut out, and
force them to modify cultural practices associated with a "deficient"
and segregated past.[25]

Until Jews finally realized full political and legal rights in the
1860s and 1870s, the legislation and edicts promulgated in the German states and in the Austrian territories reflected the reformist
and culturally conformist assumptions inherent in the recommen-
dations made by Dohm and others like him. To varying degrees they
all carried out their prescriptions. In Berlin, Breslau, Dessau, See-
sen, Frankfurt am Main, and Wolfenbüttel, for example, as well as
in Vienna, Prague, and Pressburg, state-controlled schools were established and Jewish children were required to attend them.[26] Although these educational institutions differed from place to place in
organization, curriculum, and pedagogical methodology, they all, as
Jacob Katz has indicated, "fulfilled the same historical function: they
were instrumental in breaking the hold of the traditional program
that concentrated on Jewish subjects and taught Pentateuch and
Talmud to the exclusion of all else."[27] These schools instructed Jewish children in German and encouraged them to drop their own
vernacular. They were taught to read, write, speak, and think in
the dominant language. And they were exposed to literatures, subjects, and views of the world that had previously been denied to all
but the wealthiest and most privileged among them.

Steps were also instituted to foster and compel adult Jews to conform more closely with members of the dominant culture in appearance, speech, and conduct. Thus, bearded and "strangely costumed" Jewish men in their sidelocks, wearing the traditional head covering, were presented with an alternative model of "acceptable" attire in bourgeois society, and encouraged if not pressured to "shed the more conspicuous features of their Jewishness" in order to blend in more effectively.[28] The Edict of Tolerance in the Austrian territories, as well as legislation passed by various German governments in the course of the nineteenth century, also banned Jews from using Hebrew or their "laughable jargon," *Judendeutsch*, in business and in legal documents, and required German as the language of bookkeeping and legal transaction. In this way, Jews too old to attend the secular schools were provided with a "strong practical incentive for learning German" and stimulated to integrate themselves linguistically into the majority.[29]

To be truly worthy of the civil rights of respectable citizens, however, Jews would have to be reeducated and induced to shift from what the reformers like Dohm considered to be their greatest "moral" deficiency: their almost "exclusive occupation with trade, [and] notorious propensity for haggling and usury."[30] A key goal of *Verbesserung* in Central Europe, therefore, was the effort to "normalize" the occupational structure of Jewish society by opening the way for participation by Jews in all areas of the economy, and by discouraging their *Nothandel* – their door-to-door peddling, junk-dealing, pawnbroking, moneylending, and involvement in the so-called irregular as well as the petty trades.[31] Everywhere in the German states, emancipation laws stimulated the "productive integration" of Jews into the social mainstream by providing them access to agricultural and craft occupations from which they had previously been excluded.[32] In South Germany, Baden, Württemberg, and Electoral Hessen, Jewish "moral transformation" was encouraged by legislation that granted civil rights only as a reward for occupational "reform": upon the receipt of proof that an individual had become a peasant, craftsman, or manufacturer and had shifted from "irregular" trade into a "regular" occupation.[33]

II

In drawing these broad distinctions between the "laissez-faire" and "conversionist" approaches to the emancipatory process, it is important not to exaggerate the differences between their ultimate impact on individual members of emancipated groups. Whether the attitude toward the newly emancipated was characterized by a minimalist concern for their "transformation" and societal integration, or whether it was typified by interventionist social engineering, *some amount* of social, political, and economic contact and interaction occurred between the emancipated and members of the dominant society. No matter which attitude was predominant at a given time or place, *some degree* of social change and cultural modification resulted from such contact and interaction.

Beginning early in the nineteenth century, the word "assimilation" began to be popularly used by English-speakers to describe a particular kind of change and modification among newly emancipated peoples: one that indicated the emancipated's transformation *in the direction of* the dominant group's "culture" and their incorporation into what that group recognized as "mainstream" social and political life. In German, the words *Anpassung, Angleichung,* as well as *Assimilierung* were employed – all, like their English equivalent, expressing a general sense of "conformity," of "becoming similar" to the dominant. More specifically, they also reflected the successful execution of the approach to emancipation advocated by rationalist social reformers like Christian Wilhelm von Dohm.[34]

In fact, however, both the meaning and the reality of assimilation were much more complex than either its popular, or more specific, German, usage would indicate. Instead of the absolute, all-inclusive, and unidirectional process of cultural transformation and societal integration implied in these definitions, the term was more accurately indicative of *a process of adaptation and adjustment on a continuum.* Like emancipation, assimilation encompassed a range of responses.

According to the sociologist Milton M. Gordon, three distinct "levels" of cultural adaptation and integration that can be distinguished and analyzed separately fall within the broad definition of the term "assimilation": (1) *acculturation,* or cultural/behavioral assimilation, indicating the modification of cultural patterns and symbols by subordinate group members in conformity with those of the dominant group; (2) *structural assimilation,* describing the subordinate's large-scale entrance into institutions, associations, professions, fields of economic activity, clubs, and locales from which its members had previously been excluded; and (3) *fusion,* or *amalgamation,* referring to the final, completing, stage of the continuum, when persons from the subordinate group would merge entirely with the dominant through intermarriage, losing their previous identity by becoming virtually indistinguishable from members of the society at large. Although derived primarily from evidence and the analysis of assimilation in the United States, Gordon's typology is broadly applicable to other areas of the world, as well as to the time span considered in this book.[35]

For members of subordinate groups in Europe, Africa, and the Americas, "assimilation in the direction of the dominant group" – the assimilationist process – *always* involved certain general adjustments. Even when they drifted into the process more or less inadvertently, not fully conscious of having done so, involvement in it invariably demanded some changes in their cultural values and externally observable characteristics. It required them to learn the meaning of new symbols and redefine old ones – to modify those intrinsic cultural traits that were reflected in their religious beliefs and practices, in their ethical traditions, their historical language and sense of common historical experience, in their literature and music, and in their folklore as well as patterns of recreation. The process also involved some modification in their publicly displayed cultural traits: in their fashion or style of dress, in their public behavior, appearance, and etiquette, and in their articulation and pronunciation of the ruling group's language.[36]

But the thoroughness with which individuals carried out the "adjustments," the speed and ease with which the transformation could take place, as well as the meaning of the assimilationist process itself, depended on a number of discrete factors and varied greatly. This was true, regardless of whether the adjustments were manipulated by social engineering on the part of state officials and "establishment" agencies or whether they came about through "laissez-faire," in more haphazard fashion. Thus, the measure of "successful" assimilation depended in every case on the level along the assimilationist continuum the dominant were willing to allow or encourage the subordinate to reach, and on the willingness and ability of the subordinate to attain that level. The dominant's willingness to encourage the process to move beyond "acculturation" to "structural assimilation" and to "amalgamation" was, in turn, located within a historical context that was shaped and affected by independent social, political, economic, demographic, and ideological variables that were liable to change over time. All these variables were part of what one might call the *social climate* of emancipation and assimilation.

Throughout Europe, Africa, and the Americas in the nineteenth century, the social climate in which assimilation was situated was charged with potentially turbulent disturbances. Counterforces existed everywhere, some weak, some more powerful, others gathering sufficient force and prominence to challenge and supersede the particular conjunction of elements and conditions that had initiated and supported emancipatory efforts and permitted assimilation to develop.

The conversionist vision of the British philanthropists that had led to the "Sierra Leone experiment" at the turn of the eighteenth century, for example, and that had advocated the cultural transformation of ex-colonial slaves and of Africans liberated from slave ships into "Black English," came under virulent attack when a counter-ideology based on pseudoscientific racism began to pervade the actions and policies of British colonial officials starting in the 1860s. To be sure, even the most radical among the early British conversionist thinkers had not intended the process of African "cultural transformation" in Sierra Leone to lead to "fusion" or "amalgamation" through intermarriage or cohabitation. Nor had they intended it to provide Africans access to *every* British institution of power and authority in the colony. But the racist and increasingly segregationist reaction against "Europeanized" Africans that gained prominence in the last third of the nineteenth century attacked even this restricted vision of assimilation by challenging the most basic assumption on which conversionism rested: the belief in the inherent capabilities of Africans to be culturally "uplifted," to be "Europeanized." The reaction – the change in the social climate – came to be seen by many mission-educated, "westernized" Sierra Leoneans as a betrayal of the assimilationist promise. It led some of the most prominent African "products" of the "Sierra Leone experiment" to question the conversionist effort itself, and to reconsider their own place and role within it.[37]

Central Europe provides another example. Joseph II's "assimilationist" Edict of Tolerance of 1781, which aimed "to oblige the Jews to step out of their occupational, social, and cultural isolation," and which contained far-reaching reform measures lifting long-standing restrictions against Jews, came under attack several times after the emperor's death by rulers and officials less in sympathy with the potentialities of Jewish integration.[38] Although the edict was not revoked by his successors, the execution and supervision of many of its measures varied from reign to reign in the half-century after Joseph died, and from region to region within the Hapsburg Empire. Generally, reforms concerning the education of Jewish children continued to be instituted in accordance with the original intent of the edict, and Jews throughout the realm continued to be recognized as permanent residents and legally acknowledged as "special" citizens or subjects. But the reactionary countercurrents, never eliminated, remained a potential threat to the advances of emancipation and the possibilities of assimilation. For many Central European Jews during the last decades of the nineteenth century, the air of uncertainty in the social climate of their immediate environment was a discernible feature and an influential damper on their approach to life. Even those whom one might have judged to be most successfully integrated into the bourgeois values and outlooks of the dominant society were induced to move carefully and hesitantly along the assimilationist path.[39]

In addition to the shifting social climate in which assimilation took place, moreover, the process was everywhere affected by other personal and structural factors that influenced the ability and the willingness of individuals to undergo cultural and social changes and move into the realm of the dominant. Age, gender, personality, as well as the strength and attraction of "old" traditions, and the degree and intensity of contact with the dominant culture were among these factors.

The notion of "cultural distance" – the degree to which extrinsic customs, habits, and symbols, and intrinsic values, attitudes, and beliefs resembled each other in the subordinate and in the dominant, or "core," culture – was particularly important in determining the speed and ease of acculturation. Regardless of the personal attributes of the individual engaged in the assimilationist process, or the favorable nature of the social climate in which it took place, successful and quick adjustment to the dominant culture was largely dependent upon the basic "distance" between the "old" and the "new." When this distance was great, and acculturation involved both a major modification of externally observable characteristics and a drastic revision of the value system (as, for example, was true for *adult* Africans liberated from slavery and involved in the conversionist Sierra Leone experiment, or older *shtettl* (village)-dwelling Jews legally emancipated in Central Europe), the process of change was generally slower and more difficult than when the distance was narrower.

On the other hand, acculturation became considerably easier as the similarity between "old" and "new" cultural features increased, especially in the realm of values. Indeed, for members of the second and succeeding generations following the generation of the initial recipients of emancipation – for persons already exposed to the educational system of the dominant culture, fluent in its language, and immersed in its customs – the notion of cultural distance was often much more applicable to the gap between the cultural world into which they had moved, and with which they wished now to identify, and the "old" world of their parents and grandparents.[40]

In this regard, the existence and strength of an organic "traditional" community capable of defending its way of life against assimilationist pressures and enticements was also an important factor governing the speed and degree of culture change. Generally speaking, for example, newly arrived Liberated Africans in Sierra Leone, removed from their original homes by enslavement, had less of such a community than did persons of Temne or Mende background, who were indigenous to the colony and its immediate surroundings. Liberated Africans like Samuel Crowther or Joseph May, who went to England for study as single individuals, had less still.

The age that an individual "entered" into the assimilationist process was a key determinant of the adjustment to the dominant culture. In the case of children, methods of instruction leading to socialization into the dominant culture, and their ability to absorb and learn new cultural information, differed from that of adults. It was no accident that so much of the assimilationist effort in Central Europe and in West Africa was concentrated on the young. Pedagogic theorists and reformers who considered the problem of popular education in the last years of the *ancien régime* had perceived that children learned by two fundamentally different methods: imitation or copying, and trial and error. They believed that learning by imitation or copying – when encouraged through rewards expressed in recognition, praise, and affection – generally produced results in shorter periods of time than did trial and error. They also contended that this mimetic method of learning could be channeled into direct tuition in the schools, where the values and behavioral expectations of the dominant culture could be formally presented and reinforced.[41] This method could, moreover, be further exploited indirectly by placing children in contact with adults, teachers, and other youngsters who would serve as exemplary models for imitation.[42]

Because the acculturation process in childhood coincided with this general pattern of mimetic learning, and because it did not demand a relearning or denial of long-internalized past experience, its effect on children tended to be relatively untraumatic. The thoroughness of the process for them, therefore, ultimately tended to be more complete. For adults in the subordinate group, on the other hand, the assimilationist process was quite different. Generally in adulthood, the type of rapid, intensive, learning by imitation and copying, or by trial and error, that characterized the childhood approach often failed. It was replaced by a method of learning in which new information was fitted into, or measured against, already internalized generalizations derived from past experience. For adults living within the parameters of an "old" organic cultural community (such as a *shtettl* or ghetto), this kind of learning would tend not to be particularly disruptive in a psychological sense. It could be integrated and absorbed without, or with relatively little, challenge to the individual's long-held values, beliefs, and past associations.

In an assimilationist situation, however, where separation from a "traditional" cultural community occurred, learning was often associated with more radical cultural changes – with changes in fundamental intrinsic and extrinsic cultural traits. In such a case, generalizations derived from past experiences and associations did not normally suffice as instructional referents. In order to proceed along the assimilationist path, adults from the subordinate group were forced to "regress" to a technique of learning involving imitation, copying, trial and error, which they had largely abandoned in the process of maturation from childhood.

This type of regression, in which adults "learned" about the cultural values, expectations, behavioral patterns, and symbols of the dominant culture by again becoming dependent upon others for instruction, or by imitation – *in the way that they had learned as children* – could lead to loss of self-respect, to anxieties, and to a less thorough and more difficult transformation.[43] As Jurgen Ruesch, Annemarie Jacobson, and Martin Loeb found in their psychiatric study "Acculturation and Illness":

> For a complicated [adult] personality . . . moving into a new culture means functioning at a lower level of integration, being able to carry out partial or mechanical functions only, without understanding completely the meaning of the new value system. This deficiency obviously results in a great deal of frustration.[44]

Furthermore, both the understanding of the "meaning of the new value system" and the nature of the exposure to new cultural elements would differ considerably between children and adults entering the assimilationist process at the same time. Persons beginning the "move out of the ghetto" as adults, for example, as was common in the early stages of the Century of Emancipation in Central and Western Europe, were not directly exposed to the "culture of childhood" in the dominant society – to the social and dress conventions, games, slang expressions, and to the symbolic language unique to the young. Because they, like other adults, normally learned the new culture through participation, through their "living experience" within it, their lack of direct exposure to its childhood component tended to make their "transformation" less thorough than that of the children.[45]

But, if age and "cultural distance" were important variables in the nature of individual responses to assimilation, gender played a

perhaps even more crucial determining role. This possibility was
not immediately apparent to contemporary participants in the process, nor has it been evident to its analysts today. Many assumed
that women were involved in the assimilationist process in much
the same way as men: that assimilationist efforts to move into the
bourgeoisie during the Century of Emancipation contained similar
expectations, incentives, and drawbacks, and had the same meaning,
for women as for the men. Indeed, in the case of Jewish emancipation
and assimilation in Central and Western Europe, Jewish women
"moving out of the ghetto" seemed to enjoy an advantage over their
menfolk, and appeared to make a more thorough cultural transformation. Jacob Katz, for instance, described Jewish women's transition from ghetto to bourgeois society in the late-eighteenth and
early-nineteenth centuries as follows:

> Women according to religious tradition, were exempted and excluded from
> studying the law, the main component of the Jewish traditional curriculum.
> Women did not usually attend school; they had hardly any formal education
> but absorbed what they could from their surroundings. When enlightenment
> and secular education penetrated into Jewish society, it had to compete with
> the study of the Torah that had come traditionally to occupy the whole of
> a man's free time. This was not so in the case of women. Thus the daughters
> of the well-to-do families in the ghetto were the first to benefit from the
> new opportunities. They were the first to learn the language of their neigh-
> bors, to acquire the familiarity with foreign languages and literature. They
> were also the ones to acquire the social graces that enabled them to move
> easily in a society not limited to Jews. Men found it more difficult. It is on
> record from the time of the literary salons that some of those men whose
> wives were the life and soul of social gatherings, were too embarrassed to
> put in an appearance.[46]

But, although the acculturation of Jewish women into the dominant mainstream might have been easier and more thorough in this
Central European example, the meaning of the assimilationist process itself – what the women expected from it – differed from that
of men in this case as much as in all others. Certainly, both for men
and women emerging from subordination, emancipation meant liberation from the traditional communal as well as externally imposed
social restrictions that had constrained opportunities for economic
and social mobility, and inhibited ascension into the middle class.
Both perceived it as a starting gate on the road leading into the
world of the dominant. Both took as their positive frame of reference
the values and norms of successful individuals who already belonged
to that world, and both seemed also to have recognized the corre-
lation between assimilation and upward mobility.

For the men, however, the meaning of emancipation and assimilation carried as its corollary the *promise* of eventual inclusion in *all* those spheres of public activity recognized as lying within the realm of men's privilege and right. In effect, many came to *expect* the path that had been opened for them to extend the range of social opportunities – the spectrum of options – from which they would choose. The attainment of formal education was only one such opportunity, which would provide them with the means to adapt culturally to their surroundings. But, having selected *males* belonging to the dominant society as their reference group for success, they also expected their own conformity to dominant-life styles and values to bring them acceptance and to allow them to *move into the recognized male spheres*: beyond economic activities associated with their subordinated past, into the professions, the arts, and even into the arena of politics.

The women, of course, journeyed into the bourgeois class, into the world of the dominant, in tandem with men. On many occasions, they greatly facilitated class ascension through the dowries they brought into their marriages and the economic alliances they helped to forge.[47] Like the men entering the bourgeoisie, moreover, the women adopted the manner of living and the garments appropriate to middle-class society in their respective countries. Increasingly in Europe, as they became able to afford the costs involved, they took advantage of the material benefits associated with bourgeois life; rented apartments or purchased houses in the "better" neighborhoods; filled them with solid furnishings and a mass of objects symbolic of their status and achievement; and spent leisurely hours at entertainments, afternoon teas, cultural offerings, or strolling on the avenues or in the parks. Some, as in Jacob Katz's example, became central intellectual figures in literary salons.[48] Others, as Egon Schwarz has argued to have been the case in Austria, were "more highly cultured" than their husbands, and "filled ... [their] children with a fanatic love for German culture and for German literature."[49]

But, although the women moved "out of the ghetto" and "up from slavery" in harmony with their men in the physical and material sense, the meaning of their experience was influenced by the development and enhancement of an ideological construct that differentiated between the sexes in the delineation of options. As a consequence of this construct, they were socialized into thinking that their choices, opportunities, and goals fell within a separate sphere of activity: a "domestic" or "familial" sphere distinct from the "public" sphere, which, theoretically at least, allowed men access to social privilege, authority, and esteem.[50] Whether in British West Africa, where both a Victorian and indigenous African notion of a gender-based division of labor was transmitted to the Sierra Leone Creoles, or in Brazil, where the nineteenth century's evolving view of separate spheres was supported by an older Iberian tradition of male dominance, or in Austria, where the roots of the notion were also deeply implanted in past inequities between the sexes, women emerging from ghetto or slave inferiority into the culture of the dominant internalized and accepted the idea of themselves as "the good angel of the house, the mother, wife and mistress." They subordinated themselves to their spouses in the public sphere, and provided the domestic anchor of stability in the home on which bourgeois family life was believed to rest.[51]

The ideology delineating sex roles and the division of labor into separate spheres was sustained with biological explanations based on women's reproductive and maternal functions, and was reinforced with the manipulation of sexual symbols to affirm women's "natural place within the home" as a necessary complement to the more competitive world of men.[52] This ideology was also supported institutionally in a variety of ways. Throughout the nineteenth century, for instance, the primary-school educational curriculum for Liberated African and Creole females in Sierra Leone featured instruction in manual skills related to housework, and placed less emphasis on academic subjects and the training associated with male endeavors.[53]

In Brazil, female education was even less academically oriented than in West Africa. The formal education of poor girls was virtually nonexistent; for middle- or upper-class girls, it was left in the hands of private, domestic, and religious instructors who stressed domestic duties and religious devotion. In the words of a contemporary observer, J. Pinto de Campos: "The new education for women today is exclusively that of dances, receptions, display; and those [women] who live outside the cities, or are not wealthy, vegetate in ignorance due to the concept that woman *per se* is nothing."[54]

And throughout Western and Central Europe until the 1870s — in England, France, Germany, and Austria — gender divisions structured on the polarity between private and public, home and workplace, were fortified by women's virtual exclusion from higher education and by the prescription of "correct" feminine values and behavior in textbooks and instructional materials.[55]

For most women, therefore, the meaning of emancipation and assimilation did not include the same corollary promise as it did for the men. Unlike "assimilating" men, *women did not expect their passage into the world of the dominant to include access to that world's prestigious sphere of public and professional activity.* Confined to their own sphere by the evolving ideology of capitalism and the social structuring of gender roles, they sought to fulfill their aspirations for the status and material advantages of life through their fathers, husbands, and sons.

III

It is important to stress that, even in those situations in Europe, Africa, and the Americas where assimilationism was not an articulated ideological component of emancipation, individuals attempted and succeeded in making the move from subordination into the world of the dominant. In nineteenth and early twentieth-century Brazil, for example, despite officialdom's laissez-faire attitude and the harsh economic difficulties encountered by the vast majority of emancipated slaves and their offspring, many Afro-Brazilians did manage to improve their status as well as economic situation and penetrate into the ranks of the bourgeoisie.[56] They did so by moving on a path marked by prescriptions that were universally characteristic of assimilationism: through a modification of intrinsic and extrinsic cultural traits associated with the inferior existence they wished to leave behind. They often also did so by what the Brazilians term *embranquecemento*: by consciously or unconsciously engaging in a progressive effort to transform "black into white" through miscegenation and intermarriage. In this way, they provided their physically "lighter" offspring with the possibility to "escape" the racial identification associated with slavery and subordination.[57]

Whether assimilationism was actively stimulated by members of the dominant establishment, however, or initiated through the exertions of the subordinated, engagement in the process per se involved no attack on the structural arrangements that characterized the world into which newly emancipated peoples were entering, and in which fundamental economic and social inequalities among groups remained deeply ingrained. The assimilationist effort, as such, always had reformist rather than revolutionary goals. For subordinated individuals, it generally reflected an attempt to *join* and *gain acceptance* in the system as *defined by the dominant* – to move in some degree from the status of "outsider" to that of "insider." The dynamic force behind their effort derived from the promise of personal-status rewards in the future, and of social and situational improvements for their children and grandchildren.

The actual extent to which persons engaged in the assimilationist process identified with the dominant world also depended, of course, on factors of social climate – on the "historical moment" – and on many of the same personal and structural variables that influenced the thoroughness of their acculturation and place within the assimilationist continuum. But ultimately it depended on individual goals and expectations for emancipation and the assimilationist effort, and the *perceptions* each person had of his or her place within the social world *in relation to these expectations*. Consequently, individual orientations toward the dominant group – the extent to which it became the group with which the individual primarily identified – could vary from person to person.[58] It was certainly not unusual for persons to be engaged in the assimilationist process while maintaining, as Marsha Rozenblit has argued to have been the case for some Viennese Jews, a primary identification with the group from which they stemmed.[59] It was, however, also typical for assimilating individuals to disassociate themselves from their "origins" in part or whole. They rejected their "older" primary identity that was based on ethnic, religious, or racial commonality, and identified with others primarily on the basis of common educational or professional background, similar interests, tastes, and economic situation – on the basis, in other words, of those shared values and experiences that define social class.

Because, moreover, individual perceptions and expectations were "interwoven with history" – influenced and affected by the historical circumstances in which the assimilating individuals found themselves – individual orientations and identities were prone to change over time.[60] Persons who during one moment in their life history might feel comfortable and satisfied with their situation, perceive their future life-chances with great optimism, and identify thoroughly with the world of the dominant, might at another moment perceive themselves to be blocked or excluded from that world by prejudice or discrimination, and undergo a disturbing crisis of identity.

Both the nature of that crisis and the responses that it engendered were in no sense uniform. As in responses to the assimilationist process, factors such as age, gender, and race affected how they were expressed and manifested. But they did so in relation to the duration and intensity of the perceived blockage or exclusion. The life histories of members of three families – the West African May family, the Afro-Brazilian Rebouças family, and the Central European, Jewish Zweig family – illustrate both the complexity of the assimilationist experience in the Century of Emancipation, and the spectrum of responses of individuals who, perceiving themselves to be "ineligible aspirants" in the world of the dominant, realized their own situational marginality.

Chapter 2

Up from Slavery:
The May Story

...and now more than ever I think with admiration of the missionaries and schoolteachers, who, with their good wives, have all the trouble of rough-polishing these wild native children and fashioning them into that which, however removed from our ideas of what is useful and industrious, is still strikingly superior to the rudeness, ignorance, and indolence of their aboriginal state.

Elizabeth Melville, *A Residence at Sierra Leone* (1849)

On one occasion two or three of them came to me...saying that since the preaching of the other evening their house seems to be on fire, and their bodies in its flame burning, in their souls there is neither peace nor rest, but crying, Oh! Oh! what must we do to be delivered: I therefore taught them to give up all their idols, to forsake all their sin, to repent and believe in the Lord Jesus Christ, who alone is able to wash them with his blood from all their filthiness.

Letter from Joseph May, "Liberated African,"
to the Reverend Hoole, 18 December 1846

I

If the youth is indeed "father of the Man," as Wordsworth proclaims, this relationship was hardly perceptible between the thirty-year-old Joseph Boston May, newly appointed Native Wesleyan Methodist minister in Sierra Leone colony, and Ifacayeh, the Yoruba boy liberated from slavery in Freetown twenty years earlier. By the year 1847, as he was about to enter the missionary field in the Gambia after resigning as principal teacher in the highly regarded New Town West School, which he had worked hard to establish, Joseph May appeared to have rejected his earlier identity and to have become a successful member of the "black bourgeoisie" in a colonial society ruled by the British. He had changed into what his white contemporaries in Europe and Sierra Leone would describe as a "civilized African" – a person distinguished from the "common African" masses by education, conversion to Christianity, and by his

40

outward conformity to a pattern of life that was Europeanized in essence, if not totally European in detail.

The particular transformation that Ifacayeh/Joseph May underwent during this twenty-year period was of course unique to his own life experience and to the circumstances in which he found himself. But the process of assimilation – his adaptation in the direction of the dominant ideology and culture – was also reflective of a more general and widespread response of people cast as subordinates or minorities in the encounter between groups of diverse racial, religious, and ethnic backgrounds. The incentives, both personal and external, that stimulated May to seek admission to the world of the dominant had their parallels throughout Africa, America, Europe, and Asia. In this respect, an examination of his life history and its comparison with that of other assimilating individuals permits a clearer understanding of the nature of the assimilationist process itself.

• • •

Two decades after his arrival in Freetown, the Reverend Joseph May expressed himself primarily in Yoruba to fellow Liberated Africans in Sierra Leone whose ethnic background was similar to his own.[1] Through its structure and vocabulary – its kinship terminology, its forms of address, and its images – Yoruba provided him with a potential link to a cultural reality that was different from the version privileged by the white missionaries and officials in the colony. But, although he must certainly have appreciated the intricacy of his "mother tongue" and those aspects of a transposed Yoruba culture that resonated positively with the memories of his own childhood upbringing in Iwarreh, his use of the Yoruba language at this time in his life was clearly functional. It facilitated what had come to be his prime calling: his task as teacher and disseminator of the Christian message to recently emancipated persons from his old home area.

He had learned to consider English as the "proper" medium of communication in the multiethnic Sierra Leone environment, and to rank it above all other languages. He spoke in English with the white inhabitants of the colony, and wrote in this language to them and others, always in the neat, well-formed, and disciplined handwriting that the missionaries had taught him.[2] His use of English had improved considerably since he returned from London in 1841, after eighteen months of sponsored study at the Borough Road Training College of the British and Foreign Mission School Society. Rarely now did he make the grammatical errors in writing or employ the awkward phraseology that are associated with the half-learned or with those to whom English is a foreign language. If anything, his syntax had become almost overprecise – attesting, perhaps, to the care he took to discourage any possible criticism of his literacy and educational competence. For him, as for so many others removed from slavery and a past associated with inferiority, mastery over the spoken and written language of the dominant symbolically confirmed his ascension in status. It also affirmed his new identity.[3]

Indeed, by mid-century, few outward distinctions remained between May and his colleagues, the white Methodist missionaries in Sierra Leone. Like them, he dressed in clerical garb imported from England: black ankle boots, stockings, narrow wool trousers, white shirt topped by a stiff ecclesiastical collar, wool vest, and dark single-breasted overcoat of medium length. This clothing was undoubtedly hot and uncomfortable in the tropical climate of Africa's western coast, but it clearly proclaimed him to belong to the colony's "respectable" citizenry. As was also fashionable with many members of the clergy, he had his hair cut short, with the suggestion of a part on the side, and sported a neatly trimmed chin beard. Highlighted by the narrow, elliptical, gold-rimmed spectacles that he wore after his return from London, these features provided him with the dignified and solemn appearance that, nowadays, is almost stereotypically associated with men of his calling. Only the color of his skin and the physical traits associated with his race marked him externally as clearly different from the whites – a difference perhaps that, at this point in time, would have seemed less relevant to him than the characteristics that distinguished him from the "Unto Whom," the "ignorant, illiterate, pagan Africans... unto whom God swore in his wrath, that they should not enter into his rest."[4]

Having been educated by his missionary mentors to view African religion as superstition, and his previous existence in Yoruba as benighted, he was by mid-century a fervent enemy of "heathen" practices – of what he termed "sin and iniquity, misery and wretchedness."[5] He described New Town West, the area of Freetown where he lived for the greater part of the 1840s as a "place of infamy and degradation" where "idolatery [sic] and superstition abound to a great extent; polygamy, adultery, and fornication are practiced, [and] indolence and profound ignorance [are] displayed."[6] He attested to the genuineness of his own religious conversion by preaching the gospel of Christ to "unenlightened" Africans – even before he formally entered the ministry. And he displayed his missionary zeal by smashing wood carvings and ceremonial objects associated with traditional African religious worship whenever he encountered them.[7]

His activities during these mid-century years, and his relationship both with the British and with Africans in Sierra Leone, implied that he had absorbed a crucial component of the bourgeois ethic of his European models: the belief that success is due to personal merit and is achieved through a combination of abstinence and sustained effort.[8] He had learned to link education and upward social mobility and, as a resident in a colony where missionaries were responsible for secular as well as religious instruction, he clearly seemed to connect Christianity with educational enlightenment.[9] But he had recognized and accepted hard work as the key ingredient of this formula, and continued to apply himself with energy and discipline to the tasks and opportunities in his life. Certainly, his strenuous working habits – the long hours he dedicated to his own "self-improvement" and to teaching and proselytizing his adopted faith – contradicted popular European ideas about the indolence of tropical peoples and confirmed the obverse: that all men and women, no matter how humble their origin, could lift themselves through personal effort "out of the slough of demoralization on to the firm plateau of respectability."[10]

Serious, sober, highly disciplined, and methodical, he displayed the drive of a person eager to make a mark in the world and the restraint of someone determined not to be distracted by frivolity. Puritanical about "excesses of the flesh," he had returned from England as a confirmed teetotaler. An advocate of total abstinence from alcohol, he founded a Temperance Society in the colony, taught his pupils to sing "Away, away the bowl," and demonstrated through the example of his own character that it was possible to rise above the "wicked habits" of nonbelievers. "The wicked shall be turned into Hell," he had already written in 1838 to attest to his conviction. "I must be born again. Must be born again without doubt or else I shall not enter the kingdom of God."[11]

To supplement his temperance activities, and to buttress his standing as a "respectable" member of Sierra Leone's black colonial elite, May also became involved in a variety of social organizations and in projects that reflected his concerns for personal "betterment." He belonged to the National Benevolent Society and the Yoruba Society, which were Liberated African mutual-aid organizations; the Union Society, made up of small-scale African merchandise importers on whose behalf May helped to establish direct trading and credit arrangements with an English business house in London; and an informal association of Wesleyan schoolmasters who met on a monthly basis to discuss mutual concerns. He also organized a Yoruba Improvement Class, geared not toward the study and mastery

of his native language for its own sake, but to the attempt to establish a standard Yoruba orthography into which the translated
message of the gospel could be set, written down, and used more
effectively to enlighten and teach recently liberated Africans from
Yoruba-speaking regions.[12]

After his return from England, moreover, his respectability was
reinforced through his marriage to Ann Wilberforce, a young assistant teacher at the New Town West School.[13] His wife, unlike May,
had never been enslaved and was a Sierra Leone Creole. She had
been born and raised in the colony, the daughter of Betsy Ricket
and William Wilberforce, long-resident Christian Liberated Africans of upstanding repute.[14] Ann complemented Joseph in significant ways. She shared many of his values: the belief in hard work,
in personal improvement through effort and education, and in Christian salvation. As one of her sons observed after her death, she
labored along with her spouse "in all the circuits in which he trav-
elled."[15] She apparently fulfilled Joseph's dictum that wives "always
prove obedient and respectful to their husbands." She also supported
the notion of woman's "proper" place, which Sierra Leone's white
colonial masters idealized in their households, by subordinating her
sphere of activities to his at all times.[16]

In New Town West, she took charge of female academic instruction
and ran a successful evening school, in which she taught sewing,
marking, and sampling – manual skills considered basic to the transformation of young women into genteel ladies. When she gave birth
to Joseph Claudius May in 1845, the first of the couple's nine children, she retired from teaching. She then devoted herself entirely
to domestic and motherly duties and to the work of Christian prose-
lytism. Leaving few personal traces to detail her life history for
future reconstruction, she died in 1872 in middle age and faded into
the silent background of fond memory.[17]

II

Had Joseph Boston May looked into a mirror at this time in the
mid-1840s and thought back to his childhood and early life, he could
not have failed to note the profound contrast between the person he
had become and the one he had been. From his vantage point as a
mission-educated Christian convert, he would undoubtedly have
been pleased with his personal metamorphosis.

He was born, probably in 1817, in a place he described in an
autobiographical account as a "heathen nation, a country full of
Idolatry."[18] His birthplace was a town named Iwarreh [Iware] ("the

larger of two towns of the same name"), a few miles from the banks of the river Ogun, in the southeastern district of the Old Oyo Empire – in the predominantly Yoruba-speaking area of what is now the Republic of Nigeria.[19] His father, Loncola [Lonkólá], a diviner-priest (*babaláwo*) dedicated to the Yoruba god of divination, Ifá, named him Ifacayeh in honor of the deity.[20] His mother, Manlawa [Mon'lawa], whom he described as "a woman of good constitution, and a kind and peaceful disposition," was the second of Loncola's three wives, and Ifacayeh was the second-oldest of her four children.[21]

The Old Oyo Empire, by the second decade of the nineteenth century, was near collapse. The convulsions associated with its disintegration created an atmosphere of anxiety and fear among a citizenry whose personal safety was increasingly threatened by roaming gangs of bandits, kidnappers, and slave raiders.[22] The situation was in marked contrast to the security and stability that had characterized the core of the empire in the past. At its height in the seventeenth and eighteenth centuries, Oyo had encompassed an area larger than modern Switzerland, nearly the size of Nova Scotia, and had a population of well over a million inhabitants.[23] Dominated by its capital, Oyo-Ile, a great walled city on the edge of the highlands in the northeastern corner of the empire, the economic basis for Old Oyo's power derived from trade – from the direct and indirect profits its rulers earned on the exchange of local products and enslaved persons for European goods from the coast, and for horses, leather articles, salt, and other items from the north.[24]

During this period of greatness, the divine kings, the Alafins at Oyo-Ile, were able to claim suzerainty over Yoruba peoples and kings in the rain-forest area immediately to the south of Ifacayeh's birthplace. Their power was most effectively established in the physically more gentle and rolling country covered with low savanna woodland where communication was easier, closer administrative supervision of outlying districts was enhanced, and where they were able to employ their formidable cavalry to assert control over trade routes and maintain order and cohesion.[25]

It was precisely this order and security that disappeared along with Old Oyo's unity as the central authority of the empire began to decline toward the end of the reign of Alafin Abiodun, in the late eighteenth century. Following the example of Ilorin, whose ruler Afonja had successfully defied the Alafin by declaring the independence of his province, chiefs of other large towns and provinces within the empire asserted their right to be independent of the political and economic domination of Oyo-Ile.[26] In the fierce struggle for power that ensued, the Alafin lost the support of the cavalry, a loss that was paralleled by the emergence of local armies to support regional or provincial claims. These armies fought not only with Oyo-Ile's soldiers, or with each other, but also crisscrossed the land pillaging towns and villages, raiding for captives who would be held for ransom or sold into slavery.

The situation became even more ominous in the 1820s, when the rebellious Ilorin province fell under the control of Muslim Hausa and Fulbe forces loyal to the neighboring Sokoto Caliphate. These Muslims turned the province into an outpost for the extension into Old Oyo of the Hausa-Fulbe *jihad*, the reformist Islamic religious revolution that had been unfolding for more than two decades in the savanna-steppe region northeast of the empire.[27] Instead of stimulating unity among the citizens of Old Oyo to face this Muslim threat, the collapse of Oyo-Ile's central authority, and the heightened unrest and insecurity that accompanied it, triggered a state of near-panic among the general population. In the course of the disturbances during these "lawless times," many towns in the empire were destroyed or abandoned as the inhabitants fled to seek refuge in the seemingly safer areas in the rain forest. Even the capital, Oyo-Ile, was forsaken and a new one established, at the site of the present city of New Oyo, some eighty miles to the south. The contrast between the great age of the Old Oyo Empire and this era of decline was captured in the text of a Yoruba song:

> In Abiodun's day we weighed our money
> in calabashes,
> In Awole's reign we packed up and fled.[28]

Young Ifacayeh's father, Loncola, attempted to respond to the threatening situation that prevailed in the mid-1820s in the neighborhood of Iwarreh by moving his family to temporary but apparently safer residences elsewhere. He sent his second wife, Manlawa, and her children, including Ifacayeh, who was then about ten years old, to live with the mother's brother in Ikotto – evidently the town from which Manlawa had originated.[29] It is unclear why Ikotto seemed safer to him as a haven for these members of his family household than Iwarreh. Like other towns in the empire, Iwarreh and Ikotto were probably both encircled by at least one wall, perhaps as high as twenty feet, and by a deep trench to discourage access other than through the various gates, where tolls were normally collected from transient traders and market people. Ikotto may, however, have been better sited naturally for defensive purposes than Iwarreh, and may also have enjoyed the protection of a "home forest"

(*Igbo Ile*), a bush or thicket surrounding the town that offered additional security against a sudden cavalry attack.[30]

The defenses, in any case, were insufficient. Ikotto, together with Iwarreh, and the neighboring towns of Okiti, Ajerun, and Ajabe, in the Epo district, were captured in the late months of the year 1825 by the warriors of Ojo Amepo, an independent Muslim Yoruba raider who had been one of the military chiefs of the secessionist ruler of Ilorin province, Afonja.[31] Ojo Amepo, described in the oral traditions as "a good horseman and intrepid warrior," had fled Ilorin at the head of a small army after the fall and death of Afonja. He established himself in Akese, in the heartland of the Epo region, an area that then was ostensibly still under the control of Oyo Ile, and within the Old Oyo Empire.[32] Without authorization from the Alafin in Oyo-Ile, he assumed the title of *Are Ona Kakamfo* (commander in chief of the imperial military forces) and conducted widespread raids in Epo towns for captives whose redemption or sale afforded him the revenue to purchase horses for his cavalry as well as to supply and increase his fighting forces.[33]

Ifacayeh, together with his mother, brother, and sisters, were taken captive after Ikotto fell to Ojo's raiders.[34] Little detail is known about the event, except that the town "was unexpectedly besieged one night and broken up" – an understated description by the adult May of what must certainly have been a frightening, if not traumatic, experience in the life of the boy Ifacayeh.[35] If we are to judge from the recollections of other Yoruba who were captured and enslaved during this same turbulent period in West African history, raids such as this one were bloody and cruel, and not at all mitigated by the fact that predators and victims shared a common language and many religious and social values.[36] As witnessed by Samuel Ajayi Crowther, who was enslaved in 1821 as a boy of about fifteen when his hometown, Osogun, was beset by Muslim Yoruba warriors, and by Joseph Wright, who was taken away from his parents in Egba country at about the same time and at nearly the same age as Ifacayeh, the raiders preferred young and healthy captives for their obvious attractiveness as productive slaves, and excluded the rest, many of them violently. This meant that "little children, little girls, young men, and young women" were taken away, while "the aged and old people," the infirm, and the very young were left behind, sometimes abandoned or killed. Hunted by the raiders, those who were caught were led away "in the manner of goats tied together," with a noose of rope around their neck.[37] Families were forcibly separated and sometimes brutally divided among the victorious raiders, to be sold to different owners living in disparate places.

In Ifacayeh's case, the horror of the raid and the fright of captivity may have been momentarily surpassed by the good news that his father had not been taken by Ojo's men, and that the *babaláwo* had come to the raiders' camp to ransom Manlawa and the children. But Loncola's resources were insufficient to redeem both his wife and the four offspring, and he arranged to leave Ifacayeh behind with his captors, promising to return the following morning with the ransom for him as well.

How accurately the adult May remembered the details of this arrangement – how much of his description of the situation was a rationalization for what might have been a failing on the part of his father – it is impossible to judge. It is clear, however, that the ensuing farewell from his mother, father, brother, and sisters marked the beginning of a major transformation in the young boy's life. Except for a brief encounter with one of his sisters many years later in Bathurst, he was never to see any of them again.[38]

Before daybreak, and before his father could reach the place where Ifacayeh had been left, the boy was taken to another town – "carried," as he recalled, "to a very far country" [a long distance away] – and sold into domestic slavery.[39] He then lived in the household of his "owner" "as one of his four children" for nearly a year in what was probably a situation of relatively benign subordination.[40] But in June 1826, after his master's material circumstances apparently declined, he was sold again. His new owner also kept him as a domestic slave, but "professed to love him as his own child," and made him the "*aggeah*, or favorite." All the while, Ifacayeh continued to cherish the hope of one day being redeemed by his father.[41] After some three months, however, when the rainy season began to ease and journeys on foot again became possible, his master took Ifacayeh to a town five days distant and inexplicably sold him – this time not into domestic slavery, but to a merchant involved in the long-distance slave trade to the coast.

For Ifacayeh, the shock of this nightmarish experience – his forced passage from one existence into another – was profound. Later in life, he vividly recalled how bitterly he had wept during these months after being left "a helpless child among perfect strangers," and stressed the deep longing he had felt for his parents, relatives, and native country upon realizing that he would never see them again.[42] Having stripped him of his freedom, his captors proceeded to strip him of the most distinctive element of his past identity as well: his name. They renamed him Ojo, a Yoruba name normally given to a child born with the umbilical cord twined around his head but, in Ifacayeh's case, an obviously cruel joke referring to the cord of captivity with which he was tied to other slaves by the neck.[43]

In late September or early October 1826, during the transition from the late rainy to the early dry season, Ifacayeh and other slaves destined for sale abroad were marched in a guarded caravan in the direction of the coast. The exact course of the journey, which was several days in duration, is unclear. But the boy recalled passing many towns and villages, and traversing a "great forest" until he and his companions reached the Lagos lagoon. "The rays of the setting sun at evening fell upon the waters," he remembered later, presenting "an appearance which I had never seen before, and which filled my mind with terror."[44] Herded onto canoes to cross the lagoon, he was brought to Badagry, the "large slave barracoon ... where the Portugues [*sic*] are."[45] There, he was sold to a "big man" named Adalay, and confined for three weeks until he and his fellow captives were sold again – this time, indeed, to a Portuguese slave dealer.[46]

It is probable that this purchaser was the first white person Ifacayeh had ever seen. No doubt the encounter was a terrifying one. He had heard from other captives that the Portuguese bought people "and carried them to eat in their own country" – a rumor that he believed because the Europeans purchased only men, women, and children who were physically "fair, nice, and beautiful."[47] He spent the next three months confined in a barracoon in much misery, fearful of the future, uncertain of the past. The Portuguese merchant initially had him brought and locked into a yard with two men, both of whom were confined by shackles. Being young, and probably considered harmless, he was at first left loose and he "made himself serviceable by giving water and rendering aid to those who were in fetters" – prisoners whose numbers increased almost daily as the Badagry Portuguese filled their paddock of slaves in anticipation of incoming ships. Soon the number of captives increased to one hundred, and Ifacayeh too was fettered and made to wear an iron collar on his neck. By the time their numbers swelled to over three hundred some weeks later, the heat of the dry season must have made the crowded conditions of the yard nearly unbearable.[48]

Although the horrors he witnessed and experienced during this period would presumably have remained firmly imprinted on his mind throughout his life, the adult Joseph May provided few details to describe conditions in the barracoon. According to Samuel Ajayi Crowther, however, who had endured a similar tribulation a few years earlier:

Men and boys were at first chained together, with a chain of about six fathoms in length, thrust through an iron fetter on the neck of every individual, and fastened at both ends with padlocks. In this situation the boys suffered the most: the men sometimes, getting angry, would draw the chain so violently, as seldom went without bruises on their poor little necks;

especially the time to sleep, when they drew the chain so close to ease themselves its weight, in order to be able to lie more conveniently, that we were almost suffocated, or bruised to death, in a room with one door, which was fastened as soon as we entered in, with no other passage for communicating the air, than the openings under the eaves-drop. Very often at night, when two or three individuals quarreled or fought, the whole drove suffered punishment, without any distinction... The female sex fared not much better.[49]

In January 1827 the Brazilian slave-brigantine *Dois Amigos* arrived on the coast, and Ifacayeh and his companions were readied for embarkation. Their intended destination was Salvador, Bahia.[50] Chained one to the other by the neck, they were released from the yard, taken across the Ossa lagoon on canoes, and forced to walk to the beach where the loading boats waited. But, before setting off, Ifacayeh and the others had to suffer yet another painful indignity: they were all branded on the right arm or chest with a red-hot iron – imprinted with a burn-mark that identified both their owner and their subordinate status. Ifacayeh's letter, "T," which became visible and indelible in a few days, remained distinct on his chest to the day of his death.[51]

"I was in a most deplorable state," May later recalled, as he and the other enslaved men, women, and children were packed aboard the ship, "bitter weeping and mourning" for his parents, relatives, and friends, not knowing "where I am going and what shall become of poor me."[52] Conditions aboard the *Dois Amigos* were deplorable. On three previous occasions, in 1815, 1816, and again in 1824, this brig had been intercepted on the high seas by British naval patrols belonging to the Anti-Slavery Squadron, and its human cargo released in Freetown, Sierra Leone colony.[53] Its owners and captain had attempted to overcome the financial losses incurred each time this happened by increasing the number of slaves carried in subsequent voyages: from under 100 in 1815, to 148 in 1816, to 255 in 1824, to 317 in 1827, when Ifacayeh was aboard.[54] This living freight was "packed promiscuously in the hold, like bales of goods," and only occasionally, and in turns, permitted to stretch and breathe fresh air on deck. Under the intense heat and the close and putrid air of confinement, many of Ifacayeh's companions fell ill. Nine died.[55]

The luck of the *Dois Amigos*, however, remained bad. The start of the voyage to Bahia was slow, impeded by stormy seas and unfavorable winds, and, given the brig's past experiences with the British navy, the captain must undoubtedly have worried about encountering and eluding the warships of the antislavery patrol. If he had any such fears, they would have been intensified some ten or twelve days out of Badagry, when he and the crew sighted a vessel heading in their direction. He attempted to avoid the course of the oncoming ship and to outrun it by "spread[ing] all possible canvas to fly before her." But it was to no avail: the two-masted slave brigantine was no match in speed for the naval cruiser, which was by then clearly giving chase. When it became evident that the pursuer was one of His Britannic Majesty's ships-of-war, the slaves aboard the Brazilian ship "were informed that sea-robbers were after them and they were to be very quiet" – perhaps a desperate, and futile, last attempt by the captain to hide his cargo and present his ship as a vessel involved in legitimate trade.

The ruse failed. HMS *Esk*, under the command of Captain William Jardine Purchase, overtook the *Dois Amigos* at about sundown of the day the two had first encountered each other, and the crew boarded and captured the slaver soon after, apparently without meeting any resistance. Some days later, on February 8, 1827, the cruiser with brigantine in tow entered the harbor of Freetown, on the Sierra Leone peninsula, and Ifacayeh along with 307 survivors of the long ordeal on land and sea arrived at King Jimmy's Wharf.

III

Although no portrait or description of Ifacayeh exists to illustrate his appearance or illuminate his outlook when he was first put on shore in the British colony of Sierra Leone in 1827, the boy who landed in Freetown was probably little different from other Africans freshly liberated from slave vessels. Like them, one assumes, he arrived naked or nearly naked, half-starved from the voyage, and terribly frightened. He was far from home and kin, in a mountainous alien land, confused by events, and uncertain of his fate. The King's Yard – the large walled camp to which he and his shipmates were brought after the landing, and in which they lived for weeks until they were registered and resettled throughout the Sierra Leone colony – must, upon first encounter, have closely resembled the miserable Badagry barracoon in which he had been imprisoned prior to sailing.[56] The inscription over the gate, "Royal Hospital and Asylum for Africans Rescued From Slavery by British Valour and Philanthropy," would have been meaningless to the illiterate boy.[57] The white men and women with whom he came into contact, speaking a different language from that of the sailors on the *Dois Amigos*, must have seemed strange and, perhaps, as worrisome to him as the "Portuguese" slavers who had purchased him. Accounts exist of

other emancipated African children who, months after their resettlement in Sierra Leone, dreaded being left alone with Europeans
– still harboring the fear of being killed and eaten.[58]

Indeed, one wonders exactly how Ifacayeh and other captives re-
acted to their "recapture" by British antislavery patrols – to the
high-sea seizure of the vessel on which they were being shipped,
their transportation to Freetown, and confinement in the King's
Yard. Uninformed about the circumstances surrounding these actions, Ifacayeh and the others might certainly have believed the
Brazilian sailors' ruse that the British were "sea-robbers," intent on
stealing the slaves for themselves. He would then probably have
responded in much the same way as did Samuel Ajayi Crowther,
his fellow Oyo national and future mentor, who reported "little initial difference between the British seizure of his slave ship and the
many other transfers he had undergone during the period following
his original capture."[59] What the British proudly referred to as their
humanitarian "liberation" of slaves, and saw as the beginning of a
process in which freed blacks would be "civilized and Christianized,"
was thus initially perceived by at least some of the ex-slaves themselves as nothing more than yet another exchange of masters.

Traumatic as Ifacayeh's experiences since his captivity at Ikotto
and separation from his kinfolk must have been, however, he was
not a *tabula rasa* when he arrived at Sierra Leone in 1827. Uprooted
from his home, sold into bondage, marched, imprisoned, branded,
and shipped on a storm-ridden sea to an uncertain fate, his psychological disorientation was no doubt great when he entered the King's
Yard to begin a new life. But, never having been outside of a predominantly Yoruba cultural environment – even on the slave ship,
where his African companions spoke his mother tongue – he did
bring with him to Sierra Leone the imprint of the world in which
he grew up. His cultural identity and orientation, though jarred by
the ordeal that he had endured, remained that of the boy who had
grown up in a small town within the Old Oyo Empire.

Virtually nothing concrete, of course, is known about the details
of Ifacayeh's life prior to his captivity. The adult Joseph Boston May
supplied little information in his written recollections about his
natal cultural environment or upbringing in Iwarreh. In contrast
to the much fuller accounts of his enslavement and liberation, his
reticence to discuss his earlier life suggest a perhaps deliberate
attempt to avoid recalling painful memories of childhood abandonment, and to obliterate his connection with a past that, as an adult,
he had come to view as unenlightened.

When he set foot in Sierra Leone, Ifacayeh was able to communicate only in Yoruba – a language of rich imagery and great subtlety that naturally reflected the physical and social environment of his homeland – and his perception and understanding of his new situation would certainly have been shaped by this fact. He was illiterate, in the sense that his native language was still an unwritten one, but he was definitely not uneducated. The Yorubaspeaking people regarded childhood education as fundamental to a successful adult life and to the maintenance of the social order; they viewed it as a means through which the individual was made useful to himself or herself and, more importantly certainly, to the community at large. Like other children born into a culture with a strong oral tradition, he would have been instructed by his parents and elders in the rules, values, and beliefs of the world in which he grew up.[60]

From his father, Loncola, a *babaláwo* of Ifá, Ifacayeh would presumably have learned a great deal directly and through observation. *Babaláwo* literally translates from Yoruba as "father of the secrets," and priest-diviners of Ifá were required to train for many years, memorizing a vast body of poetic literature (*ese Ifá*) and divinatory material in order to "talk to the divinity" and play the role of physicians, psychologists, philosophers, and historians for the community in which they belonged.[61] Ifacayeh, although probably too young at the time of his capture to have been directly taught any of the deeper mysteries of the Ifá priesthood – mysteries that oftentimes passed from father to son – was in all likelihood exposed through observation of his father to the rituals of the deity in whose honor he had been named, and to the divinities worshiped by his countryfolk. From Loncola and other adults, the boy would have learned about the characteristics, peculiarities, and functions of the Yoruba deities: about Olódùmarè (Olorun), the Lord of Heaven and High God of Creation; 'Eshù, the Divine Messenger and Enforcer; Yemoja, the Goddess of the Ogun river; 'Ogún, the God of Iron and War; Shango, the Thunderer; Orishala, the Creator of Humankind; Odudawa, Creator of the Earth and progenitor of the Yoruba people; and especially about Ifá, the God of Divination.[62] This childhood familiarity with the Yoruba gods and religious beliefs, one would assume, Ifacayeh carried with him to Sierra Leone.

In the compound where he was raised in Iwarreh, moreover, his mother, Manlawa, and the older members of the family would have taught him the etiquette of social relations. Indeed, growing up in a polygynous household, Ifacayeh undoubtedly spent a great deal of time under his mother's care and tuition – much more than with his father. From her, he would have learned obedience, respect for the bonds of kinship, and reverence for his ancestors – belief in the power and continuing influence of the dead among the living. He would have been initiated in the Yoruba work ethic and discouraged from laziness through assigned household chores. From folktales, proverbs, riddles, and other accounts presented by Manlawa, by his father's other wives, and by his elders, he would have gained knowledge of his society's past and its legends of origin, and absorbed ideas about the responsible behavior of the individual toward his parents, seniors, and the community as a whole. As a ten-year-old male, he might also have experienced circumcision and the *rite de passage* from childhood into adulthood, and been given instruction in the practical skills required of men and women in Old Oyo's complex, urban-dwelling, predominantly agricultural society.[63]

Almost as soon as Ifacayeh entered the King's Yard in Freetown, however, and received clothing to cover his nudity as well as food to sate his hunger, the cultural imprint that he had carried with him from his land of birth began to be altered. Assimilationist in character, the process that ultimately brought about the transformation of the boy from the polytheistic and polygynous household in Iwarreh into the idol-smashing, Wesleyan missionary, Joseph Boston May, had its ideological roots in the nature of Sierra Leone colony – in the curious combination of philanthropy, humanitarian idealism, economic self-interest, and cultural arrogance that defined Britain's "civilizing mission" in this part of Africa until the latter part of the nineteenth century.

Sierra Leone, after all, had been established not only as a haven for liberated slaves and black freed men and women from Britain, America, and the West Indies, but as a social experiment as well. The directors of the Sierra Leone Company, including the noted Clapham Sect evangelicals and abolitionists William Wilberforce, Granville Sharp, Thomas Clarkson, and Henry Thornton, conceived of the colonizing venture for which they had received a royal charter in 1790 as a means to provide "the Blessings of Industry and Civilization" to Africans "long detained in Barbarism."[64] They, like many of their contemporary Europeans, considered Africans to be deprived by their environment, the slave trade, and religious error.

But, echoing late eighteenth-century thinking about the potential *Verbesserung* of the Jews, they also considered Africans to be redeemable. Their assumption that "the heathen" should and could be converted to the benefits of European culture – based on a chauvinistic conceit that equated "civilization" with their version of "Europeanization" – remained the primary ideological justification for the existence of the colony when the British Crown took over its administration in 1808. And it continued to be so until British ideas about Africans, and particularly African "educability," were modified by the rise of pseudoscientific racism in the 1860s.[65]

Implicit in the conversionist assumption was a belief in the Idea of Progress, and a faith that "civilization" could be communicated to any human being through education. In this context, the purpose of the Sierra Leone colonial establishment was to wean Africans like Ifacayeh away from the "darkness of superstition" and the evils of slavery, and to change them through schooling and less direct forms of tuition into Europeanized and, whenever possible, Christian subjects of Great Britain. "If their children are provided with the means of Christian and religious instruction," Governor Alexander Findlay wrote about the Liberated Africans to Viscount Goderich, Secretary of State for the Colonies, "as they grow up, so will religion, civilization, and industry advance and spread into the interior of Africa."[66]

For Ifacayeh, the "weaning" began quickly. He received his initial understanding of the nature of the place to which he had been brought from his own countrypeople in Sierra Leone – from several Yoruba-speaking Liberated Africans who had been freed some years before him. Visiting the King's Yard in search of relatives not long after the boy had arrived there, they congratulated him and his companions on their liberation, welcomed them to the colony, explained the humanitarian purpose of its existence, and assured them of the kind treatment they would receive at the hands of its British rulers.[67] In performing this function – calming the confused and frightened newcomers with the promise of a new life of freedom in Sierra Leone – these Yoruba-speaking Liberated Africans were the first agents of the Europeanizing and conversionist process that Ifacayeh encountered. He was soon to meet others: Christian missionaries, European officials and residents in the colony, as well as African settlers and "Recaptives" whose conversion to Christianity and education had distinguished them as "successful products" of the civilizing mission. Directly or indirectly, consciously or unconsciously, each of these would serve him as a living illustration of "civilized behavior" and appearance, and as a model for what the dominant British defined as the "more enlightened" way of life.

Like other Liberated African children, Ifacayeh remained in the King's Yard only long enough to be registered and officially emancipated, before being taken out of the walled enclave and brought to one of the several settlements in the mountains and rural areas behind Freetown.[68] It was there in a lush West African tropical setting – in the small villages whose English names, Leicester,

Gloucester, Bathurst, Charlotte, Regent, Wellington, Hastings, and
Waterloo celebrated the regal aristocracy as well as the martial
triumphs of the British nation – that colonial officials and missionaries focused their effort among the recently freed slaves to induce
the cultural and religious transformation embodied in the Sierra
Leone experiment.[69]

The government's practice of resettling newly liberated Africans
in rural communities fringing the capital of the colony was slightly
more than a decade old when Ifacayeh left King's Yard. It had been
encouraged and systematized by the energetic and forceful governor,
Charles MacCarthy, who brought about an arrangement between
the colonial government and the newly formed Church Missionary
Society (CMS) that gave the society's clergy in Sierra Leone responsibility for the schooling and supervision of the Liberated Africans at the village level.

In accordance with MacCarthy's belief that the Liberated African
population would "yield like wax to any impression," the idea in
1816, as in 1827 when Ifacayeh was sent to the mountain settlements, was to remove recently freed men, women, and especially
children, from the distracting influences of Freetown to the relative
isolation of the villages, where, through the benefit of example and
direct instruction, they would be taught the English language and
be led to acquire "habits of industry" and "a Competent knowledge
of the arts and manners of civilized life." In the village "laborato-
ries," religious and secular education were meant to complement
agricultural and technical training in shaping Africans into orderly,
morally virtuous, obedient, and productive subjects of the Crown:
to integrate them effectively into the colonial order as tractable and
stable participants.[70]

Regent, to which Ifacayeh was initially sent to live and for schooling three weeks after his arrival in the colony, had long been considered by colonial officials as the most successful village when
measured in terms of the demonstrated industry and piety of its
inhabitants.[71] Located in a beautiful mountain valley on both banks
of Hog Brook, some four and a half miles from Freetown by way of
the rugged trail over Mount Aureol and Leicester Peak, it often
reminded visitors glancing at its physical appearance and layout of
an English rural hamlet. This resemblance had been consciously
planned – as well as for the other Liberated African villages – by
Governor MacCarthy and other officials, and was particularly expressed in the dominant size and setting of its church building (complete with bell and weathercock); its neatly demarcated, squared,
and fenced property lines; and its numbered houses, constructed of
timber, clapboard, shingles, and, occasionally, of stone.[72]

Its long-resident superintendent, the Reverend William Augustine Johnson of the CMS, had for years exercised civil authority over the Liberated Africans in the village in accordance with the administrative scheme devised by MacCarthy, and had effectively used his position as village head and schoolmaster to spread the spiritual message of Christianity and to instruct "the off-scouring of Africa," as he once called the Liberated Africans, "in heavenly knowledge."[73] Laboring among his charges with diligence, if not fanaticism, he rewarded individuals whom he considered well-behaved, hard-working, and, above all, religiously devoted, with gifts of clothing, food, even land. As a result, church attendance in Regent grew steadily during his superintendency from 1816 to 1823 – so significantly that the church building had to be enlarged and improved five times while he was its minister, and it was not unusual to find between 500 and 1,000 persons, out of a village population of some 2,000, congregated at a single Sunday service.[74]

But, by the time Ifacayeh reached Regent in March 1827, both the seemingly indestructible Reverend Johnson and the visionary and dynamic Governor MacCarthy were dead – the former of yellow fever while aboard a ship returning him to England, and the latter in a war with the Asante in the Gold Coast – and the system of village administration based on missionary superintendence had effectively collapsed. The high rate of mortality for Europeans from tropical diseases and from the "cures" that were employed in the attempt to overcome them – a rate that earned Sierra Leone and the west coast of Africa the reputation as the "White Man's Grave" – interfered with the Church Missionary Society's efforts to staff the villages adequately and to comply with the administrative tasks called for in its partnership with the government. Of the seventy-nine Europeans sent out to the colony by the Society during its first two decades of involvement in this area, fifty-three died while on duty.[75]

Regent, left without the strong personal leadership of Johnson, and unable to replace him with any European missionary who survived long enough to establish his own authority, reflected the unsettled conditions that prevailed with the change in circumstances. Its population declined as numbers of resident Liberated Africans sought employment in Freetown, its church building fell into disrepair, and attendance at services dropped off. To outside observers, the village appeared as an eminently less impressive "show piece" for the "civilizing effort" than it had been a few years earlier.[76]

Nonetheless, although the system that had granted resident European missionaries both civil and religious authority in the villages did not survive long after Governor MacCarthy's death, the agents

Regent village, Ifacayeh's first home in Sierra Leone after his liberation from slavery. [From M. L. Charlesworth, *Africa's Mountain Valley* (London, 1856)]

and agencies furthering the conversionist and Europeanizing process maintained sufficient vitality to function. The schools continued as the main institutional instrument for the "civilizing mission," and remained under the control of the Christian missionary societies. Indeed, because the locale for instruction both in the colony villages and Freetown continued to be either the home of the missionary schoolmaster or the church building, and the instructional resources used were primarily the prayer-book catechism, readings from the Bible, and Christian hymns, the link between education and religion was not seriously affected by the governmental removal of civil authority from the churchmen. "In the minds of the recipients of this form of westernization," John Peterson observed, "it was hard to divide the functions of the earliest missionaries," and "the importance of the school was indiscernible from the church or chapel."[77]

The method of instruction employed at the time Ifacayeh began to attend school was the Bell, or National, system, which was also used by Anglican philanthropic and missionary groups in Britain to teach literacy to and instill the virtue of hard work and the moral principles of Christianity in members of the working class. In Sierra Leone, the system fit the prevailing conversionist ideology well. It reflected the belief that indolence and superstition rather than racial factors had impeded "progress and enlightenment," and that the Liberated Africans could be "uplifted" and "improved" in much the same way as the British lower classes. But the choice of this method was also logical in the disease-plagued environment of Sierra Leone, where it was necessary to find a pedagogical system requiring relatively few European teachers. The system's mechanics were uncomplicated and depended upon each schoolmaster's teaching the lessons of the day to "monitors" who, upon mastering the material, were each expected to instruct groups of students in turn. "I selected twelve of the most promising-looking boys and taught them the first four letters, according to Bell's System," the Reverend W. A. Johnson wrote in his description of the method. "When they knew these, I divided the whole [student body] into twelve classes, and made one teach each class. When they had taught their respective classes I taught these boys four other letters, till they had surmounted the whole Alphabet."[78]

The curriculum emphasized the traditional three Rs – reading, 'riting, 'rithmetic – plus a fourth one, religion. Its content mirrored the prevailing cultural chauvinism of Sierra Leone's colonial masters, stressing the positive values of European civilization and the Christian gospel while deprecating African beliefs and practices, particularly in the realm of religion, as heathen error. The aim was not to provide education for its own sake, but to win converts. European history, geography, and the outlooks of some of its bourgeois disseminators were reflected in the curriculum, not the past experience and physical reality of its African recipients. Its transmission was aided and reinforced by the combined application of the "carrot and stick": by the issuance of rewards and kudos to pupils who were "industrious," "well behaved," and who gave evidence of "progress," and the denial of these positive reinforcements to individuals considered intractable and stubborn.[79]

To complement and supplement this formal tuition in the schools, moreover, it remained the practice to place newly liberated children – "protected" children, as they were called – in established and "reputable" village households, either as apprentice domestic servants to resident Europeans, or among "the best conducted persons of their own country." These persons, it was hoped, "would feel a pleasure in instructing" the newcomers further in subjects introduced in school and chapel, as well as leading them to acquire "habits of industry" and "a competent knowledge of the arts and manners of civilized life."[80] The practice, which became known as the "ward system," placed great stock in the belief articulated by the Quaker schoolteacher Hannah Kilham that the poor and unenlightened learned not only through conventional schooling, but also by imitating "their superiors."[81]

When Ifacayeh arrived in Regent, he was assigned to a Liberated African family, with whom he would remain for nearly a year. Unfortunately, little is known about the members of this household. Because of the boy's Yoruba ethnic background as well as the Liberated African Department's attempt to place newcomers initially with persons who spoke their native language, it is reasonable to assume that they also originated in the Oyo region and were Yoruba-speakers. But no information exists about the length of their residence in Sierra Leone, or about their standing among Regent's inhabitants. The missionaries had created an elite within the village community by restricting actual church membership (as opposed to attendance) to the selected few who seemed most advanced in their religious and cultural conversion – a group of communicants visibly privileged by their residence on Christian Street, and by their possession of stone houses instead of the more common mud and wattle huts.[82] This elite was intended to set a standard for emulation by other village residents. At least some of the members of Ifacayeh's new "family" may have belonged to this group, but the adult Joseph May made no mention of any of them in his recollections of this period of his life. This indicated, perhaps, that they may have been humbler folk who left no lasting impression on the boy's mind.

While residing with this family, Ifacayeh was sent to Regent's school for five hours a day, from nine to twelve noon and from one to three in the afternoon. He distinguished himself quickly. "He mastered the alphabet within a week," his eldest son, J. Claudius May, later recalled, "and in about three months he was able to read easy lessons from the Holy Scriptures, such as the Parables and Miracles of our Lord."[83] His teacher, John Essex Bull, a colony-born African employed by the CMS, made him a monitor shortly afterward, and gave him the responsibility of instructing a number of his fellow Yoruba-speakers who were older than he. In a few months, it was clear that the boy needed more advanced instruction, and he was selected to be one of seven sent to a "higher school" taught by the European missionary Edmund Boston in neighboring Bathurst village.[84]

At his juncture, Ifacayeh was renamed Joseph. The change from an African to a European name, an early milestone in his conversionist process, symbolically paralleled the boy's acquisition of fluency in English, the most significant result of his first year in the villages of the colony. Until he was able to communicate in the language of Sierra Leone's rulers, his understanding of the premises and expectations of the world to which he had been brought had in large part been influenced by the skills and perceptions of Yoruba-speaking interpreters. When he learned to read, write, and speak English, his access to that world became more direct and comprehensive. It both readied him for further Europeanization and brought him a step closer to the time when he would become an interpreter himself, translating the Christian message and cultural values of his mentors for recently arrived Yoruba immigrants.

Bright, eager to learn, anxious to please, Joseph impressed his new teacher, the Reverend Boston, who took a special interest in furthering the boy's education. Indeed, when the minister and his wife were reassigned to the village of Gloucester early in 1828, they arranged that Joseph be transferred to their care, promising to provide him with room, board, and clothing in return for his services in their household.

Joseph, in turn, learned early that pleasing his mentors would bring him rewards and praise. While he was residing in Gloucester with them, an incident occurred that clearly illuminates his astuteness in this regard. As told by J. Claudius May:

Several European gentlemen went up to Gloucester [from Freetown] to spend the afternoon with [Joseph's] master, and just before sitting to dinner, it was discovered that there was no preserved sauce. Joseph was hastily despatched with a note to Freetown ... and urged to bring up a bottle with the least possible delay; he ran down the hill [a distance of approximately two and a half miles], got the bottle, and returned in such an incredible short period, found the gentlemen still at table; most of them were astonished at the lad's fleetness of foot, and if he had not brought the sauce they would not have believed that he had reached Freetown; they manifested their delight and pleasure by giving him a present, some a 1s., others 2s.6d. and the like, and he was commended for his fleetness and agility.[85]

In all likelihood, the Bostons were kind and well-meaning people, and Joseph would remember them with great fondness in his recollections of this period in his life. He received his first Bible from them, a book that, according to his oldest son, "he prized and frequently perused, and had in constant use for fourteen years, till he was able to replace it by another."[86] But, although the minister and his wife were kind to Joseph, and in some respects may have filled the parental void created when the boy was torn from his own father and mother, they unquestionably were also his "masters" and he their servant. Their relationship with him was built on the premise of their sense of his inequality, and was defined by his dependence on them. They prescribed and, to a large extent, controlled everything about his life: the clothing he wore, the food he ate, the lessons he received, and even the allocation of his leisure time. All these were regulated by them not only on the basis of affection and caring, as between parents and their children, but in exchange for service, diligence, good behavior, and the continuing evidence of his progress on the path to Christianity and "civilization." In this respect, of course, Joseph's situation vis-à-vis his missionary mentors, and his relationship to them, though unique in its specific details, was typical of the early assimilationist experience of numerous Liberated African children in nineteenth-century Sierra Leone.[87]

Joseph stayed in the Boston household for three years. In 1829 they all moved to Kissy, a rural Liberated African settlement about three miles east of Freetown, where Edmund Boston became schoolmaster. He also continued to provide Joseph with additional private instruction in academic and religious subjects, and began to hold out the possibility that, sometime in the future, he would obtain the youth's admission to the Fourah Bay College, the CMS training institution for African students that had opened at Freetown in 1828.[88] Like so many of his fellow Europeans, however, the Reverend Boston contracted a tropical disease, became seriously ill, and was unable to fulfill his promise. Although he, his wife, and Joseph moved to the Fourah Bay area of the Freetown peninsula, where Reverend Boston could be placed under the care of fellow CMS missionaries, he died in 1830. Mrs. Boston fell ill shortly after her husband's funeral and died the following year.[89]

Left without his European guardians and mentors, Joseph offered his services to his Yoruba countryman Samuel Ajayi Crowther, the first African to register and complete his studies at Fourah Bay College.[90] He moved back up to Regent when Crowther was put in charge of the village school, and spent three years with him and his wife as a servant and ward, all the while hoping to continue receiving the training that would qualify him to enter Fourah Bay as a student. But, by the time the Reverend Crowther returned to the college as a tutor in 1834, Joseph had concluded that no progress was being made toward his admission to the college: his mentor, concerned with the advancement of his own career, showed no interest in helping the young man. Disappointed and discouraged, Joseph left Crowther's household and proceeded to Freetown on his own to seek work and establish new connections. A reflection, perhaps, of the ungenerous treatment he had been accorded, Joseph in later life revealed little about his early relationship with Crowther. Nor did Crowther mention May in any of his writings.

The next two years were crucial in shaping the course of Joseph's future. Having learned to read and write English reasonably well, he possessed a skill that raised his attractiveness to potential employers, and he had little difficulty finding clerical jobs with European merchants or in branches of the colonial government.[91] The connection between European education and potential success in Sierra Leone's colonial society were thus strongly reinforced in the youth's mind by dint of his first independent sojourn into the world of the dominant, and his experiences must no doubt have strengthened his resolve to continue "improving" himself through the acquisition of more advanced instruction. Religion, however, now became the matrix of his existence – the definitive center of his concerns.

During his first seven years in Sierra Leone, Joseph's religious outlook had been shaped in school, chapel, and home by members of the Church Missionary Society who represented the Anglican Church of England, the official, establishment, denomination of the colony. When he departed from the Crowther household and moved to Freetown on his own, he carried with him a basic knowledge of the church's Liturgy and of its prayers and rituals. It was also clearly the influence of the religious instruction he had received from the Reverend Boston that had stimulated him to internalize the importance of the Ten Commandments. These beliefs led him to quit his first job in Freetown because he had not been permitted to "observe the Sabbath properly," and was forced to perform services in "direct violation of the sanctity of the Lord's day."[92]

But, in Freetown, the religious universe to which he was exposed broadened considerably. The city's population also included significant numbers of Muslims, as well as persons identifying with syncretic Afro-Christian worship or who maintained a more or less uncompromising belief in African religious deities. By far the largest percentage of the Christian inhabitants, moreover, belonged to the Wesleyan Methodists and other dissenting denominations instead of the Established Church of England.[93] Options for alternative religious affiliation thus became available to Joseph when he separated from his CMS tutors, and he soon took advantage of one of them.

Neither Islam, which some years later he dismissed as "the system of the false prophet," nor the failed gods of his Yoruba childhood, whom he had already been taught to abhor, would satisfy his need for attachment.[94] But Methodism did. Despite specific instructions from his second Freetown employer, a Mr. Baxter, that he worship only at the Anglican St. George's Church, where he would hear "a white man preach" and not be exposed to preaching by "ignorant blackfellows," Joseph was persuaded by a fellow Liberated African to attend a revival at the Ebenezer Methodist Chapel.[95] He was to recall later how the sermon by the European missionary Benjamin Crosby, based on the text "As I live, saith the Lord God, I have no pleasure in the death of the wicked," struck his "heart with conviction."[96] "The utterance, earnestness, and diction excelled everything he had ever heard in St. George's Church," J. Claudius May subsequently observed about his father's experience, "and he returned home under deep contrition."

Joseph was also deeply impressed by the positive effect that the conversion to Methodism had on his Liberated African friend, a man who had been a "most notorious swearer" and hard drinker. Touched by the emotional content of the Methodist services and moved by the enthusiastic participation and responsiveness of the worshipers, Joseph revealed that he was influenced "to seek the Lord" for the salvation of his soul.[97]

Three years later, in 1838, looking back on this twelve-month period, which began in April 1835, Joseph described how profoundly affected he had been by the fervor of the preaching in the Wesleyan chapel. Terrified "with dreadful thoughts of death, hell, and the awful day of Judgement," he told how he was left with "no peace" in his mind when the preacher repeatedly asserted that "the wicked shall be turned into Hell," and how he internalized and personalized the message: "I must be born again. Must be born again without doubt, or else I shall not enter the kingdom of God but must be damn[ed] for ever."[98]

And the attraction intensified. He ceased working in Baxter's store, and briefly set himself up as an independent petty trader before being employed in the Government Engineering Department as an overseer and shopkeeper. With his evenings free, he increased his attendance at Methodist chapel services, and was regularly present at prayer meetings. He also took additional religious instruction from Aberdeen Turner and Perry Locks, two black Nova Scotian settlers in Freetown who had become preachers in the Wesleyan mission circuit. In July 1835 he joined Mr. Turner's class group and, as J. Claudius May later recollected, "resolved to give himself up to God and be more concerned about his soul's salvation."[99]

The sudden death of a friend who, in Joseph's words, "was summoned to meet his God without finding...peace" made a deep impression on him at this time, and heightened his fear that he too might die "undelivered" as a "guilty sinner" excluded from God's kingdom.[100] In turmoil and anguish, he noted how he spent days and nights "wrestling hard in mighty prayer," repeating a verse taught him by the missionaries:

> A poor blind child I wander here,
> If haply I may feel Thee near:
> O dark! dark! dark! I still must say,
> Amid the blaze of gospel day.[101]

Finally, in the middle of the night of August 13, 1835 – a night he spent at home in fervent prayer – Joseph underwent a religious experience. "The Lord spoke peace to my soul," he related three years after the event in the stylized language of a pulpit preacher "bearing witness":

I shouted and praised the Lord...because I have found Him whom my soul loveth....He brought me up out of my horrible pit, out of the misty day, and set my feet upon a rock and established my goings. And He hath put new song in my mouth.[102]

Tears of joy running down his cheek, he shouted to inform neighbors and other members of the household in which he lived about his rebirth and conversion, and they "united with him in praising God."[103]

Within a few months, he was baptized in Ebenezer Chapel by the same Reverend Benjamin Crosby whose preaching he had heard at his first Methodist service. He received the surname May, in honor of the Reverend John May, a European Wesleyan missionary who had labored and died in Sierra Leone colony some years earlier.[104] The boy – Ifacayeh, Ojo, whose initiation into adulthood in his native land was interrupted by the ordeal of enslavement and communal separation – was born again as the Christian man: Joseph Boston May.

• • •

Joseph's readiness for a religious experience that would lead to his conversion and baptism was only in part based on pressures and influences external to himself. Certainly, the nature of the preaching and chapel services, as well as the personal example and instruction offered by peers like John Blair Campbell and by the Nova Scotia Methodists played a very significant role in shaping his outlook and affecting the state of his mind. Because of his residence with the Reverends Boston and Crowther, moreover, he no doubt also realized that the missionaries, both Anglican and Wesleyan, normally demanded that adult converts testify to their own salvation before receiving the sacrament of baptism. He would thus have known that he had to be "pricked in the heart," as the Reverend Johnson, of Regent, had phrased it, before he could be "saved."[105]

But the intensity of his religious fervor and attraction to Wesleyan Methodism must also have been affected during this period by less apparent psychological factors. He had, after all, become uprooted again. The death of the Bostons, who had substituted for his biological parents in so many respects, and his break with the Crowthers meant that he was truly alone once more. In Freetown, for the first time since he had been taken up to Regent village eight years earlier, he was left without guardians to tutor and nurture him. Like other young Liberated African wards who had been the only children in a colony household, he had established no significant alternative individual or communal ties in Sierra Leone. He was isolated, disconnected, lonely. There remained little, beyond memory, to attach him to his previous life.

But Christianity – as the Wesleyan Methodists presented it – could satisfy his need for attachment and security. It offered him an alternative haven, assuring him of God's eternal love and comfort, and providing him with a less ephemeral focus for the expression of his affection and devotion. It supplied him with a guide for personal behavior and a blueprint for happiness, both on earth and after death. And, in view of the loss of his earlier patrons, it presented him with a replacement key to the world of the dominant, making it possible for him to continue his education, Europeanization, and social mobility upward from a subordinated past. As with others in his generation who had been liberated from slavery, for Joseph Boston May the appeal of the Wesleyan religious message and the British conversionist ideology was intimate and profound.

Indeed, Joseph's eagerness for further "self-improvement" impressed the Wesleyan missionaries greatly. They agreed to his request for "biblical help" and additional tutoring in academic subjects, and were so struck by his diligence and perseverance that they offered him employment as an assistant teacher in their Bathurst Street School in January 1837. Eighteen months later, satisfied with his performance and happy that he still found time to pursue his own religious and secular studies, they allowed him to take charge of the Mission Day School in Wilberforce village. His faithful participation in all Wesleyan religious activities also led them to appoint him as assistant class leader and, in August 1838, as an exhorter.[106]

"What shall I say to the people? What have I to say?" Joseph wondered when he was granted his first opportunity to address a large congregation of African worshippers in his new capacity. His decision to intone Isaiah 61 ("The spirit of the Lord is upon me because the Lord hath annointed me to preach good tidings unto the meek") suggests that he already saw himself as an agent of conversionism long before he officially became a missionary.[107] Already, his enthusiasm for the religion to which he had converted, and his conviction about its unerring truth, led him into a zealous encounter with Wilberforce villagers who venerated the very same African deities that his father had served as priest-diviner and that had inhabited his own childhood universe. "Some of the Idolaters," he wrote in 1838 to Wesleyan authorities in London, "hated me with perfect hatred because I showed the Rev. H. Flood their god's houses and they said I brought him ... to take their gods away."[108] Threatened with a beating and expulsion by village inhabitants whom he had exposed, he was granted a transfer to a Mission Day School in Wellington, and moved there soon afterward.

The European missionaries continued to be pleased with Joseph's performance and ambition. Early in 1840 they selected him, along with Charles Knight, another young teacher and Liberated African from Oyo, to receive additional educational training in England. They did so to meet a request by the Quaker Society of Friends for "promising youths" who could be sponsored to study more advanced subject matter and taught improved British pedagogical methods for use in colony schools. The award included free passage for May and Knight, room and board, and instruction at the Borough Road Training College in London.[109]

May lived in London from June 1840 until November 1841. Although few details of his residence have survived, one can imagine how strange and different he initially must have felt as a black man in a predominantly white racial environment. Absent from Sierra Leone for the first time since he had been liberated, and having never before been away from the tropics or in a city larger than Freetown, his encounter with the British metropolis must have been overwhelming. Undoubtedly, despite all evidence of his progressive acculturation to the world of the dominant – his European clothing, name, knowledge of English, and familiarity with the manners and customs of his British mentors in Sierra Leone – his introduction to the rapid tempo and complexity of life in England must have led him to experience considerable culture shock.

He met persons from a variety of social backgrounds during these eighteen months in London. But the accounts and letters referring to this period suggest that his personal relations were predominantly with members of the middle class. His principal acquaintances were members of the clergy and their spouses, educators, and men and women such as his Wesleyan and Quaker sponsors who were interested in "the welfare and progress of the Negroes," and who would naturally look on him as a symbol of an ongoing and successful mission. His teachers at the Training College included the principal, Dr. Cornwall, joint author of a widely used arithmetic and English grammar book, and Mr. Crossley, the headmaster, whose *Intellectual Calculator* was to become widely used as a text in colony schools soon after May's return to West Africa. Among his fellow students was Joshua Fitch, who subsequently became principal of the Borough Road institution and one of Her Majesty's school inspectors. May also established a friendship with Isaac Pitman, graduate of the college and inventor of shorthand writing, for whom the youth's Yoruba-speaking ability provided an opportunity to demonstrate the versatility of the stenographic method.[110]

If May sensed any racial antagonism or discrimination from these persons, or from any others during his stay in England, he left no indication in the records. For the most part, of course, his teachers and closest acquaintances in London were true believers in the "conversionist" ideology. In this respect, they were like the missionaries who had influenced him in Africa. They were confident of the social order to which they belonged, and convinced of the superiority of their culture and the Christian religion. Yet they also believed in educating and "raising up" the "less fortunate," and invited his continuing emulation. Moderation, restraint, abstinence, respectability: these were the characteristics they projected. They presented him with a model of British middle-class behavior and of a style of life that reinforced and refined the tutoring he had received in Sierra Leone. That, however, their conversionism was rooted in cultural chauvinism and in an arrogant dismissal of alternative values and ways seemed not to occur to him – or, if it did, not to bother him. In the fourteen years since his liberation from slavery, he had absorbed their ideology and made it his own.

IV

When Joseph May returned to Sierra Leone in January 1842, he did so as a confirmed member of the African elite in the colony. He had become a "been to": one of a small fraternity of Africans who had *been to* England and successfully interacted with the dominant British on their own soil. He had met the goals of his missionary sponsors and returned to West Africa as a trained cultural interpreter on their behalf – as a teacher educated in the latest instructional techniques and materials, polished in style and public performance, and willing to disseminate what he termed "the temporal and spiritual knowledge" of his British mentors to "less enlightened" and "less fortunate" blacks than himself.[111]

Appointed as head of New Town West School soon after his return, he was charged with the supervision of seven assistant teachers as well as the primary education of nearly four hundred students and was responsible for the successful establishment of a demanding new curriculum. He was also invited to join the ranks of the Wesleyan missionaries. It was not surprising that May in the mid-1840s described himself as a person involved in "delightful labours" and appeared happy and optimistic about his future life-chances.[112]

May, however, would live for nearly another half-century after his return to Africa from the Borough Road Training College.[113] Although he perceived the world in which he found himself at mid-century to be warm and welcoming – a perception he shared with many of his Liberated African contemporaries in Sierra Leone – changes were taking place in the social and ideological climate of that world that were potentially disturbing to his future. As the second half of the century unfolded toward a new era of European imperial expansionism, racist ideas were coming into vogue to justify and support both formal and informal European domination of peoples throughout the non-European regions of the globe. Increasingly, as European physical anthropologists proclaimed the inferiority of the "colored races," and Darwin's work was being misinterpreted and used to bolster the proposition that superior races were marked by their material superiority – especially in the technological and industrial realm – racism and the "White Man's Burden" came to displace the ideal of equality through conversion. In Sierra Leone, the emerging "new" racism challenged the key assumption on which this West African social experiment had originally been founded: the belief that Africans could be culturally transformed through Christianity, education, and legitimate commerce – that they could be converted and "civilized" to be like Europeans.

Joseph May and other "successful" first-generation products of the intensive conversionist effort in Sierra Leone were clearly vulnerable to the changing social and ideological climate. No matter how effectively they manifested their Europeanization in their dress, their language, and in their conformity to the cultural practices and values of their British models, as black persons they also exhibited the extrinsic physical characteristics that indelibly marked them as racially different from the dominant whites. It was precisely Europeanized Africans like themselves who, as the century unfolded, became the brunt of "aping-the-white man" insults, and the subject of racially motivated discriminatory actions and exclusionary incidents.[114]

But it is perhaps illustrative of the intense degree to which the conversionist ideology had been absorbed by first-generation emancipated Africans like May – particularly by those who had been liberated as children or young adults – to note that he would remain largely unshaken by the changing ideological atmosphere, and would continue to maintain faith in the premises and promises of the conversionist experience that had molded his life history. Although his climb to the highest levels of the missionary establishment open to "Native Brethren" was curtailed by British missionary authorities in the 1860s, and he was relegated to the diminished and low-salaried status of "supernumerary" in the 1870s – years earlier than he felt was justified – he seemed not to draw a connection between these limitations on his personal professional ambitions and the growing antipathy on the part of many whites to the possibility of African professional and social advancement within the colonial system.[115]

On only one occasion, late in life, did he complain to Methodist headquarters in London of having been treated unfairly by his white missionary superintendent in Sierra Leone "because I am . . . a black-man." He appended a verse by Cowper to his letter of grievance as if to remind church authorities in England that:

Reverend Joseph May in 1887, after the curtailment of his ministerial activities and three years before his death. [From C. Marke, *Origin of Wesleyan Methodism in Sierra Leone* (London, 1912)]

> Fleecy looks and dark complexion
> Cannot forfeit nature's claim;
> Skins may differ, but affection
> Dwells in white and black the same.[116]

Even then, however, he considered this incident an example of aberrant behavior on the part of a single individual, and trusted in the goodwill of his missionary mentors in London to set the situation straight.

To the extent that his own writings and the recollections of others who knew him offer accurate insights into his reality, the summary picture of May's world view during this half-century of change in British attitudes reflects the determinant role played by *perception* in triggering individual responses to exclusion and in influencing the nature of individual identity. His view attests to the connection, in Peter Gay's words, "between what the world imposes and the mind demands, receives, and reshapes."[117] And his view situates perception in relationship to the peculiarities of the individual's life-history experience – influenced not only by the circumstances of the present or visions of the future, but also by the memory and experience of the past.

Consequently, despite the apparent growth in a catalog of actions indicating that official British support for conversionism was waning, despite personal disappointments and unrealized hopes within a missionary establishment that increasingly discriminated against – *but not totally blocked the opportunities of* – its black members, May continued to have faith in the conversionist idea. He continued to consider his personal situation, not in relation to a blocked and potentially unrealizable future, but in relation to a "heathen" past that had pained and scarred him, and from which he gratefully believed himself to be eternally saved. For the remainder of his life, his primary orientation remained along lines that were characteristically closer to class than to ethnic or racial criteria. He continued to identify primarily with persons who were Christian and "civilized" like himself: with individuals belonging either to the colony's ruling group or to the European-educated African elite. For him, as for others of his generation who had experienced slavery, liberation, and the intense conversionist "transformation" in Sierra Leone, the thought of a different orientation – of one that might challenge both discrimination and colonial domination on the basis of a new collective ethnic or racially based identification – was as yet unimaginable. But members of the subsequent generation of Sierra Leoneans, including some of May's own children and grandchildren, would respond to the world in which they found themselves in a very different manner.

Chapter 3

Into the Bourgeoisie:
The Zweig and Brettauer Story

A "good" [Jewish] family ... means more than the purely social aspects which it assigns to itself with this classification; it means a Jewry that has freed itself of all defects and limitations and pettiness which the ghetto has forced upon it, by means of adaptation to a different culture and even possibly a universal culture.

Subconsciously something in the Jew seeks to escape the morally dubious, the distasteful, the petty, the unspiritual, which is attached to all trade, and all that is purely business, and to lift himself up to the moneyless sphere of the intellectual, as if – in the Wagnerian sense – he wished to redeem himself and his entire race from the curse of money. And that is why among Jews the impulse to wealth is exhausted in two, or at most three, generations within one family, and the mightiest dynasties find their sons unwilling to take over the banks, the factories, the established and secure businesses of their fathers.

Stefan Zweig, *The World of Yesterday*

I

Stefan Zweig – essayist, novelist, biographer, librettist, and for some years one of Europe's most widely read and most translated authors – was born in Vienna in 1881. His great-great-grandparents had been born in small-town Jewish ghettos in Moravia and in the Vorarlberg nearly a century earlier. That four-generation, hundred-year span between his birth and theirs incorporates the history of the emancipation of Jews in Central Europe and their integration into modern society.

A collective portrait of Stefan Zweig's family during this century of change illuminates various aspects of the Jewish response to the emancipatory process. It highlights the steps and strategies in the journey from humble beginnings into middle-class affluence – the economic move upward into the *haute bourgeoisie* – that nineteenth-century industrial development and modernization permitted to some of the more energetic and enterprising among them. The portrait also illustrates the physical and social move outward from the restricted Jewish ghettos of the Hapsburg Empire into Vienna and other European cosmopolitan centers. And it details aspects of the assimilationist path by which some Central European Jews, in the course of their emancipation from a situation of subordination, entered into the world of the dominant – the "world of security," as Stefan Zweig called it – to seek a place and identity therein.

• • •

By the middle of the eighteenth century, the Jewish quarters of Prossnitz (Prostejov), where Stefan Zweig's paternal great-great-grandparents, Moses Josef Zweig (c. 1750–1840) and Elka Katti Spitzer (c. 1757–1817), were born, was slightly larger and perhaps a trifle more prosperous than neighboring Jewish urban settlements in the Margravate of Moravia.[1] Like all the others, however, it was a segregated and restricted ghetto, a crowded and unsanitary location. The inhabitants had no permanent residential rights within the town or legal claim to acceptance or toleration beyond the protection granted them in letters of patent (*Schützbriefe*) from the local feudal lord, the Prince of Lichtenstein, who held title to the Duchy of Plumenau, in which Prossnitz was located. Jews had already been living there for at least three hundred years in the 1750s. But their community in this important commercial and marketing center was of relatively recent vintage when compared to the much older *Judenstadt* in Prague, where Jews had resided since at least A.D. 906, or to some dozen other Jewish settlements in Moravia and Bohemia.

The founders of the community had fled to Prossnitz from nearby Olmütz, which, like many other Central European towns in the 1450s, had expelled Jews in the wake of the anti-Jewish hysteria triggered by the firebrand preaching and successful rabble-rousing of the Italian monk John of Capistrano.[2] In 1584 Jews were officially granted the right to reside in the town, albeit limited to a small area. Although the natural increase of their population was small – discouraged both by the authorities and the harsh conditions of life – the size of the Prossnitz community was augmented rather significantly in the 1650s by persons fleeing the Chmielnitsky pogroms in the Ukraine, and again in 1670 by Jews expelled from Vienna.[3]

The *Judenstadt* of Hohenems, which in the last quarter of the eighteenth century became the home of the Brettauers, Stefan Zweig's maternal ancestors, was not as old or as large as its Prossnitz counterpart. Located in the agricultural and pastoral region of the Vorarlberg (in present western Austria), some 750 kilometers to the

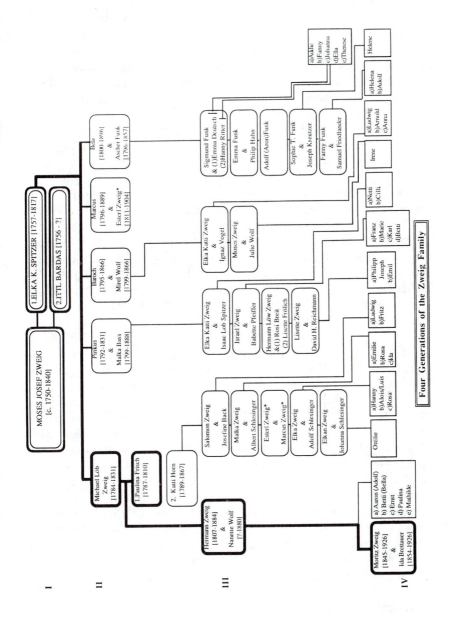

Four Generations of the Zweig Family

I   MOSES JOSEF ZWEIG [c. 1750-1840]   LELKA K. SPITZER [1757-1817]   2.ITTL BARDAS [1756 - ?]

II

- Michael Löb Zweig [1784-1831]
  - 1.Paulina Frisch [1787-1810]
  - 2. Katti Horn [1789-1867]
- Pinkus [1792-1831] & Malka Bass [1799-1888]
- Baroch [1795-1866] & Mirel Wolf [1799-1866]
- Marcus [1796-1889] & Esterl Zweig* [1811-1904]
- Bela [1800-1896] & Ascher Funk [1796-1857]

III

- Hermann Zweig [1807-1884] & Nanette Wolf [?-1880]
- Salomon Zweig & Josefine Back
- Malka Zweig & Albert Schlesinger
- Esterl Zweig* & Marcus Zweig*
- Elka Zweig & Adolf Schlesinger
- Elkan Zweig & Johanna Schlesinger
  - Ottilie
    - a)Hanny b)Alois/Luis c)Rosa
- Elka Katti Zweig & Isaac Lob Spitzer
- Israel Zweig & Babette Pfeiffer
- Hermann Löw Zweig &(1) Rosi Breit (2) Lisette Frölich
- Lisette Zweig & David H. Reichmann
  - a)Emilie b)Rosa c)Ida
  - a)Ludwig b)Fritz
  - a)Philipp Joseph b)Emil
- Elka Katti Zweig & Ignaz Vogel
- Moses Zweig & Julie Wolf
  - a)Netti b)Cilli
  - a)Franz b)Marie c)Karl d)Betti
- Sigmund Funk & (1)Emma Deutsch (2)Hanny Ritter
- Emma Funk & Philip Hahn
- Adolf (Aron)Funk
- Sophie T. Funk & Joseph Kreutzer
- Fanny Funk & Samuel Friedlander
  - a)Adèle b)Fanny c)Johanna d)Ella e)Therese
  - a)Helena b)Adolf
  - a)Ludwig b)Arnold c)Anna
  - Irene
  - Helene

IV

- Moritz Zweig [1845-1926] & Ida Brettauer [1854-1926]
  - a) Aaron (Adolf) b) Betti (Bella) c) Ernst d) Paulina e) Mathilde

southwest of Prossnitz, Hohenems was a small market town ruled
by Reichsgraf Casper when its first twelve Jewish families arrived
from Rheineck, near Lake Constance, and were granted permission
to settle in 1617. Involved mainly in commerce and particularly in
the horse and cattle trade, they became moderately prosperous. In
the next half century, the number of Jewish families grew to approximately thirty. But the pressures exerted by Christian inhabitants, who complained about competition in the cattle market, led
Reichsgraf Franz Carl to expel all Jews from the town in 1676.
Although readmitted twelve years later, many of the original settlers chose not to return, and the number of Jewish families de-
creased to twenty. By 1725, the year the wealthy merchant Jonathan
Uffenheimer moved from Innsbruck to Hohenems, the size of the
community had still not recovered fully. It was only in 1748 that
the old number was surpassed with the immigration and settlement
of Jews fleeing from persecution in nearby Sulz. In 1773, eight years
after Hohenems fell under the control of the House of Hapsburg and
the year Herz Lämle Brettauer settled in town, 227 Jews lived in
the *Judenstadt in* twenty-four houses.[4]

• • •

It is not clear where the parental ancestors of Stefan Zweig had
lived before settling in Prossnitz in Moravia, nor is the date of their
arrival in this community indicated in the available sources. A Jew
carrying the ubiquitous forename Moses, the earliest recorded member of the family, had already lived in the town from approximately
1680 until his death around 1740. Little else is known about him.
His son Josef took Petrowitz as a family surname – and this suggests
that Moses might have been born in a place with that name and
settled in Prossnitz as a young man. Starting in the late sixteenth
century, Jews often chose patronymics like Wiener, Prager, Lem-
berger, and Austerlitz, which referred to their geographical origin.
Because twenty-six villages in Moravia and Bohemia and in neighboring Silesia were called Petrowitz, however, this inference – even
if correct – sheds little specific light on Moses's earliest residence.[5]

Slightly more information exists about Josef Petrowitz, who was
born in the 1720s and died in the 1780s. He was a dealer in sec-
ondhand dry goods – one of those Jews who wandered through the
countryside, peddler's pack on his back, selling old, reconditioned
clothes.[6] Because sons tended to follow the paternal occupation in
that era, peddling would probably also have provided a livelihood
for Josef's father, Moses. Late in life, Josef became a prominent
member of the Prossnitz Jewish community, serving as *Judenrichter*
– a judicial position to which he was elected by his fellow Jews and

endorsed by the Gentile authorities – and was recognized as *Landesältester*, one of a handful of elders consulted by Jewish leaders on matters of communal concern. But, without more detailed source material, it is difficult to know precisely how he managed to reach his prominent status within ghetto society.

As elsewhere in the pre-emancipation era, attainment of high standing in the Jewish community was possible either through wealth or talmudic learning. It is not clear that Josef qualified on either of these counts. Although he was an observant, perhaps even pious, Jew and likely to have been literate in Hebrew, no evidence exists that he was knowledgeable about talmudic law, or able to employ it to adjudicate in matters like marriage, divorce, inheritance, and others that fell under the jurisdiction of the *Judenrichter*.[7] And, even though he seems to have accumulated sufficient capital to become a property owner by 1755, purchasing a section of a house in the *Judenstadt*, he died practically penniless, his family quarters lost to the communal authority in payment of debts owed.[8]

His son Moses Josef Petrowitz – who in 1787 changed his name to Zweig in response to the imperial patent that mandated Moravian Jews to adopt permanent German names – was Stefan Zweig's paternal great-great-grandfather.[9] Born around 1750, Moses Josef was the oldest of four siblings. His two brothers, Solomon (c. 1751–1809) and Israel (1756–1815), chose Löwinau as a surname, and his sister Rosel (1757–?) was known both as Zweig and Löwinau until her marriage to Jakob Salomon Steinschneider.[10] A peddler like his father, Moses Josef became sufficiently prosperous by 1784 to be able to buy back the house that Josef Petrowitz had lost through bankruptcy, and to regain a respectable, if not prominent, place in the community. His marriage to Elka Katti Spitzer produced a dozen offspring (six of whom survived childhood), and his successful though modest trading activities allowed him to maintain and support a household in humble but adequate fashion in the family's crowded quarters on the *Judengasse*.[11]

In Hohenems, in the Vorarlberg region, Stefan Zweig's maternal ancestors, the Brettauers, were also involved in commercial enterprises in the last quarter of the eighteenth century – but no longer as itinerant door-to-door peddlers dependent on purchases by local peasants and fellow ghetto Jews. By the time Herz Lämle Brettauer (1742–1802) had settled in the town in 1773, after marrying the daughter of Maier Jonathan Uffenheimer, his father-in-law had already acquired considerable wealth though his appointment as a commercial agent for the Austrian imperial court and purveyor for the military forces stationed in Vorarlberg.[12] With his in-laws' fi-

Moses Josef Petrowitz Zweig (1750–1840). He posed for this portrait at age 82, in 1832. [Leo Baeck Institute, New York]

nancial backing – support that no doubt included a respectable dowry after his wedding to the twenty-nine-year-old Brendel – Brettauer became one of the richest and most important members of the local Jewish community. By the end of the eighteenth century, this jeweler and moneylender was clearly a good deal better off financially than his Prossnitz contemporary Moses Josef Zweig.[13]

Nonetheless, despite the apparent differences in wealth, scale of commercial enterprise, and the geographical distance between their residences in Moravia and Vorarlberg, Stefan Zweig's maternal and paternal ancestors shared a number of characteristics that provided their respective life histories with a certain uniformity. As Jews in a Gentile world largely governed by feudal and corporative restrictions, they all stood outside the mainstream – distinct from the rest of the population not only through their religion, language, culture, and descent, but through legal definition as well. Within this world, all Jews, no matter how rich or poor, were classed as aliens and noncitizens. They lived in the *Judenstadt* as tolerated persons, under the protection of the Gentile authorities by virtue of letters of patent (*Schützbriefe*), contractual privileges that could be revoked at any time.[14]

The position of the Jews in these towns, as in others in the Hapsburg dominions in Central Europe, resembled that of colonies of foreigners existing on sufferance, subject to special regulations and the goodwill of their non-Jewish protectors. The growth of their population was controlled through restrictions on their freedom to marry.[15] They had no share in the administration of the municipalities in which their ghettos were located. Instead, they were organized into community corporations with an elected leadership, and were held collectively responsible for all imposts levied on them and for their social behavior and business conduct. They were generally debarred from retail trades and handicrafts, excluded by the guilds, and limited to occupations relating to commerce and the lending of money.[16]

Stefan Zweig's relatives, however, like other Jews similarly excluded from civic society, did enjoy a number of rights in accordance with their letters patent: liberty to trade in certain items over a defined territory and to engage in money transactions; protection of their person and property; protection while traveling; and freedom to practice their religion. The scope of these rights and the range of social and economic opportunities differed somewhat from place to place and over time. The differences in wealth and scope of economic activity between the Uffenheimer-Brettauers of Hohenems and the Löwinau-Zweigs of Prossnitz – and within each family branch – can

Gideon Brechergasse in the Prossnitz *Judenstadt*. Note Gustav Zweig's signpost. Gustav (1855–1925) was a lawyer and, through his wife, Helene, owner of a book-printing and book-selling shop. [Leo Baeck Institute, New York]

in part be explained by adjustments on the part of individuals to the functions permitted them as well as to the restrictions imposed upon them.[17] Their differential social mobility thus resulted from the blend of individual talent and inclination – personal striving – and historically prescribed circumstances. Additionally, as in the case of Herz Lämle Brettauer, it resulted from advantageous marriage alliances.

This combination of restriction and limited privilege was reflected in the mix of mobility and stasis – of dynamism and conservatism – that characterized the lives of Stefan Zweig's ancestors during the pre-emancipation era. The commercial activities in which they were permitted to engage allowed some to become both horizontally and vertically mobile: inside ghetto society, to the upper rungs of the Jewish hierarchy; and, geographically, within an area delimited by the non-Jewish authorities. But, in accordance with prohibitions against residential relocation, their domicile remained fixed. Of the eighteen Zweig relatives born between 1740 and 1780 for whom information exists, sixteen stayed their entire life and died in the place of their birth, either Hohenems or Prossnitz.[18] And, despite their contact with the dominant Gentile world and frequent interaction with their Christian neighbors in the economic realm, the restrictions and exclusions that had for so long underscored the "alien quality" of Jews encouraged them to turn inward to their own community for solidarity and identity. They remained firmly oriented toward the *Judenstadt*, loyal to its traditions and customs, and observant of its religious tenets and beliefs.

The Edict of Tolerance, promulgated under the enlightened rule of Joseph II in the early 1780s, sought to bring about the fuller incorporation of Jews into the dominant society.[19] It was conceived as one of a series of reform measures that would transform the state into a unified and centralized entity through the elimination of local particularisms and the barriers created by estates, corporations, and denominations. The edict relieved Jews of the obligation to wear special emblems and distinctive dress, prescribed secular and civic education for the children, and compelled Christian schools and institutions of higher learning to admit Jewish pupils. Jews were also permitted to become artisans as well as to enter the free professions, and they were encouraged to open factories. Although maintaining restrictions on their freedom to settle where they liked, to own land, and to choose certain vocations, the liberal reforms initiated by the emperor recognized the right of Jews to become naturalized subjects, provided hope for fuller citizenship privileges and greater equality in the future, and were meant to stimulate them to emerge from their occupational, cultural, and social isolation.[20]

Change, however, came about slowly. Although members of the generation of Moses Josef Zweig and Herz Lämle Brettauer "modernized" to the extent of adopting a German surname as mandated by law, the Josephine reforms induced little modification in the general orientation of their daily existence. Born around mid-century, Moses Josef and Herz Lämle's contemporaries were already too old by the 1780s to be personally affected by the new secular educational opportunities that were intended as a replacement for traditional Jewish instruction in the religious elementary schools and talmudic academies. Instead, they persisted in their adherence to the religious faith and cultural practices that had historically defined Jews, both to themselves and to the outside world, as a separate group.

Yiddish (*Judendeutsch*) remained their lingua franca, an aural symbol of their communal difference.[21] The men continued to wear skullcaps, required as a head covering for all male religious Jews, and to dress in the distinctive long coats that had been de rigueur in the pre-Josephine closed ghetto. Married women normally kept their hair covered in public as was expected, or shaved it off and wore a wig (*sheytl*), and dressed in long-sleeved blouses and long skirts as dictated by modesty. They attended synagogue on a regular basis, the men physically segregated from the women during the prayer services. They celebrated the Sabbath, observed the special days of feast and fast, supported a rabbi and cantor, and kept the Jewish dietary laws (*Kashrut*).

They belonged to organizations like the *Khevre Kedische* and *Khevre Dovor Tov*, which provided charity for the poor, ministered to the sick and dying, and maintained the Jewish cemetery.[22] Their male offspring were circumcised eight days after birth. In childhood and adolescence, they continued receiving religious and Hebrew instruction – communal when possible, private when necessary – in order to supplement the required secularly oriented instruction in the state-controlled German language schools. At age thirteen, the sons were welcomed to adulthood and full religious responsibility in a *bar-mitzvah* ceremony; the daughters, limited in rights and responsibilities within the synagogue, continued their informal education toward their recognized role as helpmates to their future husbands and as household managers and mothers.[23]

But signs of a new orientation began to appear even among members of the generation of Stefan Zweig's great-great-grandparents. A number of them demonstrated a patriotic allegiance to the state in which they resided – an identification with Crown and imperial cause that transcended the confines of their ghetto world long before they were actually considered citizens with full legal and political equality in the Hapsburg lands. Early in 1793, for example, a year after the outbreak of the War of the First Coalition against revolutionary France, Solomon Löwinau, a brother of Moses Josef Zweig and superintendent of the Jewish community, proposed that all Prossnitz Jews make a voluntary financial contribution to the war effort. Despite their relative poverty, the inhabitants of the *Judenstadt* heeded the appeal and pledged a generous sum of money. At the same time, the chief rabbi (*Landesrabbiner*) of the Moravian communities to which the Prossnitz congregation belonged asked all Jews to add a special prayer to the daily early morning services. In it, they were to invoke the health of Emperor Francis II and victory for the Austrian cause.[24] Similar support – both financial and patriotic – was provided by the Jews of Hohenems and the neighboring towns in the Vorarlberg during this conflict and, especially, during the course of the subsequent Napoleonic wars.[25]

To be sure, some of the Jewish monetary contributions and declarations of patriotism were calculated to educe the emperor's pleasure and to ensure "a peaceful and safe existence for God's People in the Diaspora," as Salomon Löwinau so shrewdly observed.[26] But, their defensive nature notwithstanding, these steps were clearly also indicative of efforts of at least a few Jews in that generation to break out of the social seclusion associated with ghetto existence and, even if only symbolically, to integrate more completely into the world of the Gentile majority.

• • •

Although a reaction against the liberal policies of Joseph II took place under his immediate and less enlightened successors, the Edict of Tolerance was not withdrawn. Imperfect as it was regarding the issue of Jewish citizenship and full equality, the edict, and the subsequent *Judenpatent* (1797) of Francis II, did slowly bring about an increase in social and economic opportunities for many Jews, including those in the Zweig and Brettauer families.

The gradual lifting of the restrictions that had limited Jewish economic activities encouraged members of the generation of Stefan Zweig's great-grandparents to expand both the scope and nature of the enterprises in which they were involved. The brothers Raphael (1782–1859) and Simon Brettauer (1788–1865), sons of Herz Lämle, revived their maternal grandfather's business in the cattle and horse trade – an enterprise that Maier Uffenheimer had abandoned in the 1770s after his privileges to deal in these commodities were re-

scinded for the Alpine territories outside of Hohenems. In partnership with his oldest brother, Ludwig (1768–1837) – Stefan Zweig's
great-grandfather – Raphael also established a firm that specialized
in the export of locally made stockings and coarse cloth (*Barchent*)
and the importation of goods and fabrics originating in the British
and Dutch colonies, as well as cloth, linen, and calico from Switzerland and other European countries.[27]

These business enterprises did not differ fundamentally from
those of the previous generation. But the new freedoms allowed
Ludwig, Raphael, and Simon to buy and sell over a wider geographical area – in urban centers and regions of the empire from which
Jews had formerly been excluded – and to establish bases outside
of Hohenems that might serve as potential business branches in the
future. Most importantly, by utilizing and building on capital inherited from their parent's efforts, *and by pooling their financial
resources through family partnerships and alliances based on marital
ties*, they took advantage of the expanded opportunities and entered
new fields of activity: in manufacturing and industrial production.

At least six of Herz Lämle and Brendel Brettauer's eight children
followed their father's example by marrying the offspring of well-
to-do members of the Jewish community. Fanny Wolf, Ludwig's wife
and Stefan Zweig's great-grandmother, was the daughter of Mannes
Wolf and Ester Maier Moos – the latter, a member of one of Hoh-
enem's prominent commercial families. Sybillia Brettauer's husband, Jonas Brentano, was her first cousin – the son of Nathan Elias
Brentano, who had made a considerable fortune pioneering the cotton textile trade in Hohenems. Klara married Seligman Bernheimer, a member of the Levi Levi family, involved in extensive
wholesaling and retailing businesses. Zihr and her sister Sarah Brettauer married Uffenheimers – their cousins Josef and Abraham –
further strengthening economic ties between these two families.
Simon Brettauer married Eleanor Rosenthal (1799–1868), the
daughter of Urban Veit Levi Rosenthal (1765–1826), a highly successful dry goods dealer and wholesaler whose business undertakings ranged widely within the Vorarlberg, the southern Tirol, and
northern Italy.[28]

Not long after Urban Rosenthal's death, Simon formed a partnership with his two brothers-in-law, Philipp (1801–1859) and Joseph (1805–1862), and transformed the elder Rosenthal's *commercial*
enterprise into an *industrial* concern focusing on the spinning, weav-
ing, and dyeing of cotton textiles.[29] Given the substantial initial
capital investment necessary to establish a cotton textile mill, their
action became possible because they willingly combined portions of

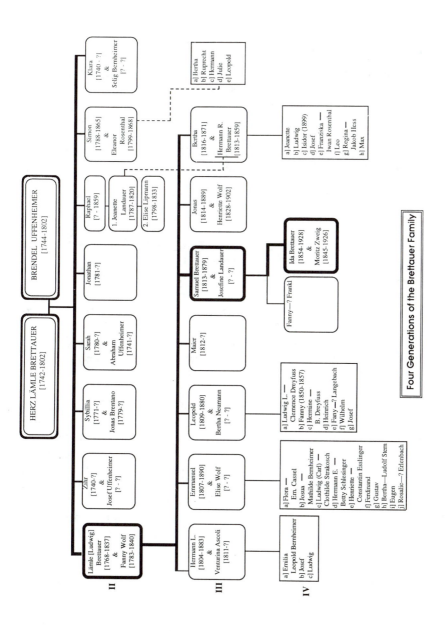

Four Generations of the Brettauer Family

their assets for mutual benefit – a willingness ostensibly lubricated by the marriage of one partner, Simon, to Eleanor, the sister of the other two. As in many other early nineteenth-century instances in which manufacturing enterprises were established in Central Europe by Jews, this one was also a clear illustration of the combination and transformation of merchant capital into industrial capital.[30]

• • •

The increase in wealth and the move away from enterprises that directly involved trade intensified in the next generation – among Brettauer family members born between 1804 and 1834 – a group that included Samuel Brettauer (1813–1879) and Josefine Landauer (1815?–?), Stefan Zweig's grandparents on his mother's side. Samuel's oldest brother, Hermann Ludwig, began his business career in a textile wholesaling firm owned by Salamon Bernheimer, his aunt Klara's father-in-law. When he founded his own import–export business in the 1830s, Hermann Ludwig followed Bernheimer's successful example and set up branch warehouses in Ancona, a port city on the Adriatic coast of central Italy, and in St. Gallen, Switzerland, relatively near Hohenems. Both these cities functioned as entrepôts for the importation of English cotton textiles, hides, and other goods, and as export and marketing centers for products from the Hapsburg Empire.

After Stefan Zweig's maternal grandfather, Samuel, joined the "H. L. Brettauer Firm" as a partner and resident manager of the Ancona operation, however, this business underwent a major change. Not only did its headquarters switch from Vorarlberg to Italy within a few years, but the nature of the enterprise underwent a metamorphosis as well – *from commerce to banking*. By the 1850s, the brothers Hermann Ludwig and Samuel were primarily known as successful bankers; they were persons of substance and wealth who counted even the Vatican among their financial clients.[31]

This generation, however, also included individuals such as Emmanuel (1807–1890) and Jonas Brettauer (1814–1889), brothers of Hermann Ludwig and Samuel, and Josef Landauer, brother of Stefan Zweig's maternal grandmother. They departed more drastically from commercial trade and occupations depending on the investment of money – into skilled handicrafts. Emmanuel and Jonas apprenticed to be tanners, and eventually owned a large tannery specializing in colored hides, and Josef became a baker and pastry-maker.[32]

It had, of course, been one of the expectations underlying the Edict of Tolerance and the subsequent laws which eased restrictions against Jews, that many would leave their traditional occupations

Josefine Landauer Brettauer (1815?–?), maternal grandmother of Stefan Zweig. [Zweig Collection, State University of New York-Fredonia]

Samuel Brettauer (1813–1879), maternal grandfather of Stefan Zweig.
[Zweig Collection, State University of New York-Fredonia]

and become artisans and agriculturalists.[33] But impediments against this type of change had remained. Hohenems, with its relatively small population, was able to support only a limited number of skilled tradespeople. Other than the butchers who supplied the community with kosher meat, the town had no Jewish artisans at the beginning of the nineteenth century. New competition from Jews in occupations that had been the preserve of Gentiles was not readily tolerated, which resulted in Josef Landauer's abandonment of baking in favor of tavern- and inn-keeping.[34] Generally, moreover, only well-to-do Jews like Ludwig Brettauer could afford to lose their sons' earning during the long apprenticeship period required for craftsmen. Not until 1840 and the establishment in Hohenems of the *Israelitischen Handwerker-Verein*, an organization that aided poor Jews to train as artisans, was this situation alleviated somewhat.[35]

The pattern of development was quite similar among Stefan Zweig's paternal ancestors. With them, however, the movement from trade and related undertakings into new branches of economic activity was slightly slower than among the Brettauers. This, no doubt, reflected the Zweigs' relatively less affluent situation at the end of the eighteenth century, and the greater difficulty they may initially have had in accumulating the surplus capital necessary for investment in new ventures. Certainly, Stefan Zweig's great-grandfather Moyses Löb Zweig (1784–1831) and his brothers Pinkus (1792–1831), Baroch (1795–1866), and Marcus (1796–1885) – all born after the promulgation of the Edict of Tolerance – adapted well to the somewhat more liberal times, and improved on their father's financial circumstances. They abandoned peddling for shopkeeping and merchandising, trading in textiles and in a variety of commodities, including tobacco, salt, grain, wine, shoes, and inexpensively produced clothing. They also seemed to have earned sufficient profits to purchase and enlarge their residences on the *Judengasse*.[36] But, despite the fact their fellow Jew Feith Ehrenstamm had established a large textile factory in Prossnitz as early as 1801, built a machine-driven cotton mill and dyeing plant a decade later, and that their town became a center for Austrian clothing manufacture during their lifetime, they seem not to have had the desire or capital resources to switch from commerce to industry.[37]

A marked change, however, can be discerned in the occupations of the children of Stefan Zweig's great-grandfather Moyses Löb Zweig and his four siblings. Of the thirty-two born between 1807 and 1841, twenty survived into adulthood: ten males and ten females. Five of the men, including Stefan's grandfather Hermann (1807–1884), became owners and co-owners of textile mills that produced twilled cotton fabrics and silk cloth; one was a milliner; and one, Elkan (1840–1906), Germanized his first name to Eduard Zweig and became the first in the family to earn a professional degree as a lawyer.[38] Two of the women, sisters Elka Katti Zweig Spitzer (1823–1896) and Lisette Zweig Reichmann (1830–1900), broke with the tradition restricting female participation in business management and earned their livelihood as dry goods dealers; two married textile merchants; one married a pawnbroker; and five became the spouses of men who owned industrial establishments: breweries, purse and drape factories, and a textile mill.[39]

Part of the explanation for this predominant shift towards industry can be found in the diversified nature of economic modernization in the Hapsburg lands. Vorarlberg, home of the Brettauers, had developed a small textile industry beginning in the late eighteenth century, but it was Upper Austria, Bohemia, and to a lesser extent, Moravia, that became the most important industrial workshops for the empire. The big landed proprietors in these areas showed themselves readier than their counterparts in the Alpine provinces to accede to the wishes of the Hapsburg rulers for industrialization, and were generally more receptive to the development of large-scale production for profit by modern means.[40] In addition, the various privileges by which the state authorities hoped to encourage persons to engage in manufacturing and industry – privileges registered in the Edict of Tolerance and reiterated in subsequent patents – provided a distinct opportunity for Jews. When they possessed the requisite investment capital, many moved into areas of economic activity where the old guild restrictions did not apply, and direct competition with their Gentile neighbors was minimal. This seems to have been the case with Stefan Zweig's grandfather Hermann, and with others of his generation.[41]

Until Jews in the Hapsburg lands were officially granted the free choice of residence in the aftermath of the Revolution of 1848, however, even the most affluent and mobile entrepreneurs among them remained bound, both in a physical and psychological sense, to the Jewish communities into which they had been born. Secular education, and greater everyday contact with the culture of the non-Jewish world, had certainly expanded their outlook and modified aspects of their social behavior. The extent of their integration into the dominant environment was reflected in their willing adoption of the majority language – German – for business, accounting, documentation, and for conversational as well as literary expression.[42] It was also reflected outwardly in the clothing they wore: in their

Hermann Zweig (1807–1884), paternal grandfather of Stefan Zweig.
[Zweig Collection, State University of New York-Fredonia]

conformity to the fashions of their Gentile economic peers, and in
the elimination of costumes that had distinguished Jews in the past.

But, without the removal of further barriers to their integration
into civic society, the feeling of belonging to a socially deprived and
legally inferior group seemed to stay alive within them. They remained sojourners in the dominant world, not full members of it.[43]

Nanette Wolf Zweig (?–1880), paternal grandmother of Stefan Zweig.
[Zweig Collection, State University of New York-Fredonia]

Despite the great distances that many of them had traversed – geographically, economically, and culturally – the members of the generation of Stefan Zweig's grandparents were not fundamentally
different from their ancestors in the pre-emancipation era. They did
not deny their religious identity as Jews, continued to belong and
to play an active role in the life of their home community, and

maintained an almost defensive sense of special obligation toward each other.

Examples abound. In Prossnitz, Hermann Zweig, his brother Salomon, and their uncle Marcus carried on the family tradition of leadership in the *Judenstadt*. Each, in turn, served the Jewish community in a judicial capacity as *Judenrichter*, and as an overseer (*Vorsteher*). Each also remained observant of Jewish religious practices, supportive of biblical, talmudic, and Hebrew instruction for the young, and involved in organizations concerned with aid to the poor and infirm.[44] Similarly in Hohenems, Leopold Simon Brettauer and his cousins – the brothers Emmanuel, Leopold, and Jonas Brettauer – served as members of the board governing the internal affairs of the community at various times. The wholesaler and banker Hermann Ludwig Brettauer was also on the governing board in the 1840s, in spite of his long absences from town during his business involvement in Switzerland and Italy. His wife, Venturina, became a director of the *Israelitischer Frauenverein* (Jewish Women's Association) and, in that capacity, concerned herself with the care of the sick as well as the welfare and education of indigent young women. Indeed all these Brettauers and their spouses, including Stefan Zweig's maternal grandparents, were recognized for their personal involvement in charitable associations, and for providing generous financial help for needy Hohenems Jews. All, moreover, continued to support Jewish religious institutions in their community – contributing for the renewal of the synagogue building and upkeep of the Jewish cemetery – and helped to sustain a rabbi and Hebrew teacher.[45]

• • •

But, although the partial lowering of restrictive barriers seems not to have effectively weakened the bond between these Zweigs and Brettauers and their religion and community, the completion of the legal process of emancipation in the ensuing years stimulated more varied responses.

Thus, the enactment of the *Freizügigkeit* in the wake of the Revolution of 1848–9 granted Austrian Jews the freedom to move about and *settle* where they wished. In 1867, after Austria's defeat by Prussia and the introduction of a liberal constitution for Austria-Hungary, Jews officially received full civic equality within the empire.[46] The attainment of these rights extended the range of social opportunities for the generation of Stefan Zweig's parents, and provided its members with the possibility of integrating more fully into the world of the dominant majority. The cost was a more complete physical and psychological break with the past.

On a symbolic level, this break was indicated by this generation's distinctively "modern" first names. Instead of the Germanized but recognizably Jewish names of biblical or postbiblical origin that had been most common even with members of the previous generation – names like Joseph, Ester, Leib, Samuel, Sarah, Israel, Abraham, Solomon, Chaim, and Moses – the preferred names were now Moritz, Heimann, Hermann, Henriette, Ida, Fanny, Ludwig, Gustav, and Max. Indeed, even ultra-Teutonic names such as Siegmund, Siegfried, and Clothilde could be found among the siblings and cousins of Stefan Zweig's parents.[47]

In the occupational realm, the tendencies evident in the preceding era also intensified. Vocational information exists for thirty-six of the forty-eight persons in the Brettauer and Zweig lineage born between 1845 and 1875.[48] Nine of twenty-three (39 percent) Zweig relatives – siblings and cousins of Stefan Zweig's father, Moritz – were owners of industrial plants, either directly or through marriage; eight (35 percent) were involved in some aspect of commerce, usually wholesaling; and six (26 percent) were in the professions: two doctors of medicine, two lawyers, one actor, and one engineer. Nine of thirteen (69 percent) Brettauers – siblings and cousins of Ida, Stefan Zweig's mother – were directors, or married to directors, of banking houses; one was a lawyer; two were medical specialists (23 percent), an eye surgeon and a gynecologist; and one married an industrialist.[49]

The growing number of doctors and lawyers in this group reflected the beginning of a trend that would grow among members of Stefan Zweig's own generation: what he called the "desire to rise above mere money" and described as the "move away from the occupations associated with the ghetto experience," into the liberal professions.[50] This trend, of course, also reflected the increasing choices available to Jews during this heyday of liberalism in Austria, as legal barriers fell and official discrimination against them in noncommercial fields waned. Nor is the large percentage of bankers and industrialists in this group surprising. The years between 1848 and the mid-1870s, as Eric Hobsbawm has argued, was the "period when the world became capitalist."[51] Any male who had accumulated surplus wealth – through personal effort, inheritance, or marital connection – found himself in ideal circumstances to take advantage of this era of economic expansion and heightened industrial development. Although peddling, pawnbroking, and moneylending had been looked on with suspicion and a certain amount of disdain by the Gentile majority in times past, banking and factory ownership carried much more prestige during the Age of Capital.

Moritz Zweig (1845–1926) and Ida Zweig shortly after their wedding in
1878. [Zweig Collection, State University of New York-Fredonia]

The freedom of occupational choice, moreover, was now also accompanied by the right of free settlement (*Freizügigkeit*). In impressive numbers, Jews left their residences in the small-town
ghettos and moved to places where they had formerly not been permitted to live. Many individuals and young couples migrated on a
permanent basis to cities like Prague and Vienna, and to the new
industrial centers of the empire where economic and cultural activity was rife. The size of the Viennese Jewish community, for in-

stance, increased dramatically, from 6,200 in 1860 (2.2 percent of
the population) to 72,600 in 1880 (10 percent of the total).[52] This
geographical mobility was clearly evident among members of the
generation of Stefan Zweig's parents.

Only ten of the thirty-five (28 percent) persons in the Zweig lineage born between 1845 and 1875 resided in Prossnitz after the
Freizügigkeit was enacted. Two (6 percent) moved nearby, to Olmütz;
one (3 percent) settled in Hamburg; seven (20 percent) moved to
Vienna; and 15 (43 percent) were born in the Austrian capital (or
in its immediate vicinity) after their parents had settled there.[53]
Among the Brettauers, Stefan Zweig's mother, Ida (1854–1938), and
her sister Fanny (1852?–?) were born in Ancona and moved to Vienna with their parents in the early 1870s, after Samuel's liqui-
dation of the banking house in Italy. Hermann and Venturina's three
children, Emilia, Josef, and Ludwig settled in Trieste. Two of Emanuel and Elise's sons, Josua and Hermann Emanuel, remained in
Hohenems, where they directed a banking and currency-exchange
bureau. Their brother Ferdinand and cousin Heinrich moved to Bre-
genz where, in partnership, the two established another branch of
the family's banking business. Eugen Emanuel became a lawyer in
Vienna. Heinrich's older brother, Ludwig, left to settle in Switzerland, founding yet another bank in Zurich. Leopold and Bertha's
daughters Hermine and Fany married and moved, one to Basel and
the other to Worms. Their brother Josef became a medical doctor
and eventually emigrated to New York.[54]

II

By leaving the confines of the Jewish quarters in Prossnitz and
Hohenems permanently, these members of the Zweig and Brettauer
families severed their ties to the old communal structures and organizations in an irrevocable manner. The nature and direction of
their identification and primary orientation shifted from *shtettl* to
Grosstadt. Unlike their parents and grandparents, who had merely
sojourned uneasily in the non-Jewish world because of residential
restrictions and legal limitations, many in this generation felt freer
to take fuller advantage of the cultural and material opportunities
available to Austrian middle-class society, and to commit themselves to their new milieu in a more permanent manner.

Indeed, if one were to judge aspects of the assimilationist experience as they were manifested by many Zweigs and Brettauers
belonging to the generation born in the third quarter of the nineteenth century – if one were to evaluate the thoroughness of their

acculturation to dominant values through their external behavior, outward appearance, and use of language – one might reasonably infer that the emancipatory avenue that had initially been opened by Joseph II's Edict of Tolerance had succeeded in attaining its goal. On the basis of bourgeois standards of "cultural refinement" as well as economic and professional achievement – on the basis of *Verbesserung* – many Zweigs and Brettauers had met, if not surpassed, the hopes of liberal social reformers. By the time Jews were granted full legal emancipation in Austria in 1867, they seemed to have fulfilled the wish that they would no longer be differentiated from other citizens except by their faith. But such an inference would fail to take into account aspects of their social and psychological adaptation which, directly or indirectly, addressed the fact that opposition to Jewish emancipation and advancement had never disappeared during the nineteenth century – that, indeed, anti-Jewish prejudices were very much alive, insidious, and growing ominously stronger.

The orientation of Stefan Zweig's parents, Moritz and Ida, for example, had unquestionably shifted away from the Jewish experience in the communities of their family origin; they had immersed themselves into the cosmopolitan atmosphere of the Viennese metropolis that they now called home with energy and enthusiasm. In their case, the end goal of this shift and immersion was clearly not intended as a flight from Judaism toward Christian baptism. Although Vienna had the highest conversion rate in Europe by the end of the nineteenth century, neither they nor any other Zweig or Brettauers of their generation abandoned the Jewish religion by converting to Christianity. Nor did any of them marry outside of the faith – as a number of their children would do.[55] No doubt for Moritz and Ida, as for other Zweigs and Brettauers, the very decisiveness of mind that the act of religious conversion required, and the finality of rejection that it symbolized, was a move too measured and too radical. As Albert Memmi has indicated in his insightful *The Liberation of the Jew*, conversion called for "the irreversible passage from one community to another, from one ideological universe to another"; "in one stroke [it] proclaim[ed] the failure of the group" from which the convert originated.[56] This "passage" and "proclamation" had been characteristic of the religious conversion to Christianity of Joseph May in Sierra Leone and of many Jewish contemporaries of Moritz and Ida Zweig in Vienna. The Zweigs and Brettauers, however, seemed unwilling to take such a decisive, unequivocal, step.

To be sure, Moritz and Ida Zweig were much more highly secularized than their own parents. They were largely emancipated from orthodox Jewish religious practices. They were, according to their son Stefan's description, "passionate followers of the religion of the time, 'progress.' " Yet they also remained Jews in more than a nominal sense. They were married by a rabbi; maintained a membership in the *Israelitische Allianz*, the Viennese Jewish community organization; and had both their sons circumcised. Despite an absence of day-to-day religious observance on their part, they seemed also to have fasted on Yom Kippur, the Day of Atonement and holiest day of the Jewish year, and recognized Stefan's and his brother Alfred's symbolic passage into Jewish manhood with a *bar-mitzvah* ceremony at the time of their sons' thirteenth birthday.[57]

But, although Moritz and Ida's unwillingness to abandon Jewish religious practices and communal connections altogether can be viewed as a reflection of their desire to keep their Jewish identity and heritage alive, their continuing identification with *Judaism* did not carry through to *Jews in general*. In spite of their membership in the *Israelitische Allianz*, they distanced themselves socially and symbolically from the Jewish hoi polloi: the large number of poor, less educated and less sophisticated, Jewish immigrants who were flocking to Vienna from the Hapsburg provinces and the *shtettls* of Eastern Europe.[58]

Indeed, both in relation to their Jewish connections and to the conventions of the dominant culture, they positioned themselves carefully within their Viennese surroundings. They acquired a series of elegant apartments in the better neighborhoods of the city; furnished them with material possessions in keeping with contemporary bourgeois tastes; and publicly showed themselves at the theater, opera, coffeehouses, and at those cosmopolitan activities associated with the "more refined, better bred" members of capital society. As was true with other assimilating aspirants for whom the integrationist promises of emancipation had not been blocked, their primary social identification and orientation was with others of their *class* – with persons among whom many were Jews to be sure, but who also included liberal Austrians not Jewish in religious orientation. Publicly, as Stefan Zweig remembered his parents, they made an effort to display the very best qualities envisioned in the emancipatory *Verbesserung* ideal: they showed themselves off as persons who seemed truly worthy of the legal and social position that the naturalization of Jews into Austrian citizenship had made possible.[59]

Similarly, as Stefan Zweig indicated about his parents, Moritz and Ida also sought to disarm potential hostility to their own economic success by belying the stereotype of the money-grubbing Jew, of the avaricious Shylock who provoked envy and hatred on the part of the Gentile majority. In spite of their considerable fortune – Moritz had become a millionaire textile industrialist and was "counted among the very wealthy, even by international standards" – they presented themselves as no more than ordinary members of the "good Viennese bourgeoisie." They diverted attention from their "difference" – from their Jewishness and their wealth – by downplaying their money and remaining discreet, restrained, and largely unostentatious in their personal appearance and style of life. Moritz dressed simply, usually in a "neat and sober black coat and striped trousers," traveled second-class on trains, rented a horse-drawn carriage occasionally for transport but did not own one, and smoked only cheap cheroots instead of imported cigars. Ida generally dressed more elegantly, in lace and satin, and wore jewelry as well as an elaborate, fashionable hairstyle. But, despite her wealthy family background and affluent situation in the 1880s, she did not appear to be particularly more extravagant in manner or costume than other ladies of the Austrian middle class; and, in every other respect, concurred with her husband's temperate taste for the well-ordered and unobtrusive public life.[60]

It is of course not difficult to understand why such highly acculturated and well-to-do individuals as Moritz and Ida Zweig adjusted to the world of the Gentile majority in Vienna with such caution and circumspection. As their contemporary Arthur Schnitzler observed in his memoirs: the steadfastness of anti-Jewish prejudices in the aftermath of the granting of full emancipation in 1867 made it difficult for Jews to forget that they were Jews – even if they had been inclined to do so.[61] In large part, throughout most of the nineteenth century, and even in the aftermath of the 1873 banking crash and economic depression that had catalyzed the emergence of a virulent anti-Semitic movement in neighboring Germany, anti-Jewish prejudice had remained on the fringes rather than within the central pattern of the Austrian social fabric.[62] Inasmuch as they were associated with free enterprise and capitalist investment, however, Jews were targeted in the reaction against the prevailing liberal order, and efforts were made to exclude them from university student unions and to limit their participation in the medical and legal professions.[63]

Much of the anti-Jewish propaganda and sentiment that had called for a halt, if not for a total withdrawal, of the rights granted by the process of emancipation was considered extremist and reactionary by significant elements of the dominant liberal establishment. It was ideologically associated with the Catholic right wing, and viewed by many assimilating Jews as an anomaly – in Jacob Katz's words, "as a backward cultural phenomenon that was bound to disappear in the course of time."[64] But the centuries-old notion of the *Jew as alien* – as a foreign, unnaturalizable, social entity – had persisted throughout the emancipation era along with the newer undercurrent of resentment against Jewish economic and professional advancement.

It was this notion that in the 1880s became the central principle of a new, racist, now truly *anti-Semitic* rather than merely *anti-Jewish* ideology. It viewed Jews as "a unique species with marked physical and moral characteristics" – as a "race" whose inferiority, according to one of its influential proponents, Eugen Dühring, was immutable, "unchanged and unchangeable."[65] This anti-Semitism, based on a widespread and highly influential ideological premise that viewed races as "distinctively different" and that posited an inherent, biological, connection between race and human capabilities and behavioral traits, made it possible to maintain that Jews, a "Semitic race," were *by nature* permanently unassimilable into the "Aryan" dominant population: that even baptism could not eradicate the Jews' inherently "inferior" characteristics.

• • •

The emergence of this racist anti-Semitism in Austria, at about the same time Stefan Zweig and his generation were born, marked the beginning of a break from the relatively mild anti-Jewish prejudice that had characterized Jewish emancipation throughout the greater part of the nineteenth century. Although the practical consequences of the racist attitudes were initially minor, in the ensuing decades they would continue to penetrate and spread within the fabric of Austrian political and social life. They would culminate in the horrors of Nazi genocide.

Nonetheless, in contrast to the cautious but determined journey along the assimilationist path taken by his parents and by earlier members of his family, Stefan Zweig and his generational contemporaries entered into the realm of the Austrian-bourgeois mainstream with greater confidence about their place within it and right to belong. From our hindsight on twentieth-century Jewish historical experience in Europe, this confidence now seems deeply paradoxical. Examined from the vantage of an earlier time, however, the contrast between the responses of Stefan Zweig and those of his parents and grandparents, illuminates the key problematic this book explores: the uncertain interplay between individual perception and historical circumstance.

Chapter 4

Into the White World:
The Rebouças Story

"Branco é quem bem procede."
"Negro na côr, branco nas ações."
"Negro por fora, branco por dentro."

"A white is one who behaves well."
"Black in color, white in deeds."
"Black outside, white inside."
Popular Brazilian sayings

*"Mas quais são os iguais a mim: os que têm a mesma côr ou os que têm
o mesma educação?"* ("But who are my equals: those who have my skin
color, or those who are educated like me?")
Quoted in Costa Pinto,
O Negro No Rio de Janeiro

The range of what we think and do
is limited by what we fail to notice.
And because we fail to notice
that we fail to notice
there is little we can do
to change
until we notice
how failing to notice
shapes our thoughts and deeds.
R. D. Laing, *Knots*

In the 1780s, not long after Gaspar Pereira Rebouças, a down-on-
his-luck tailor, emigrated to Bahia, Brazil, from São Tiago do Fontão,
in northern Portugal, he met and married Rita Brasilia dos Santos,
a dark mulatta freedwoman – a woman "of comely appearance," as
she was later described, who had been born a slave.[1] Together, the
young Portuguese immigrant and his Afro-Brazilian spouse founded
a family that would be widely recognized by the dominant elites in
Brazil for the accomplishments of many of its members – a family
that would include a number of important actors in some of the most
significant episodes of modern Brazilian history.

The children of the couple would play a role in the Brazilian movement for independence from Portugal, in the founding and establishment of the Brazilian Empire, and in the consolidation of centralized political authority during the regency and under the young Dom Pedro II. Their grandchildren would become agents furthering the progress of Brazilian industrial and technological modernization in the second half of the nineteenth century. They would be important participants in the planning and construction of a national transportation network, proponents of land reform, theoreticians of agricultural development, and would serve as leading propagandists and tacticians during the successful campaign to abolish slavery.

Although the range of public involvement and the degree of personal success achieved by the children and grandchildren of Rita Brasilia dos Santos and Gaspar Pereira Rebouças was extraordinary, the family pattern of social mobility, as well as adjustment to color-based discrimination, was not unusual in Brazil. This approach resembled that of many other Brazilians of mixed racial background, and reflected that particular feature of Brazilian race relations which Carl Degler has so aptly identified as the "mulatto escape hatch."[2] It involved a climb "up," from dire poverty and subordination based on color prejudice and origins in enslavement, into the class and cultural realm of the predominantly white Brazilian elites. It was generally undertaken with intense personal effort, applied intelligence, and the judicious exploitation of opportunities for economic and social advancement. These opportunities derived from the fact that social acceptance within the dominant Brazilian "white" world was easier for mulattoes and lighter-skinned "persons of color" than it was for blacks.[3]

Characteristically, moreover, it was marked by a degree of conformity with the cultural values and economic standards defined by the dominant group, and by a rejection of practices and attitudes considered by the dominant standard-bearers as "inferior," "backward," and "atavistic." Indeed, in a broadly conceived structural and strategic sense, the pattern of social ascension tread by the Rebouças and other Brazilian *pretos* and *pardos* had much in common with the postemancipation "up from slavery" and "out of the ghetto" pattern followed by Ifacayeh May and other Liberated Africans and Creoles in Sierra Leone; by the Zweigs, Brettauers, and other Jews in Hapsburg Central Europe; and by numerous other individuals striving to overcome their subordinate status in Europe, colonial Africa, Asia, and the Americas.

But the Brazilian pattern, like all others, also contained features

that were unique and special, derived from the particular assimilationist ideology that had evolved within the context of the country's
own historical and cultural reality. Although Christian conversion
and Europeanization had thus been the keys to initiate penetration
into the world of the dominant in early nineteenth-century Sierra
Leone, and *Verbesserung* (self-improvement) had opened doors for
Jews in Hapsburg Central Europe, in Brazil chances for admission
to that world and class mobility within it were controlled and determined by an ideology based on cultural and somatic criteria that
came to be known as *embranquecemento* (whitening).[4]

I

Despite the paucity of detailed information about the lives of Gaspar
Pereira Rebouças and Rita Brasilia dos Santos, it is not difficult to
imagine reasons why their racially mixed marriage took place. Certainly, although casual out-of-wedlock interracial sexual encounters
and miscegenation occurred far more frequently than marriage in
colonial Brazil's multiethnic and multiracial slavocratic society, the
fact of racial intermarriage was not unusual in itself. The *Registro
do Casamentos* (Marriage Register) in the *Arquivo da Curia* in
Salvador, Bahia, contains numerous eighteenth- and nineteenth-
century entries listing *pardas* (mulattas) marrying whites.[5] Demographic realities would undoubtedly have played an important role
in these situations because white males of marriageable age seem
to have significantly outnumbered white women in Bahia throughout the entire colonial era.[6] Moral pressures applied by the Catholic
clergy on parishioners would also have been influential inducements
to the formalization of wedlock. But for Rita Brasilia dos Santos and
Gaspar Pereira Rebouças, as for other interracial couples, the decision to marry would also have been influenced by subtler social
and economic factors.

Throughout Brazil's colonial period and well into the nineteenth
century, as A. J. R. Russell-Wood and others have persuasively demonstrated, the situation for a free person of color like Rita Brasilia
dos Santos was an ambiguous and insecure one.[7] To be sure, the size
of the free colored population, and especially the number of mulattoes, within the overall population of the country did increase considerably during the second half of the eighteenth and the first
decades of the nineteenth century. But this demographic growth
occurred within a context of discriminatory laws and practices that,
in intent if not always in actual fact, restricted the legal, social,
economic, and political rights as well as opportunities of persons

identified as members of the free colored social group.[8] In the wording of colonial legislation that aimed to fortify the dominant position of the white minority, free persons of color were often coupled with black slaves. They were forbidden to hold high public office in the service of the crown, state, or church, and until 1759 were prohibited from carrying weapons and from exhibiting "marks of gentility [in their dress] which might tend to place them on a level with the Whites."[9] Colored freedmen were also actively discouraged, by whites fearing their competition, from involving themselves in commerce, the skilled trades, and the artisan professions. They were, moreover, commonly subjected to popular stereotypical representations and prejudices that, in their negativity and exclusivity, complemented the severity of official policy and discourse.[10]

In effect, however, although all persons of color would certainly be compelled to recognize the white minority's power to define the norms governing social conduct and social acceptance in colonial Brazil, official color-bar legislation was often more of a theoretical than practical barrier to "restricted" social arenas. The reality of Brazilian demography and settlement patterns during the colonial era – in particular, the relative scarcity of "pure blooded" whites in rural areas away from the coastal urban centers – influenced the actual application of discriminatory laws. The degree of tolerance of the social and economic involvement of "free coloreds," and of their class ascension, thus tended to vary from region to region and over time.

Although whites consistently monopolized positions of influence throughout Brazil, a minority among the population of free persons of color was able to penetrate into the realm of the dominant in every region of the country, and was able to attain a measure of acceptance and, on occasion, even economic and social prominence. In general, in those places where demographic imbalances were not sufficiently marked to create a natural need for the active participation of persons of color in officially or unofficially restricted areas of society, patronage from some well-disposed member of the white elite would aid their admission and help eliminate impediments to their acceptance. Talent and money would also buy them admission and position, and would influence white perceptions about them once they were inside.

But, consistently throughout the colonial period, and everywhere in Brazil, *the critical determinant of their acceptance and integration within the dominant world was skin color*: mulattoes, on the whole, were preferred over blacks; lighter mulattoes were more acceptable than their darker-skinned brethren.[11] *"Branco é filho de Deus,"* popular folklore proclaimed,

> *Caboclo é seu irmão,*
> *Cabra ainda é parente,*
> *E negro, filho de cão.*

> The white is a child of God,
> The copper-colored backwoodsman
>   is his brother,
> The mulatto is a relative yet,
> And the black, a son of a dog.

This somatic, color-linked criterion for social acceptance and advancement was the foundation supporting the ideology of "whitening," which would dominate Brazilian elite thought about race until the mid-twentieth century.[12] Its proponents, although firmly anchored in the universal racist conviction that members of the "white race" were "superior" and "more advanced" than members of other racial groupings, privileged and rewarded persons whose physical characteristics were closest to the "Caucasian" ideal: to the white "somatic norm image," in Harmannus Hoetink's words.[13] In so doing, as Thomas Skidmore has indicated in *Black into White*, they discarded two of the main assumptions usually present in racist ideas outside of Brazil: beliefs in the "innateness of racial differences" and in the "degeneracy of mixed bloods."[14] Acknowledging the already existing multiracial reality of their country, they departed from European and North American notions that stressed racial purity and exclusivity. Instead, in "whitening," they postulated an integrative dynamic process in which the "superior" white race would steadily assimilate the "inferior colored races" within Brazil, ultimately erasing them from the population. They thus accepted interracial coupling and miscegenation as evolutionary means toward a positive end: as assimilationist vehicles leading to a physically whiter and culturally superior Brazil.[15]

For persons of color – aware of the superior position of whites in Brazil's slavocratic colonial society, and of the existence of a somatic and cultural bias that provided greater social and economic opportunities to individuals who came closest to "looking" and "acting white" – "marrying lighter" was therefore a logical strategy toward greater social prestige and higher social ascension. Certainly, from the perspective of a mulatta freedwoman like Rita Brasilia dos Santos, linkage with the race of the dominant group through her marriage to Gaspar Pereira Rebouças provided public evidence of movement away from a black-African slave past, and attested to her successful penetration into a "lighter," more socially prestigious world.

In Rita's particular case, no documentation exists to reveal how long she had been free from slavery when she married Rebouças, or how she had secured her liberty. Opportunities for manumission were certainly greater in Brazil than in other New World slave-holding societies, and the process of individual emancipation accelerated at the turn of the eighteenth century.[16]Although the exact number of freed women and men living in the captaincy-general of Bahia de Todos os Santos when Rita married is unknown, it is estimated that free blacks and mulattoes already outnumbered slaves in the city of Salvador by almost 10 percent.[17] Liberty could legally come to slaves by testament in a master's will, by baptismal declaration or, most commonly for adults, by self-purchase. In urban and mining areas especially, where slaves could more easily amass the necessary capital to buy themselves out of bondage, manumission through self-purchase was a frequent practice.[18] But the "mixed-blood" offspring of a master and slave were sometimes also granted their freedom, and it is quite possible, as is believed by some of her descendants nowadays, that Rita Brasilia dos Santos received her liberty in this manner.[19]

In order to bring about her marriage to Gaspar Pereira Rebouças, Rita Brasilia dos Santos no doubt took advantage of a means of social ascension – of an aspect of the "mulatto escape hatch" – that was uniquely available to women of color in Brazil. This "female strategy" played on the erotic fantasies of white males, and was succinctly reflected in Capistrano de Abreu's ditty:

> Uma mulata bonita
> Não carece de rezar:
> Basta o mimo que tem
> Para a sua alma salvar

> A pretty mulatto girl
> Need not practice devotion;
> She offers her dainty self
> Toward her soul's salvation.[20]

It is thus quite possible that, for Gaspar Pereira Rebouças, Rita's race and physical appearance may in themselves have been attractive forces, and consciously or unconsciously she may have taken advantage of this attraction. The alleged erotic appeal of mulattas, in contrast to that of white women, was certainly already well established in popular Brazilian belief by the beginning of the eighteenth century, and Gaspar would have been exposed to its expression in proverbs, songs, poetry, and in everyday street talk. He would have heard the popular assertion *"é a mulata que é Mulher"* ("it is the mulatta who is the *real* woman") and have listened to Bahian *cantadores* sing a *Lundú* like:

> *Do Brazil a mulatinha*
> *É do céo dôce maná;*
> *Adocicada frutinha,*
> *Sabroso cambucá.*

> *É quitute appetitoso,*
> *É melhor que vatapá;*
> *É nectar delicioso,*
> *É boa como não ha ...*

> From Brazil the *mulatinha*
> Is heaven's sweet manna;
> Candied fruit,
> Tasty myrtle.

> She is an appetizing tidbit,
> She is better than *vatapá*;
> She is the delicious nectar,
> Delectable like nothing else ... [21]

The bias favoring *mulatinhas* reflected a demographic reality: the relative numerical scarcity of "available" white women. But it also had its roots in practices that had evolved in the patriarchal, slave-holding society to which Gaspar had emigrated: in the domestic segregation of white women and their elevation to an almost unattainable pedestal that made them platonic rather than erotic objects. And, of course, it was also founded in the power over women that patriarchal slavocracy granted to white males in general and gave them easy access to women from subordinated racial groups for satisfaction of the pleasures of the flesh.[22]

But Gaspar's social background and economic standing were undoubtedly also very important elements in his choice of mate. The circumstances of his emigration from Portugal, which he left together with his brother, Pedro, are somewhat mysterious, and seem to have been such that they permitted him to carry little or nothing of material value to Brazil. It is likely, of course, that the Rebouças' departure for America from their home in the beautiful village near Ponte de Lima may simply have been stimulated by a desire to improve their economic lot in the seemingly wealthier New World.

For them, like for so many of their countrymen in the last quarter
of the eighteenth century, this desire would have developed in pro-
portion to the diminished economic opportunities at home following
the devastating earthquakes and agricultural shortages of the mid-
1750s.

But other reasons may explain the accelerated nature of their
emigration as well. The family name, Rebouças – for which variant
spellings Reboussa, Rebouça, Rebossa, Reboça, Reborsa, and Reborça
also existed in Portugal – is believed to be of Sephardic origin, and
suggests that Gaspar and his brother descended from Portuguese
Jews who had been forcibly converted to Catholicism in 1497. Although no conclusive evidence exists to prove that they were indeed
Christãos Novos (New Christians) – and none to indicate that their
departure from São Tiago do Fontão was at all influenced by existing
prejudices against the *defeito de sangue* (defect of blood) associated
with a *converso* background – the possibility that some form of social,
or perhaps even political, pressure sparked their emigration can
certainly not be discounted either.[23]

Arriving in Bahia as a poverty-stricken tailor, Gaspar was undoubtedly not much better off economically than the freedmen mulattoes and blacks who plied the same trade in his newly adopted
land. He did, however, possess one advantage over most of the tailors
with whom he would have competed for work: his color. And, although neither his artisan status nor his lack of wealth would have
been at all attractive to the eligible daughters of the better-off members of white Bahian society, he would certainly have been considered an excellent marital prospect by the comely *mulatinha* Rita
Brasilia dos Santos.

Little can be said about the couple's life together. Only vague
descriptions exist depicting their outward appearance, and not much
is known in detail about their personal histories and accomplishments. We do not know if either of the two was more than super-
ficially literate, involved in any of Bahia's numerous social and
mutual-aid organizations, or affiliated with Catholicism in more
than a token fashion. We know nothing definite about their likes
and dislikes, their friendships, or their relationship with each other.

But we do know that they both moved from Salvador, the capital
of Bahia, to Maragogipe, a small town in the sugar-producing Recôncavo region of this royal captaincy, before their first son, José
Pereira Rebouças, was born in the late 1780s. We also know that
they had at least nine offspring (five daughters and four sons) who
survived childhood; that by 1798 Gaspar was a "well-regarded" master tailor who had "earned the esteem of the most influential citizens

of the area"; that, despite his profession, he did not take part in the 1798 Bahian "Conspiracy of the Tailors," a failed mass rebellion influenced by Enlightenment and French revolutionary ideas; and that, some ten years after Rita's death, he was still alive when his grandson André was baptized in November 1840.[24]

Because the couple left no direct evidence to indicate their perceptions about the society in which they lived, we cannot ascertain if their lives were in any manner impeded by overt racial or social prejudice, nor can we assess the degree to which, if at all, they felt dissatisfied or discouraged with their personal lot. Although they were certainly poor, they were not among the poorest in their society. Given Gaspar's Portuguese birth and his professional contact as a master tailor with the middle and upper classes, it would not have been extraordinary if he and Rita had aspired for some greater recognition from their social peers than was merited by their actual financial circumstances. Nor would it be surprising if they had chosen to protect their upper-stratum artisan status by maintaining their social distance from those beneath them on the social ladder.

They would have realized these two aims by adopting and internalizing some of the material and cultural values of their social "betters," and by shunning possible association with Bahians belonging to the free and unfree menial laboring groups. No doubt, they might also have attempted to project their status through their external appearance and through their public manifestation of elite values: in the type and quality of the clothing they wore, and in their general outward demeanor. Because of Rita's color, moreover, her public projection of status and class achievement would also have required a conscious avoidance, if not outright denial, of cultural and religious practices prevalent among the lowest-class "persons of color" – and especially prevalent among slaves, the group within the Afro-Brazilian community from which she had managed to escape.

All this, however, is speculation. It was only in the generation of Gaspar and Rita's racially mixed children that the Rebouças' pattern of social ascension into the elite world of the dominant took form in greater detail. Physical "whitening" through miscegenation remained a consistent element in this pattern. At least four of their nine children wedded "light," marrying either a person identified as a "fair mulatto" (*pardo claro*) or a white.[25] This practice, which may indeed not have been consciously calculated on their part, was a testament to the hegemonic power and pervasiveness of the dominant racial ideology among Brazilians: to the inadvertent complicity of subordinate "colored" individuals in the maintenance of an ideological construct furthering the interests of the dominant "white" elite. Marrying "lighter" reproduced their mother's marital arrangement – distancing them, like her, from the "darker shades" associated with subordination. It also promised their own children an even better chance of somatic escape from the stigma of blackness.

But, although somatic "whitening" was a critical element within the dominant Brazilian ideology of assimilation, the Rebouças' pattern of social ascension also included its requisite cultural complement. As was true for other Brazilian "persons of color" who moved "upward" from subordination into nineteenth-century bourgeois society, it was the acquisition of formal education that further enhanced the admission of the Rebouças to the higher-status professions, freeing them from manual labor and offering the possibility of greater affluence. In this respect, of course, the assimilationist strategy that they and other "colored" Brazilians employed was hardly different from the one utilized by Liberated Africans and Creoles like the Mays in colonial Sierra Leone, or by Jews in Hapsburg Central Europe.

Generally speaking, those children of Gaspar and Rita who received the greatest amount of formal schooling studied during a period when significant educational reform and reorientation was taking place in Brazil, particularly in the urban areas. Early in the nineteenth century – beginning with the arrival of the Portuguese court at Bahia in 1808, and the introduction of a new current of pedagogical thought influenced by the ideals of the French encyclopedists – the scope and emphasis of the educational curriculum broadened throughout much of the country. Besides the subjects that had constituted the traditional curriculum for secondary education – grammar, Latin, rhetoric, poetry, philosophy, and theology – some of the Rebouças' children also began to receive instruction in living languages and modern literatures like French and English, as well as in natural and physical sciences and mathematics.[26]

This instruction, however, though revolutionary in its departure from the religious and literary-oriented pedagogical and curricular tradition that the Jesuits had introduced and disseminated throughout Brazil during the colonial era, in no sense challenged dominant cultural values and ideas about race relations.[27] Indeed, despite its growing emphasis on scientific and technical instruction, the ideological and symbolic content of the "new" education continued to reinforce a bias that held up "white" European cultural attainments as the superior standard for emulation. It also supported the "whitening process," both in its somatic and cultural dimension, as the proper assimilationist vehicle for the attainment of Brazilian social integration and national development.

The use that the Rebouças' children were able to make of education for purposes of social ascension, moreover, differed according to the level of school instruction that each individual was able to attain. Certainly, because the acquisition of formal education for Brazilian women was generally impeded by sexual bias, Rita and Gaspar Rebouças' daughters had less of a chance than their brothers to employ it for class mobility. Escolastica, Luisa, Maria, Anna Rita, and Eugenia Rebouças received little schooling beyond the most elementary instruction, and were probably barely able to read and write. Had they been female offspring of a wealthier family, they might have received private tuition in music and been instructed somewhat beyond the level of rudimentary literacy. Because they were not, however, they were no doubt trained in the domestic arts only, not academically: to cook, sew, mend, and care for their spouses, children, and male relatives.

Their social status came to depend in great part on the position and mobility of the men they married and served. In this regard, of course, they were no different from their mother, nor from the majority of women of similar background throughout the male-dominated, patriarchical, society in which they lived. At the turn of the eighteenth century and well into the nineteenth, an old Portuguese saying was still relevant in Brazil: "A woman is well enough educated when she can read correctly her prayers and can write her recipe for *goiabada* [a kind of guava jelly]. More than that would be a danger to the household."[28]

Although differences in class, status, and between rural and city residence influenced the degree of personal freedom and the independence of movement that women could attain by the early nineteenth century, they largely continued to remain in a situation of legal and customary inferiority to males, and their roles were generally still restricted to domestic functions and activities.[29] In this respect, women of color like the Rebouças' daughters were subjected to prejudices that were based on race as well as on gender – from the dominant elite in general, but also from men in particular – and it is of little wonder that they took advantage of male belief in the supposedly spicy and fiery sexuality of *mulatas* for personal "advancement."

Their brothers, however, had greater opportunities to affect their own destiny. Even Manoel Pereira Rebouças, the least successful of the four males – and the one about whom the least is known – was sent to primary school by his parents until his early teens. Although Gaspar and Rita could not afford to support him beyond this age, he managed to acquire the necessary academic skills to qualify as a clerk in the office of a public notary, a position of sufficient status to permit his marriage to a *parda clara* (light mulatta) from a family belonging to Bahia's lower bourgeoisie.[30]

Mauricio, the next-to-youngest brother, also received primary schooling before finding it necessary to seek employment. Like Manoel, he too qualified to work in a notary's office, first in nearby Jaguaripe, in the southern Recôncavo, and later in Salvador and the wealthiest Recôncavo town, Cachoeira. His ambition, however, went beyond that of his brother. After a stint as an army volunteer on the nationalist side during the Brazilian struggles for independence in the early 1820s, he managed to scrape together enough money to continue his studies in Paris, capital of the land that the Brazilian elite associated with the epitome of cultural achievement. There, he earned bachelor's degrees in arts and sciences, as well as a doctorate of medicine.

In 1832, after returning to Bahia, he obtained the chair in botany and zoology at the newly established medical college in Salvador, and built a distinguished reputation as a medical doctor and academician. His career, as such, exemplified another instance of the extraordinarily important role that free persons of color played in medicine throughout colonial and nineteenth-century Brazil. He wrote books and articles about medicine and medical education, received various commissions from the government during his lifetime, and was especially noted for lending his services without remuneration during an epidemic of yellow fever and outbreak of cholera morbus.[31] He was rewarded with the title *Cavalleiro do Imperial Ordem do Cruzeiro* (Knight of the Imperial Order of the Cruzeiro), and with the honorific position of *Conselheiro* (Counselor) to the emperor.[32]

The oldest brother, José Pereira Rebouças, complemented his early elementary school education with musical training. He learned to play the violin and piano and, after some years of clerical employment and military service in which he managed to accumulate the necessary funds, he also left Bahia in 1828 to continue his musical education in Europe. He studied instrumental music in Paris, received a master's degree in harmony and counterpoint from the Conservatory of Music in Bologna, and returned to Brazil to become conductor of the *Orquestra do Teatro* in Salvador. Playing on a Stradivarius fiddle that he had acquired in Europe, he earned a reputation as one of Brazil's finest violinists and was a frequent soloist at state occasions as well as at the Imperial Palace.[33]

It was Antônio Pereira Rebouças, however, the youngest of Gaspar and Rita's nine children, who seemed especially determined to use education as a complement to the "mulatto escape hatch," and as a stepping-stone to raise himself above his parents' social standing. Born in 1798 at Maragogipe, he learned to read and write and began his primary schooling in that Recôncavo town. Although given musical instruction as a child – in hope, perhaps, that he, too, might choose music for his future career – he wished to continue his academic instruction on a more advanced level. Until 1813, he studied Latin and Portuguese grammar at the newly established Public School in his native city. But without sufficient personal or family financial resources to support his formal study at an academy of higher learning, he was forced to rely on himself – on his considerable intelligence, drive, and determination to succeed.

He left his parent's house in Maragogipe and moved to Salvador in 1814, where he briefly apprenticed as a bookkeeper in a commercial establishment. Then, following in the footsteps of his brothers Manoel and Mauricio, he apprenticed in a notary's office. Within months of his arrival in Bahia's capital, however, he found a position as a clerk in the office of a "lawyer of major reputation," and quickly took advantage of the opportunity for professional elevation this employment offered him. The high status enjoyed by men trained in the law could not have escaped his notice. Because no law school existed in Brazil as yet, he concentrated on mastering the technical and practical aspects of the legal profession by watching his fellow clerks, and by pushing himself relentlessly both at work and at home.[34] In his spare time, he read legal literature voraciously, focusing especially on the most up-to-date juridical texts. He also instructed himself in Greek, Latin, and classical literature – the "expression of the highest level of European civilization," as he called them – because he knew they were recognized as a badge of refinement. He also taught himself "French, Logic, Ethics, Rhetoric, Geography, and History" from the books of his financially better-off student friends in Salvador.[35]

Not long after he undertook this disciplined effort, he began to be entrusted to prepare legal cases for his employers. By 1820, he had so impressed some of the leading lawyers in the city with his juridical knowledge that they "willingly and enthusiastically" supported his petition to the authorities in Rio de Janeiro that he be granted a license to practice law in Bahia. A year later, after successfully

Antônio Pereira Rebouças in 1838, the year the Sabinada revolt in Bahia was suppressed. [From A. Rebouças, *Diário e Notos Autobiográficas* (Rio de Janeiro, 1938)]

passing the required examination, Antônio Pereira Rebouças was formally recognized as a member of the legal profession.[36]

But, although drive, perseverance, hard work, and the acquisition of academic refinement and professional recognition were certainly instrumental in Rebouças's cultural "whitening" and in his climb into the bourgeoisie, the speed of his ascent and the level of his ultimate attainment were also a function of his political astuteness, luck, and willingness to become totally identified with the values of the predominantly white Brazilian elite, and with court society. He had an incredible talent for being in the right place at the right time, and in supporting the ultimately triumphant side in politically and socially conflictive situations.

In 1821 and early in 1822, for example, a major crisis occurred in Brazil's relation with its mother country, Portugal. King Dom João VI, who had moved the Portuguese court to Brazil in 1808 in the wake of the Napoleonic invasions of his homeland, was recalled to Lisbon by a newly convened, liberal representative assembly, the Côrtes. Although he had left his son, Pedro, as regent with authority over the internal affairs of Brazil, the Côrtes ordered the prince to return immediately to Portugal as well. The aim of the Portuguese representatives in the assembly – a group constituting the majority of the body – was to nullify Dom João's 1815 elevation of Brazil to the status of kingdom, and to return it to its colonial status quo ante 1808. To do this, the Côrtes attempted to strip Brazil of its royal presence, and to decentralize it by establishing governing juntas in the various provinces that would be directly dependent for orders on Lisbon and not on the Brazilian capital, Rio de Janeiro.

Prince Pedro took up the challenge from the metropolitan assembly and, defying its demands, decided to stay in America. His backers included those within the society who had benefited most from the arrival of the Portuguese court in Brazil, particularly from the Crown's abandonment of mercantilist policies that had restricted the country's access to international markets and thus limited its economic growth. Members of the Brazilian landed gentry and rising urban bourgeoisie, whose social prestige and economic standing had risen dramatically with the court's presence, were especially determined not to let Brazil be reduced to colonial subservience once again. When Prince Pedro attempted to establish a government and gain recognition for his regency, therefore, he received support and declarations of loyalty from key elements of the population in Rio de Janeiro, São Paulo, and Minas Gerais, three of the economically most powerful provinces in the country. Other provinces with strong Portuguese garrisons, however, including Bahia, were forced to fall in line behind the Côrtes, and established ruling juntas, tied to Lisbon, that disavowed Pedro's authority.[37]

It was in the midst of this situation that Antônio Pereira Rebouças, twenty-three years of age and only recently licensed as a lawyer, took the first of a series of decisive steps that would identify him with the nativist side in the Brazilian independence movement, and link him to the group of individuals who would emerge as the nation's ruling political elite. Because of his own humble origins, he was perhaps especially sensitive to the economic and social benefits of the royal presence in Brazil – in particular, to the increased opportunities for upward social mobility that this presence, and the economically expansionist policies associated with it, made possible for free persons of color anxious to improve their status.

He began to take an active role in the attempt to rally his native province to acclaim Pedro's regency. Within a relatively short period, however, feeling thwarted in these efforts by the Portuguese control of Salvador, he decided to carry on his activities in Cachoeira, the largest town in Bahia's Recôncavo region. He correctly assessed the strategic importance of this town – its location, which was central yet protected against invasion by land or sea – and the strength of anti-Portuguese sentiment that existed there. In his *Recordaçoes da Vida Patriotica* (Memoirs of a Patriotic Life), which was published more than a half-century later, he recalled taking an oath upon his departure from Salvador in February 1822, swearing not to return until the "Lusitanian stain" had been "expurgated" from the province.[38]

Within days of his move, he organized and became actively involved in clandestine "patriotic conferences" that attracted considerable support from the leading inhabitants of Cachoeira and neighboring villages in the Recôncavo, such as Santo Amaro and São Francisco. He was again quickly recognized for his legal skills, and asked by his fellow conspirators to draft a document, modeled on one issued some weeks earlier in Rio de Janeiro, that recognized Pedro as regent of Brazil and repudiated the legal standing of any body that did not do likewise. This "Act of Acclamation," as the document he drafted became known, was clearly intended as a direct challenge to the Lisbon-affiliated junta in Salvador. It was written into the official record of the Cachoeira Municipal Council on June 25, 1822, signed by its members and president, by council employees, by local military officers loyal to Dom Pedro, and by forty-three "citizens" attending the ceremony convened for its proclamation. Antônio Pereira Rebouças was also elected secretary "with full voting powers" of a five-man "provisional government," the *Junta In-*

Rua Direita, Rio de Janeiro, in the 1830s. [By Johann Moriz Rugendas, *Voyage pittoresque au Brésil*, plate 3/13]

terina, Conciliatoria e de Defeza, which was established at a large
gathering of "patriots" the day after the signing and public proclamation of the Act of Acclamation. This "government" was set up as
an alternative to the junta in the provincial capital, and was intended to function until the authorities in Salvador acknowledged
Pedro's position and submitted to the governmental orders issued
by the court in Rio de Janeiro.[39]

In no sense was Antônio Pereira Rebouças a Jacobin in sentiment
at this juncture. He and his allies wanted nothing more than to
engineer Bahia's official acclamation of Prince Pedro's regency and
to reject the Côrtes's efforts at recolonization – and they planned to
accomplish this, as he later recalled, "without any apparent symp-
tom of a revolutionary break."[40] They advocated no radical structural changes in Brazilian society, nor in the country's relationship
with Portugal. In contrast to the Portuguese Côrtes, which, by mandating a return to the pre–1808 colonial situation, had taken a
reactionary stand, their position was clearly a conservative one. But
the nonrevolutionary character of their activities would not have
prevented their arrest, imprisonment, even execution, had the
Côrtes been able to impose its will on the Brazilians. Rebouças and
his fellow "conspirators" became "patriots" precisely because the
Portuguese failed. Not only did Brazil not return to a subordinate,
colonial, position, but it was declared fully independent from its
mother country in September 1822 – becoming a sovereign "Empire"
with Pedro, crowned "Constitutional Emperor and Perpetual De-
fender," its ruling head.

Rebouças had clearly taken a risk in supporting Dom Pedro so
actively and openly during the crisis. In the aftermath of independence, the Act of Acclamation, which he had written and signed,
and the *Junta Interina,* on which he had served, were acknowledged
to have been crucial in rallying Bahian resistance to the recolonization of Brazil by the Portuguese. For his services, he received
recognition and gratitude from some of the most powerful men in
the country, including José Bonifácio de Andrada e Silva, the Minister of the Kingdom; Diogo Antônio Feijo, who in the 1830s would
serve as Minister of Justice and Regent; and even from the newly
acclaimed emperor, Dom Pedro I.[41]

In gaining the notice and support of these leading members of the
dominant elite, Rebouças succeeded in penetrating the informal, yet
extremely pervasive, vehicle of Brazilian social elevation: the system of clientele and patronage. This system, rooted in feudal an-
tecedents and in the patriarchal social and cultural realities of a
slaveholding society, was based on the reciprocity of favors – on the

exchange of personal loyalties and services by individuals from the lower societal ranks for privileges and benefits granted by patrons from the dominant classes. For talented free blacks and mulattoes like Rebouças, the benefits accrued from involvement in these relationships were insurance against potential discriminatory impediments to "normal" upward social mobility acquired through direct competition within an open market; they provided yet another path of escape from subordination. But, as Emilia Viotti da Costa has indicated in her insightful discussions of clientele and patronage, the cost of their involvement in these relationships also included an element of cooptation: it demanded their active acceptance of the dominant elite's standards and values, and their identification with its ideological prescriptions.[42]

In October 1823, when Dom Pedro visited Bahia, Rebouças was awarded a medal and had conferred on him the title *Cavalleiro do Imperial Ordem do Cruzeiro* (Knight of the Imperial Order of Cruzeiro) in "compensation for his services to the cause of Brazilian independence."[43] At the end of the same year, he received the first of series of political appointments: as Secretary of the Government of the Province of Sergipe, a post in which he occasionally carried out the functions of Provincial Chief Executive. He also received the right to practice law throughout the empire. After his return to Bahia and a brief stint as a practicing lawyer, he was nominated in 1826 to serve as Alderman Judge for Salvador's Municipal Council. In 1828 his acquaintances urged him to stand for political office, and he was elected as a Deputy to the National Assembly, in Rio de Janeiro, as well as a Provincial Councillor.[44]

II

So successful was Antônio Pereira Rebouças, so steady his social climb upwards, so seemingly secure his position among the country's ruling elite, that the fact he was a mulatto in a land dominated by whites might appear irrelevant to his life history. But this interpretation would be in error. He lived – and died – in a slaveholding society with a long tradition of color prejudice. And this reality could not, and did not, escape him personally.

During the course of his early career as a public official, he was the victim of several racially motivated attacks, including one that was particularly vicious. While he was serving as Secretary to the Government of the Province of Sergipe in 1824, acting as its executive officer in the absence of the Provincial President, a number of white property owners associated with local sugar plantations and

Antônio Pereira Rebouças in the late 1860s, wearing the medal he was awarded when Dom Pedro I conferred on him the title of *Cavalleiro do Imperial Ordem do Cruzeiro*. [From A. P. Rebouças, *Recordações da Vida Partamentor*, vol. 1 (Ri de Janeiro, 1870)]

opposed to the establishment of the regency and its new administration, publicly accused him of persecuting "pure-blooded" citizens and of secretly masterminding a plan for a slave uprising. The aim of Rebouças's clandestine efforts, according to the charges leveled against him, was to bring about the "general massacre of all whites" and the establishment of a "frightful system like on the island of Santo Domingo."[45] Such an accusation was especially malicious in light of the white minority's long-held dread of slave rebellions. This fear had intensified greatly as the number of small-scale slave uprisings in the plantation and urban areas of the Brazilian northeast increased during the eighteenth and early nineteenth century, and news of the successful Haitian revolt reached the region.[46]

Within the context of this atmosphere of growing fear and instability, the white minority had attempted to safeguard its dominant position by influencing the passage of a number of decrees and local laws prescribing harsh punishment, including the death penalty, for any black or mulatto, slave or free, convicted of instigating or participating in a slave uprising.[47] The allegations against him thus placed Rebouças in a position of considerable personal danger. They were meant to be more than merely a tactic of intimidation; they were intended to hurt.

Rebouças was eventually cleared of all charges in this matter after a lengthy public hearing. But he must undoubtedly have felt insulted, if not wounded, by the racially linked calumny. Despite his education and the signs of his personal success – despite his erudition, legal training, official status, and his conservative style of life and political outlook – for his white accusers in Sergipe he represented not only the challenge of new political authority but, as a person of color he was also a potential racial threat. In their eyes, he was indistinguishable from the mass of enslaved blacks whom they feared and sought to control.

It is enormously revealing, therefore, that mention of this racist incident is entirely absent from Rebouças's own published and unpublished writings. He did *discuss* the Sergipe accusations and other discriminatory episodes with his son André many years after their occurrence, indicating in *oral recollection*, that race prejudice did in fact leave an internal mark on him.[48] But his "silence" about Sergipe – indeed, about the subject of racism in general – within the *written* public record of his life history, may be viewed as a key to the success of his social adaptation. At one level, one can certainly argue as Daniel Goleman does, that such silence performed an important psychological function: the mind, by "dimming" pain, protects itself against anxiety. In this sense, Antônio Pereira Rebouças's long-term response was one of unconscious denial.[49] More than mere denial or repression, however, his "silence" seems to have functioned as a deliberate strategy: on a general level, as a reflection of his wish to minimize the existence of discrimination within the positive vision of Brazilian social evolution that he had come to accept; and personally, as a measurement of the small importance he wished to assign racism as an impediment blocking the rising trajectory of his own public career.

Indeed, unlike many other individuals of similar background who had also faced discrimination, it is clear from the biographical evidence about Antônio Pereira Rebouças, that experiences with racism did not lead him to allow the color of his skin, nor the slave origins of his mother and maternal ancestors, to act as a paralyzing disadvantage. On the contrary, his difference from the dominant whites in physical appearance and in family background seemed to serve him as a dynamic, motivating, force – as a driving engine – that mobilized, and fundamentally influenced him to try to achieve his personal, professional, and political choices in life with even greater determination.

In this respect, his response affirmed an important insight of Adlerian psychology: the sometimes mentally and physical energizing, rather than disabling, consequences of individual confrontations with prejudice and with accusations of inferiority.[50] By transforming the potentially negative, paralyzing effect of racism into a positive stimulant motivating both his penetration into the world of the dominant and his social climb within it, Rebouças was able to continue to believe in the feasibility of a "mulatto escape hatch." Instead of being turned against the system by his experiences with racism – instead of questioning his own place within this system as a person of color, and possibly challenging the conventions and realities of Brazilian social and racial relationships – he was able to continue to accept and support the fundamental ideological premise governing assimilation: he was able to maintain faith in the dominant group's hegemonic notion of cultural and somatic "whitening."

But, no doubt, other factors were also at play. The social and economic rewards that Rebouças earned by passing through the "escape hatch," and by his involvement in the process of *embranquecemento*, also reinforced his motivation to continue his striving drive within the dominant realm, and influenced him to identify less with the world he was leaving behind. Throughout his adult years, he consistently avoided siding or identifying with persons of color solely on the basis of "racial kinship," and generally associated with individuals who were on his level or above in class-standing and education and who shared his societal outlook. In the 1820s, the social makeup of his closest associates during the regency and independence crisis in Bahia were either upwardly mobile members of the small but growing bourgeoisie – merchants, clerks, civil servants, and professionals – or, like his fellow members of the *Junta Interina*, they were well-to-do property owners eager to maintain the economic and social benefits that had come to them with the arrival of the Portuguese imperial family in Brazil. Some of these persons were mulattoes; many, perhaps the majority, were white.

By the mid–1830s, as an elected deputy to the provincial assembly of Bahia from the Conservative party, he demonstrated little sympathy for the economic and social woes of the less-privileged inhabitants of the province, the predominantly black and mulatto class of freed men and women from which he himself had originated. The employment opportunities of this group had been severely curtailed as a combined consequence of a general fiscal depression and of unfavorable commercial agreements, forced upon the Brazilian central government by Great Britain – agreements that allowed for the importation of cheaper, factory-made European goods and that discouraged local production.[51]

Although Rebouças now consistently argued for the abolition of the imperial decrees mandating the death penalty for any slave participating in a rebellion – a stand that may have been influenced by his own experience in Sergipe – and, though he now advocated greater representation in the ministries and general councils for mulattoes who had "attained a high degree of intelligence and civilization," he emphatically did not wish to be considered as a representative of the less-educated, lower-class, free "persons of color," and certainly not as spokesman for the slaves. In fact, even though he was later in life to become an advocate of abolition, it was during this decade – after his marriage to Carolina Pinto, the only daughter of the well-to-do merchant André Pinto de Silveira – that he and his wife acquired a number of domestic slaves.[52] By becoming a master, he underscored the distance he had traveled in his own social elevation.

It was, however, the active part that Rebouças played in the suppression of the Sabinada revolt of 1837–38 – a role in which he sided with the Bahian planters, with the upper bourgeoisie, and with the authorities representing the centralizing imperial government – that most clearly demonstrates the degree to which class rather than race had come to form the basis of his social allegiance. This violent revolt, calling for a semiautonomous "Bahian Republic" and for radical social and economic amelioration, attracted considerable support from among the "colored" unemployed and discontented masses, and took five months to crush. Rebouças became energetically involved in rallying the less-disaffected inhabitants of the sugar- and tobacco-producing Recôncavo region of the province behind the imperial government. In addition, he aided "loyalist" Bahian civil authorities to sustain themselves in the towns of Santo Amaro and Cachoeira after being driven out of the provincial capital by the rebels. He also served as Confidential Adviser and Secretary to the Provincial Vice-President, José de Barros Paim, the official in charge of stemming the tide of the rebellion.[53]

Even though he was not a personal participant in the fighting, which was most heavily concentrated in the major center of the disturbance, the city of Salvador, it is inconceivable that news about the brutal character of the revolt's suppression by government troops – a suppression in which impoverished black and "colored" inhabitants were the predominant victims – could have escaped his notice.[54] The government forces employed widespread intimidation, even torture, to flush out rebels and inhibit their support, and were involved in bitter house-to-house fighting throughout the city. According to one secondary account, government soldiers

showed little mercy for the the colored masses, many of whom were noncombatants. Hundreds of women, children and old people were killed in a surge of hatred and barbarity. So thoroughly were fire and sword applied by the legalists to the colored population that the recurrent "Negro problem" of Salvador ceased to be one after the revolt ended.... The once proud and defiant black peoples of the city...[were]...thoroughly cowed and decimated.[55]

But, although Rebouças might be criticized for his unquestioning allegiance to the dominant political establishment, and faulted for his lack of empathy with the sufferings of the nonwhite Bahian masses during the bloody suppression of the Sabinada, his political stand in this episode was certainly consistent with his position during the struggles against Portuguese recolonization in the 1820s, and with his long-declared support for centralized royal authority in Brazil. The Sabinada, moreover, had challenged the power of important men in official positions who had become his personal patrons; it had attacked the authority of individuals who, from the elevated perspective of his own situation in life, could be viewed as having had a positive influence on the social acceptance and rising status of "deserving" persons of color. His firm support of the dominant establishment in this event, therefore, may be interpreted as yet another confirmation of the extent to which his perceptions re-

garding *his own* rise and achievement in Brazilian society had come
to influence his actions, social orientation, and values.

Despite his personal experiences with racial prejudice, his own
life-chances had clearly *not* been blocked, and his beliefs in the
universally ameliorating possibilities of hard work, discipline, perseverance, and talent – beliefs that the dominant ideology projected
and the dominant discourse touted – had consequently not been
diminished. Finding himself to have been rewarded, rather than
shut out or excluded, by the influential persons with whom he had
sought to identify, he seems to have perceived no need to seek an
alternate identification with the group with whom he shared some
affinity of color, but from whom he had managed to distance himself
socially and economically with such evident success.

Clearly, for Antônio Pereira Rebouças, acceptance by the ruling
elite testified both to the viability and desirability of *embranquecemento* as a strategy of ascension from subordination. If the price
for this acceptance was to be paid in unquestioning allegiance to
this elite and in a certain amount of denial of contradictory evidence,
the rewards seemed high enough for him to be willing to place his
stake in the game.

III

From the vantage point of a late twentieth-century perspective informed by the insightful revisionist studies of Brazilian race relations of Florestan Fernandes and the generation of social scientists
writing after World War II, it is not difficult to identify the ideology
and practice of "whitening" as a major buttress for the structures
of domination empowering the white upper classes in Brazil.[56] In
Fernandes's words:

The political philosophy of the solution to the Negro problem was based on
the old pattern of gradual absorption of black people through the selection
and assimilation of those who showed themselves to identify most with the
ruling circles of the dominant race and manifest complete loyalty to their
interests and social values. [57]

"Whitening" upheld the dominance of the white elites in a number
of ways. Its penetration into the general realm of Brazilian popular
mythology as an evolutionary vehicle promising class elevation and
fuller economic as well as political participation helped to feed the
notion of an evolving Brazilian "racial democracy" and to dampen
existing polarities in race relations. As such, it also helped to defuse
the potentially explosive inequities associated with racial discrim-

ination and to inhibit the likelihood of racial confrontation. Moreover, by removing individual, culturally and somatically "qualified"
persons of color from the ranks of the subordinated blacks and encouraging their identification with the dominant elites, "whitening"
made it more difficult for blacks and mulattoes to develop a joint
sense of subordinate group identity. It thus checked the formation
of a potentially united "black power" opposition to white elite
hegemony.[58]

But, despite this now obvious link between the function and effective results of "whitening" and the structures of domination, it
would be a mistake to attribute purposeful ideological manipulation
to the dominant whites, or to infer conscious intentionality on their
part.[59] No single identifiable group existed within the dominant
classes deliberately manufacturing an ideological buttress for their
position. Indeed, the strength of "whitening" as an ideology of assimilation – like that of *Verbesserung* in Hapsburg Austria or "Europeanization" in Sierra Leone – lay in its relative invisibility *as
ideology*. It was transmitted in the schools, the family, and in numerous institutions that helped to inculcate Brazilians of all social
strata with dominant values and beliefs. Like all ideologies, moreover, as Louis Althusser has argued, what this ideology represented
was "not the system of the real relations which govern the existence
of individuals, but the *imaginary* relation of those individuals to the
real relations in which they live."[60]

In this sense, both to the dominant elites and to persons of color
like Antônio Pereira Rebouças, what mattered on a day-to-day basis
was not the ideology of "whitening" per se, nor the "real" conditions
of prejudice and discrimination in the country, but their *perception*
of their own particular relationship to these conditions. Although
for Brazilian "persons of color" the "real relations in which they
live[d]" would not alter significantly in the nineteenth century with
respect to the persistence of prejudice and discrimination, André Rebouças – Antônio's son – would eventually come to perceive
these conditions through a different lens than did his father or
grandparents.

PART II

THE PREDICAMENT OF MARGINALITY
1870–1945

Chapter 5

The Marginal Situation, Individual Psychology, and Ideology

In each mind there is the conception of a [fictional] goal or ideal to get beyond the present state and to overcome the present deficiencies .... By means of this goal, the individual can think and feel himself superior to the difficulties of the present because he has in mind his success in the future.

Alfred Adler, *Individual Psychology*

It is the individual who participates extensively and intimately in the culture of the dominant group who, when he is rejected, becomes the extreme type of marginal person. The depth of his assimilation measures the depth of his psychic identification, and this in turn measures the severity of the mental shock when he experiences the conflict of cultures as it bears upon his own social acceptability.

Everett V. Stonequist, *The Marginal Man*

"[Ideology is] the system of representations by which we imagine the world as it is."

Louis Althusser

If one compares the Zweig and Brettauer family movement "out of the ghetto" with Ifacayeh May's conversionist journey, as well as with the social ascension of the children of Gaspar Pereira Rebouças and Rita Brasilia dos Santos, a number of important common features emerge.

The first of these is *structural*, and it concerns the character of the social situation that modern emancipation and assimilationism produced in all three cases. The concept of the "marginal situation" incorporates the general elements of this feature, and serves as a useful descriptive device for purposes of comparative analysis. As defined by the sociologist H. F. Dickie-Clark, the essential hallmark of a "marginal situation" is a hierarchical social structure marked by "some inconsistency in the ranking of matters regulated by the hierarchy."[1] It reflects the existence of at least two social strata –

one subordinate and the other superordinate or dominant – and is characterized by the conjunction of two factors:

1. The dominant stratum's *possession of the power to regulate access* to spheres falling within its control, such as political and legal rights, economic opportunities, as well as admission to its institutions, associations, professions, and other spheres of social interaction.
2. The existence of some sort of *barrier* which maintains the hierarchical nature of the situation and is sufficient to prevent the subordinate's enjoyment of the full privileges of the dominant, but which does not necessarily prevent the subordinate's absorption of the dominant's cultural values and outlooks.[2]

The second, related, feature common to the Zweig, Brettauer, May, and Rebouças experience is a *psychological* one. Its characteristics correspond to two key theoretical propositions of the system of Individual Psychology developed by Alfred Adler and are encapsulated in his concepts of "striving" and "the fictional goal." According to him, the predominant dynamic force behind all human activity is "striving from a felt minus situation towards a plus situation, from 'below' to 'above,' from a feeling of inferiority towards superiority, perfection, totality."[3] The character of this compensatory striving, Adler proposes, is in large part individually determined, receiving its shape and specific direction from an "individually unique goal or self-ideal" – a goal that, though influenced by biological and environmental factors and by a person's past experiences, is ultimately a "fiction," the subjective creation of the individual. Although the goal may only be "dimly envisaged" and not always consciously apparent, it acts as a determinant principle of unity and self-consistency in the individual's personality structure – as a frame of reference for orientation in the world, and as an influence on behavior and style of life.[4]

One need not, of course, accept Adler's dynamic psychological principle of compensatory striving as a *universally* valid one to appreciate the important insights Adlerian theory provides for an understanding of the psychology of the assimilationist experience and of the contextual nature of individual responses to it.[5] Certainly, one would be hard put to universalize the "striving for superiority" (as Adler terms the process) of Joseph May, Antônio Pereira Rebouças, and numerous nineteenth-century Zweig and Brettauer family members into an innate human quality – into what Adler called "an intrinsic necessity of life itself" – removing it as such from its particular historical connections to the "Century of Emancipation" and the assimilationist ideologies that accompanied that era's legal and social changes.

But the Adlerian notion of striving from an "inferior" to a "superior" situation, from "below" to "above," from an "outsider's" to "insider's" position, does address two of the key elements implicit in the structure and opportunity of the emancipatory and assimilationist experience: hierarchy and mobility. In broad terms, it does describe the psychological dynamic of individual engagement in the process of mobility *from* subordination *into* a bourgeois world, even though Adler does not tie this process to any specific social or historical context.

Every member of the May, Rebouças, or Zweig and Brettauer families for whom life-history evidence exists was in some degree motivated to move from an "outside," "minus" to an "inside," "plus" situation. Indeed, this motivation and pattern of mobility was also characteristic of Alfred Adler's own life history and to the nineteenth century up-from-the-ghetto-into-the-bourgeoisie ascension of his Jewish family in Austria.[6] In general, as the life-history accounts in Part I of this volume illustrate, the pattern of mobility – or of *desired* mobility – was from subordination to participation within the world of the dominant for those in the *first emancipated generation*. As Chapter 6 illustrates, it went from participation to greater acceptance, equality, belonging, and fulfillment for those in *subsequent* ones. Always implicit for individuals involved in this move were two hierarchical points of reference: *the situation* of inferiority from which they were emerging, or in which they still felt themselves to be, and which they were striving to overcome, and *the goal* that provided them with the "superior" alternative and with a basis for comparison.

As Adlerian theory suggests, both the "feeling of inferiority" motivating the compensatory striving of persons in these families, and the "superior" goal toward which it was aimed and which provided them with the alternate comparative referent and "forward orientation," were *in part* constructs ("fictions" – to use Adler's term) subjectively created by each individual.[7] To call them "constructs," however, is not to imply that the "inferiority" of a recently liberated slave like the young Ifacayeh May, of a *Judenstadt* dweller like Josef Moses Zweig, of a mulatto in Brazil, of a black African in colonial Sierra Leone, of a woman, or of anyone in a situation of subordination, was not also a "reality" that could be "objectively" measured and described in relation to a variety of economic, political, and social standards. Nor is it meant to preclude the possibility of "objectively" defining the attainment of a final goal for the process of emancipation by general consensus – for example, through the establishment of a set of measurable criteria that, when met, would indicate arrival at the end point of the emancipatory and assimilationist journey.

Such criteria would no doubt specify the receipt of full social and political rights by the previously subordinated, and would require the legal elimination of prejudice and discrimination. Certainly, moreover, a variety of "objective" factors could be identified – hereditary, environmental, and historical in origin – that, in the cross-cultural instances considered in this book, influenced the Mays, Rebouças, Zweigs and Brettauers' sense of self in relation to their present, past, and future. Race, religion, gender, cultural background, level of education, and economic position would be of crucial importance among these factors.

But it was not these "objective" factors – neither the externally defined "real" situation in which individuals in these families found themselves at any particular moment in their life history, nor past experience, nor a goal objectively defined through consensus criteria – that ultimately triggered and determined the nature, character, and range of their responses to exclusion. What did so instead was what Adler identifies as the dynamic relationship between the individuals' *subjective* notion of *self-in-the-present* with their notion of *self-in-the-future* – an interpretive, changing, relationship based on the individuals' *perception* of their past and present situation at a given moment in time *in relation* to their *construction* of the future.

It is essential to stress, however, that these individual perceptions and constructions themselves were not made-up fantasies culled from the imagination. As the May, Rebouças, Zweig, and Brettauer histories in the first part of this book indicate, they were profoundly embedded in social life and influenced and affected by external political, economic, and societal changes. And, as their accounts also illustrate, in the experiences of assimilating individuals in the nineteenth and twentieth century, they emerged from within social contexts in which the ideology of a dominant bourgeoisie was in the process of becoming – or had become – hegemonic.[8]

This bourgeois ideology, as Louis Althusser argues, exists in all that is "obvious to us" – in philosophical and religious systems, as well as in the truisms of "ordinary life" – and is presented through a variety of distinct and specialized institutions.[9] By the mid-nineteenth century, it had already manifested itself not only in the European capitalist class-societies into which the Zweigs and Brettauers were rising, but also in the recently independent and colonial societies in which members of the Rebouças and May families lived. The schools and universities, which played such a central, enabling, role in the assimilationist process and in the social mobility of individuals in these families, were the main vehicles for the dissemination and inculcation of the dominant ideology. They were the places that taught children and young adults to read and write in the dominant language and that, through this language, shaped their conception of the world.[10] These institutions provided them with elements of the dominant scientific and literary culture and with its versions of history, instructed them in the rules of acceptable behavior and morality, tutored them in civic responsibility, and instilled respect in them for the sociotechnical division of labor.

The educational institutions, moreover, were aided in their task of ideological inculcation by other institutions within the dominant society: by the family, the law, the media, and the arts. Together, these "Ideological State Apparatuses," as Louis Althusser calls them, helped to represent and reinforce the values, outlooks, beliefs, and myths that defined the world within which Mays, Rebouças, Zweigs, Brettauers, and other assimilating and socially mobile individuals were attempting to locate themselves.[11]

To indicate the ubiquitousness of bourgeois ideology and its influence on individual psychological perceptions and constructions is, of course, not meant to suggest that this ideology was a "set of deliberate distortions" imposed on gullible class aspirants by a calculating and cynical bourgeoisie.[12] Bourgeois ideology, like all ideologies, reflected a particular social formation and mode of production located in time and space; it was not *created* by any single, identifiable, agent. Far from being its conscious purveyors, members of the dominant group were also *within* this ideology, subjected to it, and influenced by its representations.[13] The life histories of many members of the three families demonstrate, moreover, that the hegemony of bourgeois values and outlooks was in no sense produced by brainwashing nor, for that matter, by coercion. Generally, as Antonio Gramsci argues, it was established without force: through the "spontaneous consent," given by individuals emerging from subordination, "to the general direction imposed on social life by the dominant fundamental group."[14]

That this "spontaneous consent" appears, at times, to have been given uncritically, and with much enthusiasm – as, for example, Antônio Pereira Rebouças's role in helping to crush the Sabinada and Ifacayeh May's enthusiastic "idol"-smashing illustrate – explains why its existence as a feature of dominant-subordinate relations has been interpreted as reflecting complicity by subordinates in their own victimization.[15] More accurately, however, it points to the "success" of what Louis Althusser calls ideological "interpellation": to the fulfillment of the *real* function of ideology, which is to *construct individuals as subjects.* In Althusser's words: "...*the cat-egory of the subject is...constitutive of all ideology insofar as all ideology has the function (which defines it) of 'constituting' concrete individuals as subjects.*"[16] In effect, by "interpellating" individuals as subjects – be they within a political structure, a belief system, an economic order, a system of social relationships – ideology serves to maintain and perpetuate social formations.[17]

One should not think of the content and expression of bourgeois ideology as unchanging, uniformly coherent, without contradiction. Although its primary, overriding function is to ensure the repro-duction of capitalist relations of production, a variety of approaches toward this end exist – both over time, and within relatively au-tonomous political, cultural, economic, as well as public and private spheres. The change from a predominantly assimilationist to a racist ethic, for example, was accomplished in the late nineteenth century within "bourgeois ideology" without the total elimination of assim-ilation as an attainable idea. This clearly illustrates the suppleness and multifaceted character of this ideology, and its ability to accom-modate contradiction.

At the same time, however, it is clear from the experiences of members of the Zweig and Brettauer, May, and Rebouças families that the thoroughness of ideological inculcation varied, as did the degree of socialization that this inculcation engendered in individ-uals. This variation, together with the inconsistencies and contra-dictions in the content of bourgeois ideology, left space for the emergence of what Gramsci terms "contradictory consciousness": an "alternative" consciousness based on heritage and history, on sen-timents, values, attitudes, cultural symbols, ways of looking at the world, and on expectations that differed from the dominant ideology.[18]

For Central European Jews, especially in the first half of the nineteenth century, this alternative consciousness derived from folk-ways associated with the "inner life" of individuals and with com-munal ritual and practice: from the persistence and strength of customs associated with birth, marriage, death, and burial; with food and drink; with the synagogue, Sabbath, and festivals; and with child-rearing and religious education.[19]

For Liberated Africans and Creoles in Sierra Leone, the sources of alternative consciousness lay in the deep-seeded beliefs and folk practices, concerning ancestral power and the life-cycle for example, of the various African peoples from which they originated, as well as from the customs of groups indigenous to the colony and its hin-terland.[20] It was "contradictory consciousness" that provided individuals with the alternative comparative referent against which to measure themselves in relation to a future goal and past orientation.

• • •

By acknowledging the key role played by subjectivity in causality as well as the ideologically embedded nature of individual perceptions and intellectual constructions – by recognizing the dynamic, interpretive, character of individual frames of reference regarding past, present, and future – it becomes possible to attain a deeper understanding of changes in individual responses over time, and of the similarities and differences between them. A comparison of life-history accounts in Part I of this book demonstrates that the end point of the emancipatory journey – of what it really meant to "move into the world of the dominant" – differed in its particulars from person to person and within the course of a person's lifetime.

These accounts particularly highlight the crucial analytical necessity to differentiate between the various *marginal situations* in which these individuals were all located and the potential *psychological* and *social responses* of persons finding themselves within such situations. The accounts demonstrate, in the experience of Joseph May, Antônio Pereira Rebouças, and various Zweig/Brettauer family members, that assimilating individuals within a "marginal situation" *did not automatically perceive themselves to be marginals* – they did not necessarily view themselves as blocked, excluded, denied, ineligible aspirants to dominant privilege and power. They did not automatically display the various personality traits, including "inner strain and *malaise*, a feeling of isolation, of not quite belonging," ascribed to the so-called "Marginal Man" in the earliest sociological literature on marginality.[21]

The May, Rebouças, Zweig and Brettauer histories, moreover, illuminate our understanding of that distinctive feature of dominant-subordinate hierarchical differentiation: the *barrier*. Their accounts confirm that any of a number of criteria – from biologically determined physical appearance to culturally related symbolic expressions like language, dress, as well as religious and social customs – have been used by members of the dominant stratum to limit or prevent access to dominant privileges.[22] The histories also confirm that such barriers could change over time and differ in scope, ranging from subtle prejudice expressed on a person-to-person basis, to overt officially supported discriminatory exclusion.

Barriers, in other words, could vary in the comprehensiveness and effectiveness of their exclusionary function; depending on the circumstances of their existence, they could be "complete," and as such act effectively as a block to integration into the dominant stratum, or they could be "permeable" or "surmountable."[23] In their *perme-ability*, as differences in the status attained by individual blacks, Jews, or mulattoes indicate, barriers might screen out *some* members of the subordinate stratum *but not others*. They might permit *partial* but *not total* participation in the dominant's system of social relations, and be permeable with respect to some powers and privileges, but not others. They may also allow significant aspects of the dominant culture to "seep through" to the subordinate while selectively denying the rights and status recognition associated with the possession of this culture. The *surmountability* (or transcendence) of the barriers, on the other hand, is reflected in the phenomenon of "passing," or of "posing" – in the possibility of escaping the barrier and the subordinate situation altogether through a kind of subterfuge or deception.[24]

But what the May, Rebouças, and Zweig-Brettauer accounts demonstrate most convincingly is that it is not the *existence* of the barrier per se that engenders the subordinate individuals' responses and adjustments to exclusion. Instead, it is their *perception* of the barrier and its effectiveness that is the key determinant for action. The barrier is thus both a *structural* and *psychological* phenomenon; it is both *objective* and *subjective*. It can also change over time in its "objective" characteristics (from mild prejudice, to selective discrimination, to total exclusion), but also in the way individuals perceive it at different moments within their own lifetime.

These factors help to explain why individuals located within the subordinate stratum of the same "marginal situation" – of the same situational universe – often failed to respond, or responded in different ways, to circumstances that an outside, "objective" observer would identify as discriminatory or rejecting. For some of these individuals – Joseph May and Antônio Pereira Rebouças, for example – whose own life ambitions seemed largely to have been met through opportunities that emerged in the aftermath of emancipation, any barrier was perceived as permeable if not inconsequential. Not expecting to accomplish more through the assimilationist process than they had already attained, they did not question their own social identity or the incompleteness of their own integration into the world of the dominant, even though they themselves were excluded from many of its powers and privileges. Having been able to elevate themselves socially and economically from conditions of slavery and dire poverty, they assessed their attainments in relation to a past that they were happy to overcome rather than in relation to a potentially ideal present or future situation – one in which they would be indistinguishable in privileges and life-chances from members of the dominant bourgeoisie on whom they modeled themselves and with whom they identified. In Gramsci's formulation, they continued to grant their "spontaneous consent" to the dominant, hegemonic order.

By the late 1870s, on the other hand, Moritz and Ida Zweig were clearly conscious of their own location within a marginal situation. Despite their own economic accomplishments and their respective families' successful journey from ghetto disenfranchisement into participant citizenship, they were aware that the social acceptance of Jews within the dominant Gentile society in Austria continued to be impeded by the persistence of anti-Semitic stereotypes and prejudices. Although the positive aspects of their own social integration led them to view "the barrier" against Jews as permeable, they were also cognizant of efforts that threatened to transform it into a completely exclusionary one. Their attitudinal polarity – expressed in efforts to achieve an unobtrusive external conformity to Austrian middle-class values while maintaining an ongoing but ambivalent connection to Judaism and the Jewish community – reflected their uncertainty about the barrier's future nature and attested to the sense of marginality that their consciousness of potential exclusion called into being.

The life histories of André Rebouças, Cornelius May, and Stefan Zweig, examined in the following chapter, further illuminate the dynamic causal interplay among marginal situation, barrier, and individual perception, and highlight the particular complexities and profundities of a variety of responses to the predicament of marginality.

Chapter 6

"I belong nowhere, and everywhere am a stranger": The Predicament of André Rebouças, Cornelius May, and Stefan Zweig

The Jew is one whom other men consider a Jew.
Jean-Paul Sartre, *Anti-Semite and Jew*

We were aborigines, found upon our own soil, strangers to the white man, and certainly different from him if not in all, in many things. The position between himself and us was that of master and subject, ruler and ruled. We saw him in all the majesty of an alien civilization and we observed that as he either flitted past us, or dwelt in our midst, he had, invariably attending him, comfort, light, liberty, contentment. Did ever unsophisticated humanity dwell amid conditions stimulating admiration without seeking to conform itself to these conditions? Our forebears of 50 years ago, so near the primitive conditions of native life, and who sought to reproduce the European method of living which they admired were not to blame....The white man came to them and was to them as a demi-god; his own civilization appeared to give him the supremacy which he enjoyed; the black man also noticed that unless he "conformed" he could not be admitted into confidence, nor thought to be anything in the new European order.
Cornelius May, *Sierra Leone Weekly News*, 6 August 1910

My blackness was there, dark and unarguable. And it tormented me, pursued me, disturbed me, angered me ....
Frantz Fanon, *Black Skin, White Masks*

"Ah! Saudosos tempos que hoje relembramos como um sonho paradisíaco." ("Ah! Nostalgic times that today we remember like a paradisiacal dream.")
André Rebouças to Visconde Taunay, 8 November 1896

I

It was natural for Stefan Zweig, Cornelius May, and André Rebouças to proceed along the same paths their elders had pioneered. Indeed, although their parents had adapted themselves deliberately and even with cunning to the milieu of the dominant people in the countries where they lived, both out of a profound internal desire for acceptance and a longing for security, the sons immersed themselves in this world with more assurance and with a deeper sense of belonging.

Unlike their parents, all three received either a university education or professional training in their own countries and abroad. Rebouças, who was born in 1838, in the second year of the bloody Sabinada uprising that swept his native Bahia, was admitted to the civil engineering course of the prestigious Escola Militar in Rio de Janeiro after a brilliant showing on the admitting examinations. Thanks to his self-sacrificing father, who financed the journey and additional study, both he and his younger brother, Antônio, also trained in civil engineering, went to France and England in 1861 to complete their theoretical and practical instruction.[1] Cornelius May, nineteen years younger than André Rebouças, attended the Wesleyan Theological College (which later became the Prince of Wales School) in Freetown; and in 1880 went to England, where he spent seven years studying journalism and gaining advanced instruction and experience in printing.[2] Stefan Zweig attended university in Vienna and, briefly, in Berlin; he earned his doctorate in 1904 with a thesis on the French philosopher Hippolyte Taine.[3]

In Zweig's case, academic recognition was fulfillment of his parents' desire to rise above mere money. No doubt, both the tradition of their Jewish forebears and the values of the Viennese bourgeoisie influenced them to hold learning (*Bildung*) in higher esteem than material possession (*Besitz*). But for them, as Stefan astutely observed, his success also expressed "a secret longing to resolve the merely Jewish – through flight into the intellectual – into humanity at large."[4] It was not only a testimonial to their son's admission into the elite circles of society, but also further acknowledgment of the vast distance the family had traveled beyond the "defects and limitations and pettiness" forced upon Jewry by the ghetto.[5]

Bourgeois not only by upbringing and education, André Rebouças, Cornelius May, and Stefan Zweig lived in a style and cultivated a physical appearance that conformed to the standards set by the members of the educated middle class in their respective societies. May and Rebouças were formal as well as sober in appearance, and

Cornelius May in the 1890s. The portrait was taken after he joined the Royal Empire Society, in London. [Royal Commonwealth Society, London]

their presence projected careful grooming, dignity, and order. They preferred to wear clothing made from the heavy materials imported to Sierra Leone and Brazil from European textile centers: stylish and well-cut suits, but certainly uncomfortable in their tropical environment. Both wore mustaches – small, slightly drooping, and elegantly trimmed – and cut the hair on their head very short, parting it on the side according to contemporary European fashion, consciously or unconsciously de-emphasizing its thickness, texture, and curl – physical traits linked to race. Throughout his mature life, Rebouças also wore a trim goatee of a type popular in the late nineteenth century with university-educated young men in Europe and Latin America. Of the three, Zweig alone chose to wear clothing that was light, comfortable, even careless – a reflection, perhaps, of the more casual attitude toward dress of his most immediate peers, the artists and writers of Europe. He also grew a mustache during his university days, and kept it for the rest of his life.

The tastes of the three men were those of the urbane and cultured *haute bourgeois*, far removed from those of the "popular classes" in their countries. Stefan Zweig, who even as a young man acquired an international audience for his writings, regarded himself as "a mediator in the world of European letters."[6] He knew many of Europe's intelligentsia intimately, translated a great number of their works, and corresponded at length with such luminaries as Sigmund Freud, Thomas Mann, Maxim Gorky, and Romain Rolland.[7] André Rebouças, an intimate friend of Carlos Gomes, the classically trained Brazilian composer of *O Guarani* as well as numerous operas and pieces for voice and piano, was a knowledgeable devotee of "serious" Italian and German music and frequent concertgoer. His close friendship with Alfred d'Escragnolle, Visconde de Taunay, developed from a mutual appreciation of Gomes's talent and from a shared interest in European art and in Brazilian art of European inspiration and character. He was personally acquainted with many of his country's best writers and leading intellectuals, read voluminously, and expressed himself easily and elegantly in writing. He was a talented linguist as well, sufficiently familiar with Latin and Greek to tutor them, and able to communicate in French, German, Italian, and English in addition to his native Brazilian Portuguese.[8]

Cornelius May, although not nearly as erudite as Zweig or Rebouças, was also an avid reader and wrote lucidly and intelligently on wide-ranging social, political, and economic issues for the *Sierra Leone Weekly News*, of which he was editor and owner, and for other publications. He habitually attended public and private functions where the "finer things in life" were displayed: musical entertainments and recitals, dramatic performances, poetry readings, lectures, and *Conversazione* – grand, alcohol-free, salon-like gatherings for which admission tickets were sold and at which stimulating conversation was expected to take place. He was a member of the Young Men's Literary Association, an organization founded to raise

André Rebouças, probably in the early 1880s. [From A. Rebouças, *Diário e Notos Autobiográficas* (Rio de Janeiro, 1838)]

the culture of the "corrupt" youth of Freetown, and became an organizer and officer of other clubs sponsoring lectures, plays, and recitals, both musical and literary.[9]

So long as Rebouças, May, and Zweig perceived their life and career contingencies to be relatively unhindered by factors related to the racial or religious "difference" they had inherited at birth, their principal basis for group identity within their respective societies was class and status. Their rapport and identification was with individuals like themselves, of similar life-styles and values, and not with people with whom they shared a religious background or racial appearance.

Throughout his formative years, therefore, Cornelius May found the British colonial system, of which he was a subject, generally acceptable and viewed himself as different from – and superior to – Africans who had not experienced or taken advantage of prolonged cultural contact with Europeans in order to "better" themselves. Like his father, Joseph May, before him, and like other missionary-influenced Creoles who had come to see themselves as agents, if not partners, of the British in the "civilization" of Africa, May frequently assailed "barbaric" social and religious customs among black Africans, and sought to be accepted as a successfully Anglicized Sierra Leonean – one who had much more in common with middle-class, European-educated, persons of whatever race than with Africans who were less Europeanized, "lower class," but fellow blacks.[10]

Stefan Zweig was initially unconcerned with the mass of working-class Jews coming to settle in Austria from Eastern Europe. If anything, he showed contempt for the narrow traditionalism and ghetto communalism of these Galician, Polish, and Russian proletarians of the street whose sometimes uncouth behavior contrasted so markedly to his own urbane refinement. He certainly did not identify with these and other Jews on the basis of religious kinship. His upbringing in matters of faith, as he himself recognized, was extremely lax and his feelings about his own Jewishness were weak.[11] "It has a beneficial effect on me," Martin Buber wrote sarcastically about Zweig's lack of religious commitment, "to find that it is possible for one to feel Jewry, Jewishness in such a vegetatingly matter-of-course way."[12]

The connecting thread of Zweig's life work until the late 1920s – the intellectual unification of Europe – led to meetings, exchanges, and friendships with writers and artists throughout the Continent. Some of these acquaintances were Jews as well, but Zweig's relationship with them was primarily based on mutuality of professional interest, avocation, and on a shared cosmopolitan humanism,

Stefan Zweig in 1912. [Stefan Zweig Estate, London]

grounded in a belief in progress and enlightenment. With Theodor
Herzl, for instance, a man of his own class background who as *feuil-
leton* editor of the *Neue Freie Presse* gave him his first opportunity
to be published in a famous newspaper, Zweig chose to maintain a
distant friendship based on literary affinity rather than, as Herzl
had hoped, on sympathy with Zionism, a philosophy that proclaimed
the failure of Jewish assimilation and integration in Europe.[13]

Until the end of the 1860s, André Rebouças tended to dissociate
himself from the Afro-Brazilian masses, both black and mulatto.
Following in his father's footsteps, he did take an early position

against the ongoing Brazilian slaveholding system, but did so because he abhorred both the institution's inherent cruelties and its obstruction of national modernization, not because he identified with its victims as *fellow persons of color*. His opposition, moreover, lacked commitment during this period: he employed some slaves on the customhouse and port-construction project that he directed in Rio de Janeiro, and he and Antônio Pereira Rebouças did not liberate their own last three household slaves until 1870.[14] In his early diaries, he also habitually used the descriptive terms *"o negro"* (the Negro) or *"o prêto"* (black person) with third-person detachment when referring to lower-class Afro-Brazilians – perhaps reflecting a desire during this time in his life to distance himself from the "hoi-polloi" both racially and socially. This practice contrasted greatly to the usage he would make of these same terms in the late 1880s and in the 1890s.[15] Rebouças's initial orientation, therefore, was like that of May and Zweig when they perceived no significant barrier to the assimilationist process in which they were engaged: it was directed toward the elite of the dominant society into whose world he had entered through miscegenation, tuition, and study.[16]

II

Ultimately, however, even members of this second, postemancipation generation found no guarantee in the assimilationist process to ensure their continued acceptance and security in the world of the dominant. With racism on the rise as a potentially negating barrier, it did not matter that André Rebouças, Cornelius May, and Stefan Zweig felt more comfortably rooted and more thoroughly integrated within the dominant society than their parents. When they eventually perceived themselves rejected and excluded by racism, the strength of their faith in assimilationism and the depth of their commitment to it were challenged – even more profoundly so, perhaps, than if they had been less certain about their sense of belonging. They were then plunged into a phase of considerable psychological uncertainty about their identity: a crisis period of inner conflict and disorientation during which they became conscious of their marginal position between two worlds. Scrutinizing their values and practices, questioning the validity and feasibility of the assimilationist approach, each came to ask himself: "Who am I? Black or white? African? European? Jew?" Eventually, each was influenced to explore personal alternatives to assimilation – to seek an adjustment to his situation in accordance with personal limitations and historical circumstances.

The feeling of rejection built up slowly in Rebouças. In the autobiographical notes, diaries, and letters that record his life between the years as a student in the Escola Militar and involvement in the abolitionist movement – the period from 1854 to 1880 when his inroads into the world of Brazil's elite were greatest – he cites nearly a score of incidents in which either he or his father or brother were victims of racial prejudice. He and Antônio Rebouças Filho were denied scholarships for further engineering study in Europe in 1861 as a result of overt discrimination by government officials, despite their eligibility and outstanding qualifications; and André was refused employment and blocked from academic appointment on at least four occasions of more subtle exclusion.[17] When he was finally named to head the construction of the docks for the Rio customhouse (*Alfandega*), he was paid more than a third less per year than the British engineer he replaced, less even than the preceding assistant director.[18] His enemies and rivals lashed out at him and his family during his tenure, publishing anonymous ditties about them containing blatant racial insults, and sent unsigned letters to Rebouças's white friends lamenting their association with mulattoes.[19] He encountered a great deal more prejudice in the United States, which he visited for a few weeks in 1873 after he was replaced on the dock project by his greatest professional rival, and was forced to stay in inferior hotels, denied service in restaurants, and prevented from attending a performance at the "Grand Opera House" in New York because of his color.[20]

Nonetheless, although they most certainly registered on his consciousness and would be recalled later, Rebouças did not perceive these experiences, when they occurred, as sufficiently compelling to deny the validity of the world view on which he had been raised or of the life course on which he had been embarked. His optimism remained strong: each prejudicial incident seemed to be counteracted, if not neutralized, by a positive demonstration of his acceptance. He established strong friendships during this period with a number of Brazilian nobles and persons of influence, Machado Coelho, the Barão de Estrela, and the Visconde de Taunay, Mauá, and Itaborai among them. These people appreciated his intellect, vision, and talent, and received him into the elite world of the imperial capital replete with its *salões*, parties, dances, art exhibitions, and concerts.[21]

Despite the impediments Rebouças encountered professionally and the racial antagonism he met during these years, he was appointed to consequential and prestigious posts that brought him considerable personal recognition and, rather rapidly, the financial

André Rebouças while in Paris as an engineering student, 1861. [From A. Rebouças, *Diário e Notos Autobiográficas* (Rio de Janeiro, 1938)]

means to support himself and his family in the comfortable, genteel manner of Rio de Janeiro's upper bourgeoisie.[22] Most important of all, it was during this period that he formed his strong personal relationship with the imperial family, particularly with Emperor Dom Pedro II, and open acceptance by this epitome of Brazilian high society not only flattered him but also seemed to affirm his vision of a future in a potentially good world – if not the best of all possible ones.[23]

The association with Dom Pedro had a profound psychological impact on Rebouças and would grow into an obsession in the last decade of his life. In contrast to the growing number of Brazilians favoring republican government, he identified the emperor with the best, most progressive, and liberal characteristics of the nation: a *"philosopho e philanthropo"* who staunchly maintained political liberty, order, a free press, and freedom of conscience. He found him to be remarkably approachable on a personal basis and extremely knowledgeable in scientific and cultural matters. He also saw in him a powerful ally, interested in the modernization of Brazil and the improvement of its inhabitants. And, echoing his father's judgment, he also recognized Dom Pedro and the imperial family to be *"amigos dos mulatos"* – sympathetic to people of color.[24]

Rebouças's positive identification with the imperial family intensified during the closing months of the campaign to abolish slavery. He had become passionately involved in the abolitionist struggle after the death of Antônio Pereira Rebouças in 1880 because, by this time, he was convinced that slavery and the system of exploitation on which it was based "stained the land" and acted as the major impediment to the attainment of a progressive, modern, nation in which "rural democracy, freedom of conscience, [and] free trade" could dominate.[25] Acting on his convictions, he became a founding member and officer of the Brazilian Society Against Slavery, the Abolitionist Confederation, and the Abolitionist Center of the *Escola Politecnica*, where he taught. He was also an important financial contributor, as well as a dedicated and energetic propagandist who wrote numerous manifestos and articles in support of the abolitionist cause.[26]

After slavery was finally abolished in May 1888, however, he credited the stand taken by the emperor and Princess Isabel on the issue of total emancipation for the ultimate success of the movement. "It was simply an act of courage and abnegation," he wrote in 1889, "to risk a throne in order to perform a just and equitable deed."[27] He believed that the emperor, in his heart, had always been with the abolitionists, that his sentiments had been well known despite his earlier inability to speak out publicly, and he concurred with the eulogies naming the old monarch "Patriarch of the Abolitionist Family" and his daughter the "Redeemer Princess" (*Princesa Redemtora*).[28]

Rebouças's residential proximity to Dom Pedro in Petropolis, and his frequent conversations and visits with him in the months following abolition, reinforced his sense of personal attachment to the emperor and his family.[29] When the Brazilian Empire was overthrown in the republican coup of November 1889 and the imperial family was arrested, the news was therefore more than shocking for him: it represented the rejection of his own beliefs and direction of life as well. He interpreted events as the reaction of the forces of slavery and the racist old order against the "modern" Brazil that he and the emperor had championed and for which abolition had been a crucial preliminary.[30] He also perceived the events as a negation of his own faith in assimilation: his belief in a system that would reform itself, expand, and make room for all Brazilians – in his own words, "white, mulatto and black; European, Asian, American, African and Oceanic; all equal, all brothers."[31]

Suddenly and unequivocally, the national crisis triggered a personal one for Rebouças. In the past he had always been able to overcome the racism he had encountered through his faith in the promise of Brazilian progress. Indeed, the considerable recognition earned by his father, and his own professional and academic achievements despite all obstacles, had confirmed for him the existence of a society that rewarded hard work, intelligence, dedication, and drive. But he had increasingly come to associate Dom Pedro and other enlightened monarchists like his friend Taunay directly with the racial and economic democratization of his country. When the emperor was ousted, therefore, and Rebouças's quixotic attempt to rally an antirepublican counterrevolution failed, his sudden decision to leave Brazil and accompany the imperial family into exile attested to the acute sense of discontinuity and disillusionment he suffered at this moment.[32] For André Rebouças, more than a monarch had been deposed; a vision of the world had also been shattered.

On December 7, 1889, Rebouças landed in Lisbon on the *Alagoas*, which carried Dom Pedro, the empress, the Princesa Isabel, and other members of the royal entourage.[33] In Europe, in exile, his own racial consciousness increased; his vision of himself metamorphosed. This happened not because he himself seems to have experienced any new and devastating personal encounters with racial prejudice, nor because of any factual knowledge on his part that the nature of racial discrimination had indeed drastically worsened in the months since the 1888 emancipation of the slaves. Instead, these changes occurred in him because his *perception* of the future of the Brazilian multiracial reality, and of his own place within it, had been altered by the success of the coup.

Throughout the 1870s, and during his abolitionist involvement in the 1880s, he had seen himself primarily as a modernizer whose identity as a person of color was secondary. It had been his belief that, in the new Brazilian nation he was helping to bring into being, race would ultimately not be relevant. His interpretation of the events of November 1889, however, and of the forces behind the overthrow of the empire, now led him to the opposite conclusion: that, with racism alive and ascendant, racial identity *did matter*, and *would matter*. Increasingly, in the months after his arrival in Portugal, he identified himself in public as a mulatto, as a spokesman for the "African race" – as a person of color paying homage to the ousted Brazilian imperial family on behalf of his "African brothers."[34]

Despite his growing sadness, feeling of isolation, and worsening financial situation, he described himself – in words whose very Eurocentricity highlight the identity crisis he was undergoing – as living "a Tolstoic life" after a year in exile, resisting "with the greatest vehemence" of his "African blood" the "Jacobin bacchanal" that had afflicted his homeland.[35] He refused requests from friends and family that he return to Brazil with the explanation: "Our old Emperor needs my African, very African, dedication."[36]

By the time the emperor died, in December 1891, however, Rebouças had given up hope that Dom Pedro's empire and the world it promised would ever be revived. "What illusions!" he was to write later, recalling this period: "The slaves having been restored to liberty, we believed our Brazil was about to initiate an era of peace, happiness, and unceasing progress – the 'golden age' which the philanthropists always imagined would be around the corner but which, nevertheless, is still far, very far, centuries away."[37]

His despair became intense. He began to view Lisbon as nothing but "an extension" of Rio de Janeiro, as a city frequented by the same "treacherous monsters" who "disgraced Brazil." He dreaded having to spend another winter in Europe and felt the need "to return to the Sun and fresh air of a warm climate." His odyssey, both in a geographic and in a psychic sense, was clearly unfinished. He attended the emperor's funeral, where he inscribed the card that accompanied his wreath of flowers: *"Um negro brasileiro em nome de sua raça"* ("A black Brazilian in the name of his race.") Within days, he decided to leave Europe to work in Africa.[38]

Africa, Rebouças explained in letters, was to be his "new destiny" – a place to start life afresh and calm the nerves – as well as a "hygienic necessity" to distract him from the "painful longing" (*saudades*) for his "Saintly Teacher, the Emperor" and the "horrors afflicting his unfortunate homeland."[39] It would also soothe his personal anguish. "No one knows better than Taunay," he wrote his most intimate friend, recalling memories of past incidents, "how unjust and iniquitous Brazil was for the Rebouças, from father to last offspring."[40] "It is essential," he confided, "that I wash these wounds on my African heart in the waters of the Nile, the Niger, the Congo, the Zambezi, and the Equatorial Lakes; and, if necessary, in the Mediterranean and the Atlantic Ocean and the Indian Ocean."[41]

By moving to the continent of his "African forefathers" and performing good works – sowing "the doctrine of Jesus and Tolstoi; of labor and humility; of sacrifice and abnegation" – it might be possible to reconstitute on African soil his vision of society, which the republican revolution of 1889 had destroyed.[42]

But, even though Rebouças now wished to find emotional refuge in the world of his black ancestors and to identify with Africa and Africans, his perceptions of the continent and its peoples were filtered by the cultural values and outlooks that he had brought with him from his urban, bourgeois, Brazilian-European world. His view of Africans was paternalistic; his preoccupations with "uplifting" them simply recapitulated on the African continent his Brazilian plans for the future of the newly emancipated slaves. He envisioned an African campaign that would

raise the Negro; cover his barbarous nudity; provide him with a piece of land; permit him to create a family by allowing him Rural Prosperity; accelerate his cerebral evolution through Well-Being...; teach him; instruct him; educate him in everything and with everything for the final fusion of the Great Human Cosmos.[43]

Agricultural education was to be the first step in the black Africans' accelerated evolution; instruction in reading and writing was to be delayed, so as to avoid premature enfranchisement and the potential danger of political intrigue and electoral fraud.[44] He urged that Africans be taught a "civilized language" of Europe and that the benefits of its culture be revealed to them through this vehicle. Always meticulously concerned with his own appearance, he despaired of public nudity and presented a plan to clothe "300 million Africans," explaining that the "Satanic spirit of slavery" preferred Africans naked rather than dressed in European clothing in order to justify arguments for black racial inferiority and inability to evolve to Christian, egalitarian civilization.[45]

The exploitation and enslavement of Africans on their own continent offended and discouraged Rebouças profoundly. As he had done in Brazil for the abolitionist cause, he exposed these iniquities passionately in writing. His diaries and letters reveal, however, that he had little intimate contact with the victims of this treatment: the African people. As in Brazil and Europe, his friends and acquaintances continued to be men of his own background and class: Simon Goodman, of the Royal Observatory of the Cape of Good Hope; Harold Alers Hankey, a journalist; Richard and Albert Rosenthal; Joseph Freeman; and a lawyer named Stokes.

Curiously, this group included no mission-educated black Africans, such as existed among the "school" people of Cape Colony, where he lived for six months, nor for that matter any Cape colored. Empathetic as he might be to African sufferings, a gulf existed between him and the African masses that exceeded any bonds based on racial kinship. He himself sensed this estrangement and the limbo in which it placed him vis-à-vis both Brazil and Africa when, with considerable self-sarcasm, he wrote in his *Ydillios Africanos VI*: "Blessed are they who have no motherland; they who are strangers in their own continent."[46]

Rebouças remained in Africa for fourteen months. He settled first in Laurenço Marques, Moçambique, after a brief residence in Egypt and Zanzibar, but soon left for Barbeton, in the Transvaal, because he could not tolerate the drunkenness and debauchery as well as the mistreatment of Africans by Europeans whom he had encountered in the Portuguese port.[47] He initially thought of Barbeton as "an African Petrópolis . . . only just inferior to the Eden created by the Emperor Dom Pedro II," and hoped to find rest there.[48] He was even optimistic that he could introduce coffee plants to the nearby Kaap Valley, whose red soil he found similar to that near São Paulo, the most productive coffee area in Brazil.[49] Nonetheless, after a few months of "incessant conflict" with white bigots in Barbeton, he felt compelled to move on to Capetown, considered more "liberal" in matters of race.[50] But, as a mulatto in a society where skin color rather than cultural attainment played such a crucial role in defining status, he did not feel comfortable there either. Increasingly, he realized that even in Africa, the continent of his black forebears, he was being defined from without and sealed in by his color.[51]

By June 1893, Africa had become unbearable for Rebouças. Without much explanation, he left for Funchal, in the Madeira Islands, which was geographically and spiritually a midpoint between his African and Brazilian worlds. There his financial situation deteriorated drastically, and his health, never good, degenerated acutely. He was reduced to £7 per month for expenses after a series of extraordinary drops in the exchange rate for Brazilian currency, and he suffered from severe intestinal problems that robbed him of sleep and energy. Time and again, however, he refused entreaties from friends and relatives that he return to his homeland. "I have scruples," he wrote Taunay, "I have many scruples which impede my return to Brazil. I have qualms about being inconsistent; I have qualms about debasing my personal dignity; I have scruples about shattering the integrity of my character."[52] Illusions were no longer possible: both Brazil and Africa had failed him, and he could see no hope in the future.

In May 1898 – on the tenth anniversary of the abolition of Brazilian slavery – Rebouças was found dead at the foot of a cliff overlooking the ocean near the hotel where he had resided. An early account reported suicide as the cause of death. His relatives objected to this finding, maintaining that it would have been out of character for him to end his own life.[53]

• • •

Cornelius May's sense of rejection – his disillusionment with an assimilationist ideal, as well as his perception of himself as a marginal man – was considerably more ambiguous than that of André Rebouças after the overthrow of the empire, and his responses reflect this equivocation.

By the time he returned to Freetown in 1887 after seven years of study in England, he was aware that European prejudice and discrimination against people like himself – the "educated Africans" – had grown. A new wave of racism, legitimated in scientific and academic circles, was becoming increasingly popular among British government and colonial officials as well as the public at large, and marked a clear departure from the conversionist ideology that had been the basis for the Sierra Leone experiment. As physical anthropologists and others proclaimed the inferiority of all black peoples, and Darwin's work was used to bolster the proposition that "superior races" were marked by their material and technological superiority, it was becoming clear to May and others that many Britons no longer accepted the premise on which the Sierra Leone colony had been established. These Britons, unlike their forebears, did not believe in the transformational power of European education and Christianity.[54] For them, the "lower races," biologically locked

The Reverend Joseph Claudius May (seated, center), older brother of Cornelius and first principal of the Wesleyan Boys' High School in Freetown. Here he sits with the school's teaching staff not long before his death in 1902 at age 58. [Methodist Missionary Society, London]

into their backwardness, could never grasp the complexities of European "civilization" – to say nothing of mastering it well enough to act as carriers of European culture among their fellow blacks.

The extent to which May experienced the prejudicial effects of this new racism during his stay in England is not known. But he found the changed racial atmosphere in Freetown unsettling. It was not at all unusual, by the time he returned to his homeland, for colonial officers, travelers to Sierra Leone, and resident Europeans to speak of Westernized, European-educated Africans as "apes" and "niggers" and to insult and parody them in articles and books. Richard Burton's popular *Wanderings in West Africa* and *To the Gold Coast for Gold*, G. A. L. Banbury's *Sierra Leone, or The White Man's Grave*, and A. B. Ellis's *West African Sketches* all shared a derogation of African capabilities as well as scorn for conversionism and its consequences.[55] Racial discrimination, moreover, permeated the colonial professional fields, commerce, and the civil-service bureaucracy, where African advance was being impeded and blocked. Even if May himself was not immediately touched by any of these manifestations of racism, the signs were already unmistakable to him and many of his fellow Creoles that the assimilationist ideal they had embraced was under attack.[56]

The Reverend Claudius May, Cornelius's older brother, described the situation in 1887 when he wrote in the *Sierra Leone Weekly News*:

It is a matter beyond controversy that everything today points to the fact that we are approaching a crisis in our existence as a community.... We are... face to face with a problem which has to settle the "to be" or "not to be" of the questions of our future life.... The successors of those who fifty years ago believed in giving us every opportunity to rise in the world, now believe that every effort on our part should be nipped in the bud or regarded with indifference bordering on contempt.... They treat us as puppets not as men, they look upon us as instruments which they may use when necessity requires and throw off when necessity ceases to exist.[57]

Instead of provoking a counterattack against the new racism, however, the "crisis" stimulated Creoles, including Cornelius May, to turn an introspective eye on themselves and their society. If the European world seemed to reject them, and their advancement within it was made difficult or impossible, was this perhaps because they did not belong there in the first place? Had they "perverted" their "true racial personality" through indiscriminate Europeanization, thus deserving ridicule and prejudicial treatment? May and his fellow Creoles scrutinized everything that defined "educated Africans" – not only their mode of education and subjects learned but

Address by the Freetown Freemasons, including Cornelius May, to the Duke of Connaught, 15 December 1910. [Royal Commonwealth Society, London]

also their social life and occupations, preference for European-style dress, dwellings, diet, even the manner of parting their hair – and concluded that their community had lost "the flavor of their race." Children and grandchildren of liberated slaves, they had become people of captive intellect, blindly imitating manners, and customs alien to the African environment.[58] Having acknowledged the errors of the past, they resolved to assert a new identity that was African, not European.

Their introspective approach was strongly affected by the presence of the West Indian-born Edward Wilmot Blyden in their midst.[59] A prolific writer and dynamic speaker, he had early in life fashioned an ideology that combined a teleological belief in the perfectibility of humanity with a conviction about the uniqueness of races. "Each race is endowed with peculiar talents," he wrote in *Christianity, Islam, and the Negro Race*, "and watchful to the last degree is the great Creator over the individuality, the freedom and independence of each. In the music of the universe each shall give a different sound, but necessary to the grand symphony."[60] In Blyden's conception, differences among races did not mean that any one race was inferior or superior, either physically, intellectually, or morally. Each was capable of equal, but not identical, development and progress. Europeans, in this racially determined universe, became God's rulers, God's soldiers, and God's policemen to keep order. In the divine plan, it was their role to work for the material and temporal advancement of humanity. Science and politics were their racial forte; individualism was the basis of their society.[61]

African blacks, on the other hand, possessed a different "racial personality."[62] They were members of a "spiritual race," communal and cooperative rather than "egotistic and competitive" in social organization, and polygynous rather than monogamous in family life. Unlike the whites, their divine "gift" did not lie in the realm of political life but in spiritual advancement through church, farm, and workshop.[63] And, perhaps because they were by nature the less aggressive people, the qualities uniquely inherent in their race had to be nurtured, protected, and developed if they were to contribute their share to the total uplifting of mankind. As Blyden saw it, no person benefited from the dilution or destruction of the black African personality through the wholesale introduction and acceptance of European culture.

All these ideas, of course, had particular relevance for members of the Sierra Leone Creole elite. Blyden explained the Creole lack of initiative or "African manhood," their superficial attainments, lack of progress, "artificial emotions," and their easily caricatured appearance by blaming their European education and training. Because the races were divinely ordained to move along "parallel lines," and not "in the same groove," no amount of cultural interaction or tutelage would ever make Europeans from black Africans or black Africans from Europeans.[64] At best, those Africans who thought of themselves as Europeans were imitators; at worst they became "apes" and parasites, people without an identity of their own. Speaking to the Freetown Unity Club, Blyden had made himself quite clear on this point:

Your first duty is to be *yourselves* .... You need to be told to keep constantly before yourselves the fact that you are Africans, not Europeans – black men, not white men – that you were created with the physical qualities which distinguish you for the glory of the Creator, and for the happiness and perfection of humanity; and that in your endeavors to make yourselves something else you are not only spoiling your nature and turning aside from your destiny, but you are robbing humanity of the part you ought to contribute to its complete development and welfare, and you become as salt, which has lost its savour – good for nothing, but to be cast out and trodden down by others.[65]

Blyden's efforts to make "Europeanized" West African blacks more conscious of their "true" racial identity and his challenge to their assimilation of European ways struck an exposed nerve among all Creoles concerned with the state of their own society. His uncomplimentary views hit them hard, but they were nonetheless the views of an educated fellow black and, as such, more easily received that if they had been articulated by a European. Moreover, no matter how harsh their implications for Creoles, his ideas were also extremely attractive: to believe in the distinctiveness and uniqueness of the black race and its destiny was an effective psychological salve against the pain inflicted by European insults and discrimination.

Influenced by Blyden, a number of Creoles, including Cornelius and Claudius May, founded the Dress Reform Society in 1887. Unlike André Rebouças's chimerical plan to clothe "300 million Africans," its avowed purpose was the elimination of the most obvious badge of Europeanization – Western style clothing – as a first step toward the gradual independence from all European customs. The aims of the society were set forth in the *Methodist Herald*, a newspaper founded by Claudius May and for which Cornelius briefly served as editor:

It should be presumption to state that the intended sphere of the Dress Reform Society is unlimited. It would set itself as time advances to grapple with other social and local questions. Its intention is to become the line of advance of all social improvements.... It is a society that could become more and more the rallying point for all who long for and are zealous for the independent national existence of Africa and the Negro.[66]

Within a year of its establishment, however, the Dress Reform Society was defunct, along with several complementary efforts such as "name reform." Its failure was prefigured from the start by the intellectual ambivalence of its founders: they could neither divest themselves completely of the European world into which assimilation had taken them nor embrace a solely "African" identity. At no time did Cornelius May or the other members of the society view their activity as initiating links between themselves and those some of them considered as the "less-enlightened" African peoples in the Sierra Leone colony or its hinterland. Clearly no mass mobilization across ethnic and class lines lay behind the symbolic Africanization implicit in their call for non-European clothing.

The society's wardrobe was an invention – somewhat like the short trousers and sleeveless country-cloth gowns worn by "bush" Africans to be sure, but still different enough not to be confused with them. This allowed the "reformers" both to have their cake and to eat it. On the one hand, they could believe they were no longer wholesale imitators of the Europeans and were shaping their culture more in keeping with what Edward Wilmot Blyden, who was one of their group, termed their "racial destiny." On the other hand, they avoided identification with the "barbarian aborigines"– the phrase they occasionally used for the mass of Africans from whom historical circumstances and "Europeanization" had removed them.

Dress reform was thus no harbinger of an African nationalist movement based on racial solidarity, but was rather an intellectual game. It was a sterile hybrid at the juncture of two worlds: a creation based on the illusion that clothes *can*, somehow, make the man. Its failure reflected the deep uncertainty of the membership about departing from the assimilationist path. Cornelius May himself remained uncertain. As a journalist, he was keenly aware of and sensitive to European prejudice. Yet, as André Rebouças had done before the overthrow of the empire, he also still perceived that racism only impeded mobility into the world of the dominant Europeans, made things more difficult but *not* impossible. Did not his own life and career opportunities within Sierra Leone society remain favorable? He became proprietor and editor of the widely read *Sierra Leone Weekly News*, which was relatively free from colonial government constraint. Later, he was appointed as consul for Liberia, was a member of the Sierra Leone Legislative Council, was elected as city councillor as well as mayor of Freetown, and became one of an influential elite that was occasionally consulted by British residents and officials in the colony, including the governor.[67]

Consequently, May's personal sense of exclusion from the world his European education had opened to him was transitory. Despite its increasingly overt racism and discrimination against blacks, he came to regard the colonial system of which he was a subject as blemished but not permanently scarred. He continued to question the assimilationist ideal in *Weekly News* editorials when a particular prejudicial incident or discriminatory action brought on a momentary crisis, but his predominant response for many years was optimistically reformist. His aim – whether as part of a delegation petitioning the Colonial Office, as representative from Sierra Leone to the National Congress of British West Africa, as member of the Legislative Council, or in articles written by him to criticize colonial conditions and iniquities – was to correct the imperfections in the system of which he felt himself inextricably a part.[68]

Only toward the end of his life did he suffer irremediable disillusionment. In 1926, while serving his third year as mayor of Freetown, May was arrested for "conspiracy to defraud the City Council." His trial, held without a jury, was heard by a European judge who ignored the "not guilty" verdict of the three trial assessors and who refused to allow an appeal. He was convicted and sentenced to nine months of imprisonment with hard labor. He never recovered from the indignity of the event. Having taken a stand a few weeks prior to his indictment in support of black Sierra Leone railway workers who were striking for higher wages, he considered the conviction not only to have been unjust but also motivated by racism – inspired by the colonial authorities' desire to curtail independent thought on the part of Africans. That the British used the scandal as an excuse to abolish the African-governed City Council in 1927, and to replace it with one dominated by Europeans appointed by the governor-in-council, lent credence to his interpretation. Certainly, although May could be said to have been guilty of careless management while mayor of Freetown by indirectly permitting corruption to breed among some subordinates, the evidence for his personal involvement in a fraudulent scheme is extremely weak.[69]

May was nearly seventy years old at the time of his conviction, and his health deteriorated so rapidly while he was in prison that the acting governor decided to reduce his sentence and have him released. He spent the last months of his life in an unsuccessful effort to acquire a royal pardon. Embittered and broken by his experience, he died after suffering a paralytic stroke early in 1929.[70]

The world that Cornelius May had envisaged in pursuing his

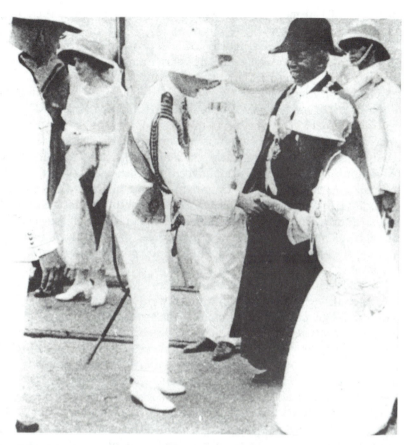

Cornelius May, mayor of Freetown, and Claribel Agnes May greeting the Prince of Wales during his visit to Sierra Leone in 1925. One year later, after a controversial scandal, colonial authorities abolished the Freetown Municipal Council and May was imprisoned for embezzlement. [Sierra Leone Museum, Freetown]

assimilationist ideal was fundamentally similar to the one for which André Rebouças had striven and worked, particularly during his intense involvement in the Brazilian abolitionist campaign. It was a harmonious and reasonable world in which neither language, race, religion, nor politics would limit individual freedom – a world, in other words, ideally suited for cultural and racial "hybrids" such as the two exemplified. But its appeal was also particularly great for urbane Jews like Stefan Zweig, who desired to move far beyond the confines of religious traditionalism and the segregated corporate communalism associated with the pre-emancipation ghettos and *shtetlekh* of Europe, and who wished to be accepted as full citizens of the societies in which they lived.

In Stefan Zweig's case, it was a world nurtured in the optimistic first decade of this century and the years immediately preceding the Great War, a period when, in European intellectual circles at least, "a community spirit" and "European consciousness" seemed to be emerging.[71] "I never loved the earth more than in those years before the First World War," he wrote in his autobiography, "never hoped more ardently for European unity, never had more faith in the future than then, when we thought we saw a new dawning."[72] His idealism was expressed in his consistent advocacy of European cultural brotherhood: a humanist internationalism that he based on the "sum of individual, personal links forged in friendship" rather than on a political program.[73] Although born in Austria to Jewish parents, he thought of himself as a "citizen of Europe," belonging to an intellectual fraternity beyond nationalism and xenophobia in which religion and race were inconsequential.

As had been the case with Rebouças and May, however, the signs of rejection were also discernible to Zweig relatively early in life. His autobiography indicates that he was aware of his parents' efforts to dispel prevailing Gentile fears of Jewish social ascendancy, as well as Gentile stereotypes about the "natural propensity of Jews for money," by not calling attention to their own economic success. He was also conscious of the active and wide-ranging anti-Jewish sentiment indicated by the emigration of Jews from Eastern Europe, the Dreyfus affair in France, and the election of the demagogic anti-Semite Karl Lueger as mayor of Vienna. And, during his days as a university student, he no doubt noticed the rising popularity among many of his Gentile contemporaries of the nationalist "race and blood" type of anti-Semitism: the pseudoscientifically backed racist ideology about Jews whose ascendance paralleled the growth of the biologically supported "new racism" against blacks and persons of color. In much the same way that the latter opposed the emancipatory and assimilationist inroads attained by "non-Caucasians," racial anti-Semitism challenged the Jews' social and political emancipation, contrasted the inferior "racial traits" of Jews to "Aryan" Germanic superiority, and advocated occupational restrictions and confinement of Jews to ghettos.[74]

But, although Zweig was aware of these signs, he preferred to be guided by the more optimistic signals that also existed and that seemed more relevant to his own personal condition. His acclaim and following as a man of letters rose steadily in the dozen years preceding World War I, and continued to climb. The decade of the

Stefan with Alfred Zweig (seated) at the turn of the century. [Zweig Collection, State University of New York-Fredonia]

Stefan Zweig (second from left) early in 1915 with colleagues assigned to "information work" at the War Archives in Vienna. Although Zweig later in life maintained that he had always been a pacifist opposed to the First World War, he was a committed and ardently outspoken patriot for a number of years after its outbreak. [Zweig Collection, State University of New York-Fredonia]

1920s marked a period of phenomenal success for him as an author and mediator in European literary and publishing circles. He introduced numerous foreign writers – among them Emile Verhaeren, Romain Rolland, Paul Verlaine, Charles Baudelaire – to a German-speaking public by translating their works or finding translators for them, publishing articles and essays, and interceding personally on their behalf with publishers. His own books, translated into some forty languages, achieved worldwide popularity as well, selling in the hundreds of thousands to a public unattracted by expressionist and experimental literature; and his writings were dramatized, read aloud publicly, made into films, and studied in schools throughout Germany and Austria.[75]

He was enveloped at this time by what Hannah Arendt has described as "the radiant power of fame" – by a success that must have indicated to him that he was accepted and his background irrelevant. Indeed, for Zweig, the 1920s seemed to recreate turn-of-the-century optimism; despite the ominous undercurrents, he believed that it was a time when "one might even dream again and hope for a united Europe."[76]

In 1931 Zweig looked upon "Jew hatred as a dying force in civilization" and on Adolf Hitler as "one of the last specimens of a rapidly dying bigotry." "There can be little doubt about it," he told David Ewen, who interviewed him on his fiftieth birthday,

today, if a Jew has a talent and ability there is nothing in the world which can keep him down. Some of our greatest literary figures . . . are known to be Jews – and are recognized and appreciated far and wide. This is a healthy sign. It is no longer an insurmountable obstacle to be a Jew. . . . With race prejudice grown negligible, the Jew will be able to continue following his religion, his beliefs, his precepts in whatever country he finds himself. And, at the same time, he can go a long way towards working for universal peace and the brotherhood of man.[77]

He could hardly have been more mistaken. Hitler's accession to power as chancellor of Germany early in 1933 marked a victory for National Socialism, a political program that fused together extreme nationalistic and racial anti-Semitic ideologies. Far from becoming a dying force, "Jew hatred" now acquired the sanction and encouragement of state officials and of the institutions under their control; with their backing, its prejudicial and discriminatory manifestations were permitted to increase and grow more openly aggressive. Zweig himself was directly and dramatically affected by Hitler's triumph. Within weeks, he and other Jewish writers were attacked in the press and radio; his books were ripped from library shelves, publicly

Stefan Zweig and his second wife, Lotte Altmann, probably in 1938.
[Stefan Zweig Estate, London]

pilloried, and burned. He shared this literary martyrdom with such eminent contemporaries as Einstein, Freud, Mann, and Werfel; and the publication of his works, as well as those of other "non-Aryan" authors, was banned in Germany, where he had enjoyed some of his greatest popularity.[78]

Almost up to the moment of the Austrian *Anschluss* with Germany in 1938, however, Zweig tried fanatically to hold on to a view of the world and an ideal of humanity that the march of events on the Continent increasingly contradicted. "We shouldn't think too much about these things," he admonished after the book-burning, and declared himself unhappy about the wide publicity the event received.[79] He left for England in October 1933 because he felt unable to concentrate on his work in his Salzburg residence amid the excitement, and looked on London as a "kind of sanatorium...miles away from politics" – sentiments that strangely echoed André Rebouças's words as he set out on his African exile.[80] But Zweig went, hopeful "that the terrible misunderstanding" would not remain "lasting and eternal" and that National Socialism as well as the anti-Semitic virulence would be transient phenomena. He did not conceive of his move as a permanent migration.[81]

He returned to Austria periodically until 1938, continued to write best-selling books and earn popular acclaim, and in mid-decade went first to the United States and then South America on immensely successful lecture tours. He alternated for much of this period between public reaffirmation of his lifelong European internationalism and silence based on the conviction that the flow of hatred and madness would dissipate if left alone. Like Erasmus of Rotterdam, whom he regarded as his spiritual father and whose biography he completed in 1934, he considered fanaticism the main enemy of reason and continued to present himself as a nonpolitical person, tied to no party or group, unwilling to be forced into any demonstration contrary to his innermost convictions.[82]

The deteriorating political situation and reports of growing anti-Semitic outrages on the Continent eventually threw Zweig into an ever-darkening mood; the triumphant entry of German troops into Austria in 1938, and the enthusiasm with which the people then attacked and humiliated their Jewish fellow citizens, transformed his growing pessimism into despair. The effect of the *Anschluss* was profound and personal. It cut him off from his homeland and literary base. His passport became void and, as he wrote in his autobiography, his status in England changed overnight from "visitor" to "immigrant" – from "gentleman . . . spending his international income and paying his taxes" to "refugee." On the day that happened, he confessed, "I ceased to feel as if I quite belong to myself"; instead, he felt "one rung lower," in "a lesser . . . category," one "of the men without a country."[83] The "fall of Austria" also signified to him, as a writer, that he was stripped of virtually his entire German-speaking public – separated by barriers erected through force and unreason from the world of his own language.[84]

As never before in his life, he was excluded and marginal, conscious for perhaps the first time that, with Hitler ascendant, Stefan Zweig, European, was being *defined from without* as Stefan Zweig, Jew. It did not matter who he was – that he was famous, cultured, and rich. His distinguishing mark, unlike that of a black or a person of color, was invisible; but it was a mark nonetheless.

Like André Rebouças after the successful anti-imperial coup in Brazil, Zweig too, plunged into a crisis of identity when his assimilationist ideal – his belief in himself as a *citoyen-du-monde* – was shattered. To Felix Braun he described himself during this period as "shaken by the times" and in the midst of the "vortex."[85] Defined by others as a Jew, he was unable to find solace in Judaism. As the epitome of the secular intellectual, he had no Jewish religious faith to sustain him – no conviction about the sanctity of traditional observance and law. The assimilationist road along which his forebears, and then he, had traveled had removed him from the faith that had sustained Jews in past times, provided them with an identity, and given meaning to their lives. "What was most tragic in this Jewish tragedy of the twentieth century," he wrote in his autobiography, in explanation of the particular dilemma of the assimilated Jew,

was that those who suffered it knew that it was pointless and that they were guiltless. Their forefathers and ancestors of medieval times had at least known what they suffered for; for their belief, for their law. They still possessed a talisman of the soul which today's generation had long since lost, the inviolable faith in their God. They lived and suffered in the proud delusion that they were selected by the Creator as a people chosen for a special destiny and a special mission and that the promise of the Bible was to them commandment and law .... But the Jews of the twentieth century had for long not been a community. They had no common faith, they were conscious of their Judaism rather as a burden than as something to be proud of and were not aware of any mission. They lived apart from the commandments of their once holy books and they were done with the common language of old. To integrate themselves and become articulated with the people with whom they lived, to dissolve themselves in the common life, was the purpose for which they strove impatiently for the sake of peace from persecution, rest on the eternal flight. Thus one group no longer understood the other, melted down into other people as they were, more Frenchmen, Germans, Englishmen, Russians than they were Jews.[86]

For Zweig at this point in his life, discovering an "inviolable faith in ... God" would have required a journey to the world of *the day before yesterday* – to the world of his grandparents and great-grandparents – to a world of religious belief and observance for which he had no affinity.

It was not true, as some of his critics have maintained, that Stefan Zweig denied his Jewish cultural heritage.[87] On occasion, he employed Old Testament themes and Jewish characters in fictional works. But he viewed his religious heritage through secular lenses as no more valid or important than any other of the major strains in the civilization of "European Man." And he used it less as an affirmation of his Judaism than as a vehicle to illuminate universal ideas. He wrote the verse-play *Jeremiah* during World War I, for example, as a condemnation of warfare; no evidence exists that he intended it to be viewed as an exploration of Jewish history in the period of the Babylonian captivity. When the play was produced again in the mid–1930s in London, and parallels were drawn between its account of persecution in biblical times and Hitler's oppression of the Jews in Germany, he objected in a letter to his wife that he had no "desire to overemphasize the Jewish aspects" of his drama.[88]

Although Zweig felt some affection for the Austrian-Jewish bourgeoisie, he did not feel strong ties to any other community within Judaism.[89] For many of the same reasons that André Rebouças had been unable to identify meaningfully merely on the basis of racial affinity with Afro-Brazilians and Africans, or Cornelius May with the "less enlightened" African masses in Sierra Leone, Zweig could not maintain a sense of identity with those fellow émigré Jews with whom had had little in common except an externally defined Judaism and a sense of the experience of persecution.

While in England, and later in the United States and Brazil, he did give financial support to Jewish refugees, worked to find shelter and employment for some of them, and helped to raise funds for relief activities. But he frequently complained of the émigrés' excessive demands, possibly sensing correctly and resenting that they too were defining him "from without" as "one of them," and seemed annoyed at what he considered their overestimation of his wealth and potential influence. By 1939, when the character of the emigration had changed to include more working-class and less-educated individuals, his willingness to help the refugees declined and he began to speak of them as "nothing but beggars, mostly second-raters, weaker brethren 'who had delayed too long.'" Feeling "pressed in" by their "endless appeals," he yearned for a means to escape.[90]

"How comfortable it would be to be a Zionist or Bolshevik or some other type of committed person instead of being tossed and driven like a plank in a flash flood," he complained to Felix Braun in October 1939.[91] But Zweig chose not to abandon his convictions and clung to the ideal of remaining above the parochialism of political involvement. As a person who throughout his life had been an internationalist, he could muster no sympathy for Zionism, an antiassimilationist *national* movement aiming to reconstitute a Jewish state through political means. Even after 1938, although he recognized the paradox in believing himself a world citizen while finding himself homeless, he could not overcome his lifelong antipathy to political action and would not use his fame to combat hatred and oppression.[92]

Unable to find a substitute for the receding world of his ideal, Zweig turned to autobiography, seeking, he explained, to recapture past times as a witness, not to his personal story, but to the history of his generation and of an era "when life was worth living and the world open and free."[93] The present intruded many times before he

Stefan Zweig in Rio de Janeiro, toward the end of 1940. [Deutsches Literaturarchiv, Marbach]

finished the book in October 1941, however, and the catastrophic news of the outbreak of war, the fall of his beloved Paris, the rapid military advance of the Germans, and the ever-worsening persecution of Jews hit him, he wrote, like "hammer blows," and plunged him deeper and deeper into despair.[94]

He abandoned England for Brazil – a country that after an earlier visit he had called "a mercy on this earth of ours . . . the only place where there isn't a race question" – and moved with his second wife, Elizabeth Charlotte Altmann, to the mountain resort town of Petrópolis, André Rebouças's last residence before exile.[95] Ironically, however, hate letters from Hitler's supporters in Brazil reached Zweig even in that haven.[96]

Like Rebouças during his last years, he became incapable of further adjustment. His autobiography was complete; *The World of*

Yesterday that he had so movingly evoked in this book was at an end, even as an act of literary re-creation. In January 1942 he also finished writing *Schachnovelle* (*The Royal Game*), perhaps his finest novella, and his only work concerned with contemporary political events. As John Fowles has insightfully observed, its story – the tale of an individual who resists relentless and torturing questioning by the Gestapo by retreating further and further into the complexities of imaginary chess games played out within his own mind – paralleled "Zweig's own habitual retreat into the imagination... when domestic or political reality threatened him too closely."[97] Read within the context of Zweig's dark world view when he wrote the novella, however, the theme of *The Royal Game* was hardly meant to be interpreted as an affirmation of survival in the face of despair. Instead, in his protagonist's descent into obsessive madness, Zweig projected his own current sense of the negative cost of this type of retreat into the mind: his pessimism about the viability of any successful escape from what he identified as the "daimons of outer unrest."[98]

And, indeed, his Brazilian exile only intensified the anguish of his marginality. "I believe I shall never return to... Europe," he wrote Friderike Zweig from Petrópolis, "and everything of mine there... is lost [including] the countries where I had a footing, for the English and American world is not my own world at all."[99] Sixty years old, tired, dejected, and unclear about the meaning of his existence, he concluded: "I belong nowhere, and everywhere am a stranger, a guest at best."[100]

• • •

On February 22, 1942, Stefan Zweig and Elizabeth Charlotte took massive doses of the barbiturate compound veronal and died at their home in Petrópolis. He left his final literary creation prominently displayed on his desk: an elegantly crafted suicide note that he had entitled "Declaração" in Portuguese, but which was otherwise written in German, the language in which he had acquired his reputation as masterful stylist:

Before parting from life of my own free will and in my right mind I am impelled to fulfill a last obligation: to give heartfelt thanks to this wonderful land of Brazil which afforded me and my work such kind and hospitable repose. My love for this country increased from day to day, and nowhere else would I have preferred to build up a new existence, the world of my own language having disappeared for me and my spiritual home, Europe, having destroyed itself.

But after one's sixtieth year, unusual powers are needed in order to make another wholly new beginning. Those that I possess have been exhausted by long years of homeless wandering. So I think it better to conclude in good time and in erect bearing a life in which intellectual labor meant the purest joy and personal freedom the highest good on earth.

I salute all my friends! May it be granted them yet to see the dawn after the long night! I, all too impatient, go on before.[101]

III

AN AFTERTHOUGHT:

A curious fact exists about Stefan Zweig's suicide note and about his explication of the event itself – a fact that was overlooked both by his contemporaries and by others who have focused on his final declaration and debated the justification of its message. All commentators neglected to see that, despite the double *nature of the Zweigs' deed, a death pact that involved both husband and wife, his note was written entirely in the* first *person singular. Elizabeth Charlotte Altmann Zweig had no existence within its carefully styled text. And Charlotte – Lotte – who had been Stefan's secretary before their marriage and continued to act in that capacity in Brazil, herself provided no separate, supplementary explanation for her decision to die at her own hands. She left no note, no declaration, no word. She was, at the very end, "the silent woman," the submerged subordinate partner to her famous but despairing mate.[102]*

When I became conscious of Lotte Zweig's omission from Stefan's suicide note and of her own silence, I realized that this woman's "voicelessness" in this dramatic instance was not a singular occurrence; that it indeed was but one other manifestation of female "silences" in my study as a whole. It brought into focus the fact that, though a broad outline of the historical experience of the women in the Zweig-Brettauer, May, and Rebouças families could be reconstructed through careful research, detailed commentary by the women themselves about crucial aspects of this experience was virtually nonexistent.

The sparsity of articulated response to marginality on the part of the women should, of course, have come as no surprise to me. Persons like Ida and Lotte Zweig, Ann Wilberforce and Agnes Claribel May, Rita Brasilia dos Santos and Carolina Pinto Rebouças, understood the meaning, and perceived the promises, of emancipation and assimilation differently than did the men in their families. Although their husbands and male relatives generally expected their emancipatory and assimilationist journey to lead to access into the sphere of public and professional activity, the women were socialized toward a different expectation. Having been relegated to a separate, "domestic," sphere by the division of labor reflected in bourgeois ideology and the social construction of gender roles, they attempted to attain the material benefits and status of bourgeois life through their link to husbands and male relatives. When they perceived exclusion from the public spheres of the dominant realm, they did so only indirectly: through the experience of their men. And because it was the consciousness of an impeded goal – of a barrier to acceptance within the public sphere – that stimulated many of the men to explore their predicament and articulate their plight, the absence of female voices becomes more understandable. For the women in the May, Rebouças, and Zweig families, marginality was thus a predicament-once-removed. From the perspective of the dominant establishment, they were not just the "Other," as Simone de Beauvoir has argued, but the "Other's Other."

Lotte Zweig's "silence" and the relative "voicelessness" of other women in the three families was thus a manifestation of a situational distance from the public arena of male expectation. This conclusion, however, derives from the particular comparative and cross-cultural focus on which this study is based. It should not lead to the erroneous generalization that all *women, rising from a situation of subordination together with their men, will necessarily remain silent about their perception and experience of discrimination and exclusion. In other contexts, many women did move beyond the confines of home and hearth into areas of social, economic, and political activity that were characteristically open only to men. When they did so, of course, emancipation and the journey into the world of the dominant acquired a similar, if not the same, meaning for them as for the men. One can assume they too then articulated their anguish when, in the course of that journey, they felt themselves to have become victims of aspirations they could not achieve and hopes they could not satisfy. Yet, paradoxically, one can also wonder: if they attained a "voice" only by becoming female versions of "marginal men," did the authentic sound of that voice actually emerge? Or, ultimately, did they still remain "silent women"?*

Chapter 7

The Way Out:
From the "Savage God"
To "Holy Violence"

> ...When the sky began to roar
> 'Twas like a stick across my back.
> When my back began to smart
> 'Twas like a penknife in my heart.
> When my heart began to bleed
> 'Twas death and death and death indeed.
>> Traditional nursery rhyme,
>> quoted in A. Alvarez, *The Savage God*

> For honor never will be won by the cult of success or fame, by cultivation of one's own self, nor even by personal dignity. From the "disgrace" of being a Jew there is but one escape – to fight for the honor of the Jewish people as a whole.
>> Hannah Arendt, *The Jew as Pariah*

> A day necessarily comes when the colonized lifts his head and topples the always unsteady equilibrium of colonization. For the colonized just as for the colonizer, there is no way out other than a complete end to colonization. The refusal of the colonized cannot be anything but absolute, that is, not only revolt, but a revolution.
>> Albert Memmi, *The Colonizer and the Colonized*

Suicide, the "Savage God," was a personal "final solution" for Charlotte and Stefan Zweig – a drastic, but certainly not uncommon, response to the predicament of marginality. One need only recall the circumstances of André Rebouças's death to confirm this observation in a different cultural and historical context. No more poignant or bitterly ironic commentary on the burden of a failed assimilationism by a marginalized individual exists than the suicide in 1915 of the Haitian writer Edmond Laforest, who tied a Larousse dictionary around his neck and then lept to his death from a bridge.[1] In Central Europe, within Stefan Zweig's circle of friends, the writers Egon Friedell, Otto Pick, and Ernst Weiss – all Jews, all acutely

174

conscious of their exclusion from a world with which they had identified wholeheartedly – killed themselves in the two-year period
following the *Anschluss*.[2]

The suicide rate among Jews in general, which had been among
the lowest in Central Europe until the 1930s, increased considerably
as Nazi persecution intensified.[3] The justification for the suicides of
the "better-known Jews," as they were sometimes called, became
matters of emotional controversy to their contemporaries. Frequently, their *selbstmord* was viewed with little sympathy. "One's
thoughts turn to those comrades who, under externally more difficult
circumstances, are obliged hourly to combat despair," Bruno Frank
wrote in the New York refugee paper *Aufbau* after news of Zweig's
death reached the United States. "Let us hold together, let us help
one another materially and morally, that no more shall fall before
we see the light."[4] "Did he regard his life as a purely private affair?"
Thomas Mann asked upon hearing of Zweig's deed in Petrópolis,
"Could he concede the archenemy such a triumph?"[5] Hannah Arendt,
even more scathing, considered émigré suicides such as Zweig's as
"abnormally asocial and unconcerned about general events." She
regarded them as instances of a senseless "kind of selfishness" based
on individualism and self-absorption – as acts that lent support to
defeatism as well as demoralization and hindered collective resistance to oppression. "We are the first non-religious Jews persecuted,"
she wrote in "We Refugees," and "we are the first ones who, not only
in extremis, answer with suicide."[6]

Seen from a the vantage point of Zweig's contemporaries – within
the context of a period of growing persecution in which, to some at
least, collective resistance and action seemed to offer the best chance
of survival – it is understandable why the decision to end one's life
"personally and individually" – to "throw life away and leave the
world," as Arendt wrote – might be viewed as a kind of betrayal.[7]
But is it really valid to judge such an intensely personal act entirely
on the basis of its political consequences for group solidarity? Can
one really ignore individual human differences – in background,
personal history, and psychological makeup – among those who committed the act? Without knowing what passed through the minds
of persons who decided to kill themselves, without understanding
the decision in terms of their life experiences and expectations, is
it fair to castigate the dead?

Indeed, by shifting the critical vantage point closer to our own
time, to a more recent perspective on the general causes and meanings of suicide, it is possible to view the drastic personal solution to
the dilemma of marginality chosen by Zweig and some of his con-

temporaries in a much more sympathetic light. "Suicide," Alfred Alvarez observed in *The Savage God*, "seems to me to be somehow as much beyond social or psychic prophylaxis as it is beyond morality, a terrible but utterly natural reaction to the strained, narrow, unnatural necessities we sometimes create for ourselves."[8] Likewise, Jean Baechler, whose massive volume, *Suicides*, provides the most comprehensive study of this subject since Emile Durkheim's classic sociological monograph, has taken issue with the commonly held conclusions about the deviancy, aberrancy, or antisocial character of the suicidal act. Instead, he has argued that "suicide is a solution brought to bear on a problem . . . a positive act, performed by a human being committed to a strategy of life."[9]

In this sense, Stefan Zweig's fatal act can be understood and judged to be *tragic* rather than the *asocial* response of a person *unconcerned with general events*. It reflected his psychological inability to modify a personal world view, and a view of himself, that was antithetical to group or national identification: a supra-national, above-politics, world view that dissuaded him from engaging in political resistance to oppression through collective action. But it was also a *positive* solution, consistent with the ideal of personal freedom that he had held and advocated throughout his entire adult life. This solution affirmed his ultimate control over his own death, asserted his freedom of choice, as well as his integrity as a thinking, feeling human being.

Suicide, to be certain, was one extreme within a broad category of "escapist" responses to the predicament of marginality: responses that centered in the individual and that remained largely particularistic, if not private, in their orientation and execution. The other extreme within this category was represented in the actions of those individuals who attempted to *hurdle* over the barriers of discrimination and exclusion altogether – who sought to *pass totally* into the world of the dominant by obliterating all signs and overt connections, cultural and physical, linking them to the subordinate world from which they had emerged.

For some individuals at this extreme, *religious conversion* became a means toward such a transformative break with the past. Among Austrian Jews of Stefan Zweig's background but mainly of an earlier generation, persons like Victor Adler, Herman Wittgenstein, Gustav Mahler, Arnold Schönberg, and Karl Kraus converted to Christianity, but fellow Viennese Jews Otto Weininger and Arthur Trebitsch went even beyond religious conversion to become virulent anti-Semites.[10] Indeed, although the number of converts probably never amounted to more than a small percentage of the total Jewish population in the city, Vienna had the highest conversion rate in Europe until well into the 1930s.[11]

For a few of these converts, no doubt, the adoption of the Christian religion was motivated by a personal estrangement from Judaism and by the spiritual attraction of the new faith. For others, perhaps for the majority, conversion was, if not a strategy for survival, a pragmatic decision undertaken for the sake of career advancement or intermarriage. It was intended to provide what Heinrich Heine had called the "entry ticket to European culture."[12] Thus, according to Marsha Rozenblit, "an extremely high percentage of male converts [in Vienna] were either civil servants or professionals, those whose careers would profit most from a convenient change of religion."[13] Gustav Mahler's formal conversion to Catholicism, linked to his appointment as conductor of the Vienna Opera, clearly fell within this category. "He had to be baptized," wrote his wife, Alma Mahler, "before he could aspire to such a high position under the Royal and Imperial exchequer."[14]

But, for all those who repudiated Judaism and embraced Christianity – in fact, for religious converts in general – conversion involved a conscious and decisive act that, in its resoluteness and implicit finality, had a curious symbolic affinity with suicide. It marked a "passage from one community to another, from one ideological universe to another," to use the words of Albert Memmi, but it was also meant to signal the conclusion of the converts' assimilationist journey and their irrevocable departure from the world of their ancestors. At the same time, however, although many religious converts in Central Europe left Judaism "to shed the stigmata that compromised their opportunities," as Peter Gay has observed, the act of conversion for some of them was generally based on a notion of reciprocity: on the expectation that conversion would bring acceptance and integration into the dominant majority as its reward.[15]

Yet it was precisely this notion of reciprocity that came under direct challenge during the early decades of the twentieth century as racial anti-Semitism gained ascendancy in the consciousness of the Gentile majority in Austria and Germany. For the generation of Stefan Zweig's parents, even for Mahler and his generation, religious conversion had still been a viable option for "escape" from Judaism. By the 1930s, however, when the ideology of "racial purity" became an instrument of Jewish exclusion and persecution throughout the German and Austrian social and political realm, this option effectively ceased to exist. Baptized or not, in the beliefs and actions of the increasingly powerful new breed of racial anti-Semites, a Jew would always remain a Jew.

Conversion to a form of the dominant religion had, of course, also been a central component of the ruling group's assimilationist plan for persons of color in colonial or multiracial societies dominated by whites. Indeed, the conversionist effort undertaken by European missionaries and agents in the Americas, Africa, and Asia induced numerous subordinated individuals to convert to Christianity. They were no doubt attracted to the dominant religion for many of the same reasons that had influenced Jews to convert in Europe. The experience of Joseph May, described in Chapter 2, illuminates the complex dimensions of this conversionist dynamic for one such individual in Sierra Leone colony.

But, in general, there was a fundamental difference in the potential benefits that religious conversion could bring to persons of color and to Jews. For individual Jews before the triumph of racial anti-Semitism, religious conversion could in fact bring about the convert's personal integration and acceptance within the dominant realm; it could achieve the virtual obliteration of his or her perceived link to a stigmatized past. The acceptance of Jewish converts was, of course, usually not an immediate one. Peter Gay has argued and demonstrated that it frequently "took more than one generation, several intermarriages, possibly a change of name and of residence, before the past of the new Christian faded into invisibility."[16] For blacks and mulattoes, however, religious conversion – even when accompanied by other evidence of cultural assimilation – could *never* itself alone eradicate the difference that set them apart from whites. Color, a *genetically* determined physical trait, was their "primordial characteristic," to use Talcott Parsons' phrase: it was a fundamental factor in their social differentiation.[17] Unlike religion, it was a visible, externally perceptible, factor – one that was less easily altered or ignored.

As a response to their particular "somatic predicament," therefore, many persons of color discovered that a different strategy was called for. They realized, on the one hand, that they certainly needed to emphasize the thoroughness of their *cultural* conformity with the dominant group. They needed to highlight their educational achievements, their comportment and manners, their compliance with dominant standards of dress and outward appearance, and their acquisition of the material objects and symbols associated with European bourgeois society. On the other hand, because their exclusion from the dominant world was specifically tied to their visible racial "difference," they also realized that they needed to overcome and escape the confinement of their color through a process of physical transformation: through the process that especially in the Americas came to be termed "whitening."

For the Rebouças in Brazil, but also for numerous other persons of color in ex-slaveholding and multiracial South Atlantic societies, physical "whitening" involved a form of long-range eugenic planning.[18] By selecting mates "lighter" than themselves, such persons of color banked on the future; they hoped – if not for themselves personally, then at least for their offspring – to bring about an escape from the somatic "prison" into which their color, and racism, had confined them. Such a long-term transformative strategy was occasionally present as an extreme response in colonial African societies as well. In Sierra Leone, for example, Joseph Renner-Maxwell, a contemporary of Cornelius May and, like him, a Creole, advocated solving what he termed the "difficulties of the Negro Question" through miscegenation and the gradual elimination of Negroid features and skin color. "If a man finds his racial circumstances disadvantageous to his interests," Renner-Maxwell argued in the 1890s, "stunting to the development of his tone and manhood, and contemptible to his neighbours, he can at least ameliorate the condition of his progeny."[19]

For some persons of color seeking quicker, more immediate, results, however, "whitening" occasionally also involved "passing." This was a subterfuge by which persons of mixed racial background consciously sought to *disguise* their ancestry by physically "blending" into the dominant white society. Because concealment was so crucial to the success of this strategy, it is difficult to know how frequently it was undertaken and how widespread its practice was. In Brazil and in those West Indian societies where somatic and other physical characteristics defining racial categories were more fluidly conceived, passing from "light mulatto" into "white" was certainly attempted by many, and was generally successful so long as those doing so also met the cultural and economic expectations of the dominant white group. The query in a nineteenth-century Brazilian anecdote – "Is the *Capitão-mor* [a militia chief] a mulatto?" – could thus receive the amusing but seriously intended response: "He used to be, but is no longer... How could a *Capitão-Mor* possibly be a mulatto?"[20]

In the United States, on the other hand, where legal and social laws classified persons of mixed racial ancestry as "black," access into the white world through passing was more difficult. Given the potential hostility against persons "transgressing" the color line, it was also eminently more dangerous. Even in the United States, however, passing did permit a small minority of "light blacks" to gain access to white privilege – a fact, and concern, that a number of Harlem Renaissance writers took up in fictional and autobiographical form in the 1920s.[21] "Then, as now," the critic Hoyt Fuller indicated in a discussion of these writers, "most Black people probably knew at least one individual or family who, for tactical or economic reasons, worked or spent some portion of time with assumed white identity."[22]

But, as was true with "whitening," and with other "escapist" responses like religious conversion or suicide, passing was by and large a personal solution to discrimination and exclusion. It was an action that, when accomplished successfully, generally divorced its individual practitioners from others in the subordinated group, and in no way challenged the ideology of racism or the system in which it was rooted. Indeed, because individuals responding to marginality through conversion, whitening, and passing could be viewed as either conscious or unwitting accomplices in their own victimization – as persons consenting to the continuing maintenance of existing inequalities and exclusionary ideologies – it is certainly understandable why they often elicited such scathing criticism from their contemporaries.

Similarly, individuals who emigrated, and who thus undertook what was perhaps the most commonly practiced form of situational modification, normally separated themselves from conditions in their original homes. The reasons for emigration varied greatly, to be sure, and were often unrelated to the discriminatory and exclusionary practices associated with marginality. Movement, transience, relocation – rural to urban, international, and intercontinental – had been characteristic hallmarks of the new opportunities that emerged with emancipation.

In the Hapsburg Empire, as the Zweig and Brettauer family pattern indicated, large numbers of Jews streamed into Vienna from the villages and towns of Moravia, Bohemia, Hungary, and Galicia.[23] In Brazil, freedmen and women abandoned agricultural and mining areas for city residence. Elsewhere, in the nineteenth and twentieth century, thousands upon thousands of persons emigrated from their places of origin hoping to improve their life-chances in different settings. Discrimination and persecution, directly experienced or indirectly witnessed, provided an additional major incentive for the permanent departure and resettlement of hundreds of thousands of persons. From Germany and Austria alone, close to half a million Jews fled the Nazis between 1933 and 1941, and countless others,

who may also have wished to emigrate, were less fortunate in achiev-
ing refuge elsewhere.[24]

Whether they were induced by a "push" or generated by a "pull,"
emigrations were often traumatic, if not devastating, experiences
for their uprooted participants, and demanded fundamental re-
adjustments in values, outlooks, and styles of life. They were also
crucial stimulants for the transfer of knowledge, talent, and experience.[25] And yet, it was in the very nature of emigrations to distance
individuals from direct engagement in the situations that they had
left behind. In that sense, the emigrations were paradoxical. They
provided hope for a better future in a new setting. In circumstances
of extreme persecution, they offered a chance, sometimes the only
one, for survival and renewal. But in removing the emigrants from
their home ground, they also removed potential challengers to the
status quo. The discriminatory and exclusionary practices that had
engendered marginality remained in place.

Direct challenges to the marginal situation, however, were present in a range of responses of persons who shifted their focus away
from individual solutions to group efforts – from the *self* to the
collective – and who attempted to turn their somatic or cultural link
to the subordinated mass into a dynamic weapon for change. These
responses were characteristically triggered in people who had come
to view the exclusionary barriers that they had encountered as im-
permeable and insurmountable. Perceiving themselves permanently blocked, these individuals reconsidered the assimilationist
ideology that had induced them to identify along class lines: with
"achievers" like themselves, and with people who shared their own
educational, social, and economic backgrounds. Having been defined
"from without" as "the other," they internalized the identity that
was being forced upon them, but came to reject the orientation that
had failed to gain them acceptance and recognition within the dominant world.

As an alternative to assimilation and a class-based identification,
they now sought to identify and to align themselves with persons
and groups with whom they shared the extrinsic reference points
that had been used to discriminate against them. They attempted
to make this connection with their subordinated "kinfolk" despite
the social and cultural distance that, in many instances, had developed between them. On occasion, such persons utilized the awareness of their own marginality, and exploited the advantage of the
dual contact that their experience and background had provided, to
become leaders of the subordinate group. Together with the group
into which they had been defined, *and with whom they now iden-*

tified, they sometimes created movements of collective action for change.

Broadly speaking, the responses in which individual "marginals" sought to reconnect and reidentify with the subordinated masses may be divided into two categories. Although certainly not mutually exclusive, these categories emphasize different approaches toward the creation of a new collective identity and to the resolution of the predicament of marginality. In the first, the reconnective efforts remained primarily *intellectual* constructs – affirmative but subjective quests in the realm of ideas, emotions, and symbolic representation. Literary, polemical, ideological, these efforts can be distinguished from the second category – from responses that were principally *political* in expression and purpose, seeking solutions for subordination and exclusion through collective political mobilization and through political action.

The common denominator of the intellectual responses – exemplified among blacks and persons of color in efforts such as those by E. W. Blyden and his Creole admirers to define the "Negro Personality" in late nineteenth-century Sierra Leone, and in the articulation of various *négritude* ideas in Francophone Africa and the Americas in the twentieth century – was the call for psychological liberation from the structures of domination and exclusion.[26] Triggered by rejection, humiliation, and by the shattering of an envisioned future, this call for a new consciousness was predominantly associated with the star products of assimilationism: with persons who had identified most closely with the values and outlooks of the dominant bourgeoisie, and whose alienation from their cultural roots was considerable. The intellectual responses were thus invariably characterized by a double quest: for self-awareness and for the ingredients of a lost collective identity – by what Abiola Irele portrayed as the "attempt to recreate an emotional . . . bond beneath the contingencies of a particularly difficult historical experience."[27] These responses were also characterized by the personal search for renewed dignity and by the determined refurbishment of tarnished pride.

In their intellectual efforts to free themselves from "the European paradigm," and in their conscious reactions to the exclusive and universal priority granted to European values in the ideology of assimilation, blacks and persons of color in Africa and the Americas employed a number of strategies. Individuals associated with "Negro Personality" and *négritude* ideas generally confronted the failure of assimilation through literary and polemical expression. Challenging the fundamental assumptions of European cultural superiority, they addressed unmet promises, blocked aspirations, persistent prejudice, and racism, by attempting to turn discriminatory stereotypes and exclusionary premises on their head.

"Listen to the white world," the Martinican poet Aimé Césaire wrote in *Cahier d'un retour au pays natal*, his classic poetic affirmation of *négritude*,

> horribly fatigued by its immense effort
> its joints cracking under the hard stars
> its steel blue stiffness piercing the mystery of the flesh.
> Listen how its treacherous victories trumpet its defeats.
> Listen to the lamentable stumbling in the great alibis.
>
> Mercy for our omniscient and naïve conquerors! ...
>
> *Eia* for those who never invented anything
> for those who never discovered anything
> for those who never mastered anything
>
> but, struck, deliver themselves to the essence of all things,
> ignorant of surfaces, but taken by the very movement of things
> not caring to master, but playing the game of the world.[28]

Endeavoring to recover self-pride for themselves and their race, *négritude* and "African Personality" writers grasped the very attributes that white racists employed to stereotype and belittle blacks – their rhythm, sensuality, sexuality, earthiness, color, orality, lack of industrialization and scientific production – and inverted them from negative to positive characteristics. Such an inversion is reflected in the contrast drawn by Aimé Césaire between the "steel blue stiffness" of a cold European scientific rationality, already defeated, and the living, pulsating, earth-connected, sensuality of blacks. It is also exhibited in his representation, articulated through the vehicle of his own persona, of the black race's sympathetic symbiosis with nature:

> ... my *négritude* is not a speck of dead
> water on the dead eye of the earth,
> my *négritude* is neither a tower nor a
> cathedral
>
> it thrusts into the red flesh of the earth
> it thrusts into the livid flesh of the sky
> it digs under the opaque dejection of
> its rightful patience.[29]

This inversion is expressed in the defiant "black is beautiful" poetic statement by Léon Damas, of French Guiana:

> The White will never be negro
> for beauty is negro
> and negro is wisdom
> for endurance is negro
> and negro is courage
> for patience is negro
> and negro is irony
> for charm is negro
> and negro is magic
>
> for joy is negro
> for peace is negro
> for life is negro.[30]

And the inversion is represented in Léopold Sédar Senghor's identification of dance/rhythm as the essence of *négritude*, in his rejection of the "pale aridity" of a European rational perspective, and in his validation of an inherently "Negro African" subjectivity based on a rhythmic, feeling contact with nature.[31] "But if I must choose at the hour of testing," Senghor thus affirms,

> I have chosen the verset of streams and of forests,
> The assonance of plains and rivers, chosen the
>   rhythm of blood in my naked body,
> Chosen the tremulsion of *balafongs*, the harmony
>   of strings and brass that seem to clash,
>   chosen the
> Swing swing yes chosen the swing...
>
> I have chosen my toiling black people, my
>   peasant people, the peasant race through
>   all the world.[32]

Instead of celebrating what they perceived as essential characteristics of the black race, as did the *négritude* writers, other Africans and Afro-Americans turned to history in search of accomplishments. Hoping to counter the racist disparagement cast on themselves and the past achievements of their race, they attempted to restore their heritage to a place of honor. In order to accomplish this – to convince their detractors of its worth, but also to reestablish their own connections to ancestral cultures from which slavery, colonialism, and the assimilationist experience had removed them – they searched back in time, employing the tools of historical reconstruction and ethnology. Through filters dictated by their own needs and expectations, they proceeded to gather evidence of great deeds and past glories.[33]

Many examples of this reconstructive use of history can be cited.

Already as early as the 1860s in West Africa, the Sierra Leone, Creole physician Dr. James Africanus Beale Horton argued in his *West African Countries and Peoples* – a book revealingly subtitled "A Vindication of the African Race" – that Africa had been the nursery of the science and literature of classical Greece and Rome, and that "tawny African bishops of Apostolic renown" had contributed much to the development of early Christianity.[34] Edward Wilmot Blyden described the splendor of black-African antiquity in his essay "The Negro in Ancient History"; and his travel account *From West Africa to Palestine* viewed "the enterprising sons of Ham," the progenitors of his contemporary "Negro-Africans," as the persons who had sent civilization into Greece and who had been teachers of the renowned poets, historians, and mathematicians of classical Europe.[35] His works, and those of J. E. Casely-Hayford from the Gold Coast, anticipated the aims, concerns, and methods employed later in books such as *Nations negres et culture*, by Cheikh Anta Diop of Senegal, and *African Glory: The Story of Vanished Civilizations*, by Charles de Graft-Johnson of Ghana.[36]

Because, however, the persons attempting this type of historical revision were also among those most exposed to Europeanization – products of a Eurocentric educational system that had provided them with little knowledge about the historical deeds of the people from whom they had descended – their search back into the past was problematic. Lacking the detailed knowledge and the linguistic tools to reconstruct the history of their ancestors and to make it acceptable on its own terms, they used the European-oriented education they had received to demonstrate, in European terms, the greatness of their collective cultural past and its germinative influence on the civilization cherished by their white detractors. But, in doing this, they remained confined within an ideological and epistemological framework they had received from the dominant culture. Having once believed that progress and technical achievement unlocked the kingdom of acceptance and modernity, they found themselves unable to present historical revisions that modified the premises inherent in the only keys they had learned to use.

In this sense, of course, the historical responses departed from the assertive inversions characteristic of their *négritude* literary counterparts. The *négritude* writings, however, were equally based on essentialist constructs. The collective they invoked – be it "Africa," "the Negro," "the Negro African," "the black people," "the African past" – was an intellectual creation that generally had little specific connection to any existing or historical group of people. Both the historical and literary expressions thus reflect the degree to which the assimilationist process had severed the connection between the highly assimilated individuals who articulated them and the cultural and historic world of their parents and grandparents. These expressions demonstrate the difficulties and dilemmas embedded within any intellectual effort to overcome the predicament of marginality – the conflicts and contradictions of any attempt to link self to collective and to re-create a lost bond with the past.

The Haitian poet Léon Laleau communicated some of the difficulties of this re-creative effort, and its emotional cost, in particularly poignant poetic terms:

> This beleaguered heart
> Alien to my language and dress
> On which I bit like a brace
> The borrowed sentiments and customs
> of Europe.
> Mine is the agony
> The unutterable despair
> In Breaking with the cold words of
> France
> The pulsing heart of Senegal.[37]

Normally, moreover, the affirmations of African history, culture, and of inherent "Negro" qualities were articulated by black intellectuals in the languages of the colonial powers. Published in books and journals not easily accessible to a less educated or less affluent general public, their rhetoric and purpose was often lost on the very masses with whom "marginal" members of the elite hoped to identify. This was particularly the case with much of the "classic" *négritude* literature produced in the 1930s by French-speaking black intellectuals that received its major creative surge in Paris within the pages of the French cultural journal *Présence Africaine*. Although the various affirmative efforts thus performed important positive psychological and compensatory functions for the European-educated minority within the subordinate group, inducing within its members a consciousness of "racial identity" with less assimilated persons on the basis of shared "racial disabilities," they did not affect the masses in similar fashion. In this respect, intellectual responses of this type were ultimately less successful than their political counterparts in mobilizing subordinated groups into effective movements for change.[38]

Modern Zionism – a response to exclusion with strong intellectual *and* political manifestations that began to gain momentum among Western and Eastern European Jews in the 1880s and 1890s – was somewhat more successful than *négritude*-type responses in bridging the elite-mass gap.[39] In part, of course, this connection was catalyzed by the Russian pogroms of 1881 and the Dreyfus affair of 1895, two specific anti-Semitic shocks during these decades that directly or indirectly touched the lives and altered the consciousnesses of large numbers of Jews from various social backgrounds throughout Europe. In the words of Arthur Hertzberg, these events helped "to transform Zionism from closet philosophy into a mass movement and a maker of history."[40] It was also made possible by the compromise that was forged within Zionism between its secular and religious constituencies – between "political" and "cultural" Zionists – based on an acceptance of the versatility of Jewish experience and on the recognition of the "distinctive unity of the Jewish spirit."[41]

In effect, Zionism, as articulated by two of its leading theoreticians, Theodor Herzl and Ahad Ha'am (Asher Zvi Ginsberg), in Western and Eastern Europe, respectively, emerged as a reaction to the perceived failure of emancipation: "its failure to occur at all in Eastern Europe, and its failure to bring full integration or to eliminate anti-Semitism in the West."[42] "We have sincerely tried everywhere to merge with the national communities in which we live, seeking only to preserve the faith of our fathers," Herzl – a highly assimilated member of Vienna's upper bourgeoisie of the generation of Stefan Zweig's parents – wrote in *Der Judenstaat* in 1896, a year after he witnessed the Dreyfus affair in Paris:

It is not permitted us. In vain are we loyal patriots, sometimes superloyal; in vain do we make the same sacrifices of life and property as our fellow citizens; in vain do we strive to enhance the fame of our native lands in the arts and sciences, or her wealth by trade and commerce. In our native lands where we have lived for centuries we are still decried as aliens, often by men whose ancestors had not yet come at a time when Jewish sighs had long been heard in the country. The majority decide who the "alien" is; this, and all else in the relations between peoples, is a matter of power.[43]

For Herzl and the other founders of modern Zionism, the "Jewish question" – the eternal problem of the Jews in the Diaspora, "the major unresolved problem of the western world" – was rooted in the persistence of anti-Semitism. "The world resounds with clamor against the Jews," Herzl observed:

The Jewish question still exists. It would be foolish to deny it. It is a misplaced piece of medievalism which civilized nations do not even yet seem able to shake off, try as they will. They proved they had this high-minded desire when they emancipated us. The Jewish question persists wherever Jews live in appreciable numbers. Wherever it does not exist, it is brought in together with Jewish immigrants. We are naturally drawn into those places where we are not persecuted, and our appearance there gives rise to

persecution. This is the case, and will inevitably be so, everywhere, even
in highly civilized countries ... so long as the Jewish question is not solved
on the political level.[44]

Because emancipation and assimilation could not provide a solution for "Jewish existence in an antagonistic Christian environment," Zionists proposed a *political* remedy for the plight of Jews:
they advocated the creation of a Jewish national homeland, a state
in which Jews could "determine their future with dignity, as equals
in the community of nations."[45] "We are a people – *one* people,"
Herzl argued, "our enemies have made us one whether we will or
not ... Affliction binds us together, and thus united, we suddenly
discover our strength. Yes, we are strong enough to form a State,
and indeed, a model State. We possess all the requisite human and
material resources."[46]

For its theoreticians in Western and Eastern Europe, Zionism was
thus intended both as an escape from persecution and as a rehabil-
itative response with potentially wide-ranging positive consequences. Convinced about the impossibility of Jewish existence in
the Diaspora, they envisioned the collective return of the Jewish
people to a lost sovereignty and homeland as a key step in their
transformation from persecuted minority to equal partners among
the nations of the world. Such a return to national existence, in a
"nation-state like all other nations," would help to terminate the
long and dark episode of Jewish "exile" in Gentile lands, and would
rectify the political and social abnormality that had characterized
Jewish experience over the centuries. It would reestablish "nor-
malcy."[47] Herzl, in particular, as Amnon Rubenstein has indicated,
viewed the "establishment of a Jewish national state and [the] emigration [of Jews] from Europe" to be "compatible with the interests
of the family of enlightened nations." In the fulfillment of the Zionist
dream,"the western world would rid itself of a painful problem" and
would acquire another "civilized offshoot" incorporating its highest
values.[48]

In addition to its function in collective political and social reha-
bilitation, however, the establishment of a Jewish state and the
Jews' "Return to Zion" was also seen by its formative theorists as
the requisite – indeed, the imperative – agent for individual transformation. It was intended to bring about that very metamorphosis
of the Jewish person that could not be achieved through assimilation
in Europe; it would liberate individual Jews from the "defects" acquired in the Diaspora – from their "parasitical" occupations and
"sickening submission to brute force and oppression" – and would
transform them from the "negative" *Yids* reviled by anti-Semites

into "positive" *Hebrews* in charge of their own development and destiny.[49] "What we see around us among Jews is merely the outcome of arbitrary action perpetrated by others," Vladimir Jabotsinsky observed in 1905 regarding the character and existence of Jews in the Diaspora: "Only after removing the dust accumulated through two thousand years of exile, of *galut*, will the true, authentic Hebrew character reveal its glorious head. Only then shall we be able to say: This is a typical Hebrew, in every sense of the word."[50] The call through Zionism was for the emergence of what might be termed "Hebritude" – the Jewish analogue to *négritude*.[51]

But, although general consensus existed among European Zionist thinkers about the need of Jews to solve their collective subordination through national and political restoration, and about the consequent transformation that would create "new men and women," divisions existed about the meaning and character of this personal and social metamorphosis. As was true with so many other persons throughout the world who had undergone the assimilationist experience and internalized the values, ideals, and promises of emancipation, it was difficult for Herzl and other highly assimilated German-speaking Jews to imagine alternatives that departed in radical ways from the world to which they had aspired, but from which they found themselves blocked.

In Herzl's view, the persons who would inhabit the Jewish state would not be "different from the cultivated Europeans": the rational, secular, liberal, progressive individuals like himself, who were products of Jewish assimilation into Western European society.[52] They would transfer the most advanced values of modern European culture into their national homeland. The Jewish state, Herzl indicated in *Der Judenstaat*, "will be carried out entirely in the framework of civilization" – by which he clearly meant "Western civilization." In this state, he argued,

we shall not revert to a lower stage; we shall rise to a higher one. We shall not dwell in mud huts; we shall build new, more beautiful, and more modern houses, and possess them in safety. We shall not lose our acquired possessions; we shall realize them. We shall surrender our well-earned rights for better ones. We shall relinquish none of our cherished customs; we shall find them again.[53]

And, revealing his bourgeois perspective, he indicated:

Those [Jews] only will depart [Europe] who are sure thereby to improve their lot; those who are now desperate will go first, after them the poor, next the well to do, and last of all the wealthy. Those who go first will raise themselves to a higher grade, on a level with that whose representatives will shortly follow. *The exodus will thus at the same time be an ascent in class.*[54]

However, in contradistinction to Herzl's largely secular notion of a Jewish state, and to his vision of a "new Jew" rooted in the progressive ideals of modern, Western European culture and society, other Zionist thinkers offered an alternative societal and personal model. As indicated by Amnon Rubenstein, this division reflected "the wide divergence between the emancipated western Jew who entered Zionism via the corridor of frustrated assimilation and the Jewish masses of Eastern Europe living under the authoritarian yoke of antisemitic regimes."[55] The latter view, cogently articulated in the writings of the Russian-born Ahad Ha'am (Asher Zvi Ginsberg),[56] argued for the necessity to maintain and foster the totality of Jewish tradition, including historical experience and religion, in the individual and the state. "Will the sons of Israel," Ahad Ha'am asked,

live in their state according to their own unique spirit and give life and develop their own national assets which were bequeathed to their past, or will their state merely be another European colony in Asia, a colony which looks up to the metropolis, seeking to imitate her in every way?[57]

Eventually, it was in the dynamic tension between these views, and in the modus vivendi that was reached between them, that a bridge was created between Jews of Herzl's assimilationist background and class orientation and the less-assimilated Jewish majority who had remained closer to Jewish *shtettl* culture with its rich religious, folkloric, as well as historical traditions. The modern Zionist idea survived – and Zionism became a widely based national movement – precisely because it was able to draw into itself diverse groups and elements within the Jewish diasporic experience. It infused into these a belief in national liberation and a faith in future transformation.

Although creating a bridge between these groups, no Zionist ideal could ultimately *resolve* the fundamental tensions between the competing visions of the character of the Jewish state. These would reemerge in Palestine, and would challenge the very integrity of the dream of a unified national revival in Israel. Nor could Zionist ideas in their actualization reconcile the inherent contradiction that emerged when the state of Israel was finally established in Palestine in the aftermath of the Holocaust. The political, nationalist, "solution" of the European "Jewish problem" did not take into account the rise of competing non-Western nationalist forces with which

Zionism would inevitably come into conflict in its Middle Eastern milieu.

Indeed, like modern Zionism, the "non-Western nationalist" or "colonial nationalist" movements, which arose in areas of the world under European imperial domination in the twentieth century, are also illustrative of the category of "reconnective," politically oriented, "self-to-collective" responses to subordination. They too were characterized by efforts on the part of Western-educated individual "marginals" within the colonial territories to forge political connections with "less acculturated" persons – to mobilize politically and act collectively with them in order to overcome what was now perceived to be mutual subjugation. Although modern Zionism, however, specifically employed a common Jewish origin and the apparent inescapability from anti-Semitism to establish the individual-mass connection, colonial nationalism used the territorial boundaries of the colonial state to define both the constituencies and limits of the connective effort.

Given the character of the European imperial division of Africa and other areas of the non-European world in the late nineteenth and early twentieth centuries, this decision was a necessary one. In the "Scramble for Africa," which began in the mid–1880s, for example, the European powers had divided up the continent among themselves, and had drawn up territorial lines for their colonial "possessions" that took relatively little heed of existing African political and ethnic boundaries. In principle, this meant that the new colonies might contain a number of different ethnic and precolonial political groupings within their territorial limits; it also meant that many ethnic groups and precolonial polities were split up and came under the administrative control of different European rulers.

It therefore generally became the task of colonial nationalism in Africa to mold a *new national* group identity from the various ethnicities and groupings within the territorial boundaries of the colonial state. Even though many precolonial groupings had met the criteria normally applied to nationhood – possessing a common culture, common territory, common language, a common historical tradition, and the institutions of a state to articulate these elements – the colonial framework that the Europeans created either contained *more than one* of these old "nations," or it destroyed them through territorial and political division.[58]

Thus, unlike the nineteenth-century Central and Eastern European quest for national self-determination, in which the definition of nationality usually coincided with ethnic identity, or in Zionism, where a people who had once been a nation sought a state in which to regain their nationhood, African colonial nationalism initiated a dynamic process in which a "new nation" was to be created within the boundaries of the colonial state. African colonial nationalist leaders thus called for loyalty to Ghana, for example, rather than to Asante or to the Fante Confederation; to Uganda rather than to Buganda, Bunyoro, or Ankole; to Nigeria rather than Benin, or Oyo, or the Sokoto Empire; to Sierra Leone rather than to a Krio, Temne, or Mende political entity. As characterized by Philip Curtin, the claim of African nationalist leaders was: "Here is a people, living within the boundaries of a colonial territory, under the government dominated by foreigners. This people has a right to an independent political life, *so that* [they] may become a nation."[59]

To be sure, although the framework of the colonial state normally set the territorial limits within which a new national identity was to be forged, the connective tissue linking "elite" individuals to the collective – as well as different groups within the collective to each other – was race. The fact that colonizer and colonized were distinguished by race within each colony – that racism was used by the dominant group, both against the African masses in general, and as a block to the aspirations of "elite" individuals who had been most strongly influenced by European institutions and liberal promises – meant that the colonized persons could attempt to use their shared racial "disabilities" to submerge, if not transcend, ethnic and class differences. Engendered in individual members of the "colonial bourgeoisie" by their experience of the predicament of marginality, this awakened sense of racial identity thus became a useful catalyst for collective social and political mobilization among the colonized.[60] Together with other perceived joint disabilities and inequities in the economic, social, and political realm, it provided a basis for interclass and multiethnic solidarity among all subordinated groups within a given colonial entity, and helped to bring about the elite-mass alliances necessary for effective nationalist, anticolonial, political action.

In their functional sense, of course, racially based *intellectual* constructs of the *négritude* or "African personality" variety resembled these *political-nationalist* efforts to establish a sense of racial identity among the colonized. In the realities of practical application, the differentiating boundaries between typological representations of response often blurred. Even though emotional and philosophical connections existed between these "intellectual" and "political" types, however, the notion of racial identity represented within each category encompassed somewhat different groupings. For *négritude* and "African personality" writers, the notion was a broad one that generally transcended national borders and included all persons of color, in Africa as well as in the African Diaspora. For them, the notion was truly Pan-African. In contrast, colonial nationalists normally focused on race as a binding element *within* existing state structures. They conceived of collective racial identity as a means toward a specific political end.

Because the prime goals of colonial nationalism were political independence and the ending of European domination, the achievement of these ends provided a potential resolution for the one type of marginal dilemma that had long haunted individual African members of the colonial elite. Within the new states, barriers to acceptance and mobility that had been based on the racial difference between the dominant Europeans and their colonial subjects were largely eliminated. Paradoxically, however, new opportunities for social differentiation and status emerged within many of these now independent states as well: opportunities that challenged the very basis of elite-mass nationalist unity under which independence had been attained. Where this happened, the pattern was similar. Class and ethnic differences which, in part at least, had been submerged in the course of the effort to eliminate European colonial domination, resurfaced. "Tribalism," reflecting "old" sentiments of loyalty to ethnic or linguistic groups within the new nation, reemerged to compete with modern nationalism.[61] State power passed from colonial authorities into the hands of an indigenous elite: to individuals and groups who, all too often, refocused their political and economic goals to advance the interests of their own class or ethnic kin, and to consolidate their power.[62] Certainly, in such places, "marginal situations"– characterized by wide hierarchical differences in privilege, wealth, and power, and by impediments to the amelioration of inequalities in status and opportunity – continued to exist. And where they existed *and were perceived*, efforts by subordinated individuals to resolve the discrepancy between their aspirations and their situational reality – to resolve their predicament of marginality – continued as well.

There was, of course, another type of response within the "political" category that, potentially at least, offered a much more radical restructuring of societal relations and existing hierarchical arrangements. In twentieth-century Europe, the classic example of this response was the Russian Revolution of 1917, which overthrew Tsarist authoritarianism, rejected bourgeois parliamentarism and the oppressive structures of the past, and attempted to establish a classless society in which social inequalities and prejudices would no longer exist.[63] The promises inherent in this revolution attracted many kinds of marginalized groups within the Russian Empire: workers, peasants, intellectuals, women, ethnic minorities, and a large number of Jews who preferred radical economic and social transformation within their Russian homeland to Zionist emigration. The promises also influenced numerous other subordinated people throughout the world.

The social revolutionary response in colonial situations was reflected in decolonization efforts of a type that Frantz Fanon calls "independence taken." In contrast to "colonial nationalist" movements like those in British West Africa in which independence was "given" to colonial peoples through constitutional, evolutionary processes, the Algerian, Vietnamese, and Mozambican revolutions, for example, involved violent struggles for "national liberation." They were also typified by an articulated ideological commitment to fundamental structural, social, and economic transformations in postcolonial society.[64]

Indeed, in Fanonian theory, *true liberation* from colonial domination could *only* come about through collective revolutionary struggle characterized by his notion of "holy violence." "Violence alone," he wrote in *The Wretched of the Earth*,

violence committed by the people, violence organized and educated by its leaders, makes it possible for the masses to understand social truths and gives the key to them. Without that struggle, without that knowledge of the practice of action, there's nothing but a fancy-dress parade and the blare of trumpets. There's nothing save a minimum of readaptation, a few reforms at the top, a flag waving: and down there at the bottom an undivided mass, still living in the middle ages, endlessly marking time. [65]

Where independence is forcefully "taken" by the masses, Fanon argues, the liberating act of violence will generate "the great shock which founds a new world"; it will bring about radical personal and societal changes and lay the foundations for a new reality. Accordingly, he notes, on the level of the individual, violent struggle performs a therapeutic function: it acts as a detoxifying, "cleansing force," freeing "colonized" persons from the "colonial neurosis" – liberating them from their "inferiority complex" and from "despair and inaction." Restoring their self-respect, it transforms them from alienated and subordinated objects into self-conscious, self-confident subjects; it *truly* emancipates them and transfigures them into "New Men" and "New Women."[66] On a collective level, the incrementally "all inclusive and national" character of "violence in action" liquidates old divisions based on "tribalism" and "regionalism," and binds its participants together into a new community. Relationships between parents and children, between husbands and wives, between the old and the young, lose their restrictive traditional character.[67] "In a veritable ecstasy," states Fanon, as he imagined the metamorphosis following the aftermath of the combat,

families which have always been traditional enemies decide to rub out old scores and to forgive and forget. There are numerous reconciliations.... There is a permanent outpouring in all the villages of spectacular generosity, of disarming kindness, and willingness, which cannot ever be doubted, to die for the "cause".... Even tribes whose stubborn rivalry is well known now disarm with joyful tears and pledge help to each other.... In undertaking this onward march, the people legislates, finds itself, and wills itself to sovereignty.[68]

To be sure, Fanon's mesmerization "by the creative power of revolution, by the purifying flame of violence" was singular in its intensity.[69] Elsewhere – in China, Cuba, Vietnam, Mozambique, Angola, and South Africa, for example – theoreticians of national liberation and social revolution had less faith in the spontaneous transformative powers of violent struggle. Where Fanon conceived of violent liberation as the *primary* vehicle for personal and collective emancipation and reconstruction, they saw the need to channel and guide the revolution into a rational and ongoing process of change. To achieve radical economic, social, and political alterations in postindependence society, they wished to perpetuate the effects of spontaneous revolutionary action through political education and the institutionalization of revolutionary ideals.[70] In the words of Che Guevara:

From an ideological viewpoint, our fundamental task is to find the formula which will perpetuate in daily life these heroic attitudes [of total commitment to the revolutionary cause].... In this period of the construction of socialism, we can see the new man being born. His image is as yet unfinished; in fact, it will never be finished, for the process advances parallel to the development of new economic forms.... This is why it is so important to choose correctly the instrument for the mobilization of the masses.[71]

For *all* theorists, however, in colonial as well as metropolitan lands, the revolutionary response was intended to accomplish more than the demolition of the political and economic structures of domination – more, even, than the achievement of personal and communal renewal. By tearing apart the fabric of values and assumptions on which domination had been built, this response was also meant to destroy the dominant group's ideological and cultural hegemony. Indeed, everywhere, revolution was intended to be the ultimate negation of the bourgeois model, the final rejection of a failed emancipatory and assimilationist promise. "Let us decide not to imitate Europe," Fanon thus urged his fellow colonial revolutionaries,

> ...let us not pay tribute to Europe by creating states, institutions, and societies which draw their inspiration from her.... Humanity is waiting for something from us other than such an imitation, which would be almost an obscene caricature.... We must turn over a new leaf, we must work out new concepts.[72]

In turning over "a new leaf," the revolutionary response was clearly not intended to be backward-looking. The ashes from which new societies were to rise and evolve in Phoenix-like fashion also included the negative remains of traditional cultural legacies. The inequities and inequalities that had resided within these legacies were to be rejected as well. In this respect, the revolutionary response was characterized by a dual iconoclasm: by the shattering of hierarchical structures and the negation of exclusionary ideologies *both in the past and present*. Situated at this critical juncture, it promised a definitive resolution to the predicament of marginality.

Naturally, the multiple promises of social revolution were ambitious and difficult to attain and realize in practice. Major disagreements about the accomplishments of the revolutionary response exist, not only among its participants and heirs, but also among its "outside" appraisers. Assessments of the correspondence between social revolutionary theory and postrevolutionary reality have been based on a variety of social indices – measurements of collective well-being in numerous sectors within the broad expanse of the economic, political, and social arena. The decline in infant mortality, the availability of food and shelter, of medical and hospital care, of goods and services, of employment and access to education and political decision-making – these are usually included among the concrete estimates of revolutionary "success." In the area of social relations, judgments about the status of women, about race relations, about the tolerance of dissent and the protection of wide-ranging individual rights and liberties have provided additional appraisals.

Generally, these assessments of collective transformation and social change have been based on "objective," measurable indicators. Estimates of changes in individual consciousness, however – in world view and in the interpretation of experience – necessitate life-history analyses that, by their very nature, are much more "subjective" as appraisals. As the focus on members of the May, Rebouças, and Zweig-Brettauer families in this book has demonstrated, moreover, such analyses reflect the voices and visions of the articulate minority: of those individuals within the group whose "mind" can be approached and probed with the help of concrete records and evidentiary materials. Although providing insights into the consciousness of some individuals, explorations employing this approach merely sample the totality of potential personal reactions – to revolution, but also to the range of other responses to marginality. Beyond this sample, a vast number of individual stories remain enveloped in silent obscurity, waiting for the teller and method that will bring them to light.

Notes

Introduction

1. Erik Erikson, *Life History and the Historical Moment* (New York, 1975).

2. See Philip D. Curtin, "'The White Man's Grave': Image and Reality, 1780–1850," *The Journal of British Studies* 1 (1961): 94–110; and P. D. Curtin, *The Image of Africa: British Ideas and Action, 1780–1850* (Madison, 1964), pp. 177–197.

3. For a discussion of the Josephine reforms, see Chapter 1 and C. A. Macartney, *The Habsburg Empire, 1790–1918* (London, 1969), pp. 1–133; William M. Johnston, *The Austrian Mind: An Intellectual and Social History, 1848–1938* (Berkeley, 1972), pp. 15–21; Wenzel Lustkandl, *Die josephinischen Ideen und ihr Erfolg* (Vienna, 1881); and Max Grunwald, *History of Jews in Vienna* (Philadelphia, 1936), pp. 145–67. For Jewish immigration into Vienna, see Grunwald, pp. 206, 207, 422; and Marsha L. Rozenblit, *The Jews of Vienna, 1867–1914* (New York, 1983), pp. 18–43.

4. Jacques Barzun, *Clio and the Doctors: Psycho-History, Quanto-History and History* (Chicago, 1974), pp. 153–54.

5. Martin Duberman, *The Uncompleted Past* (New York, 1971), p. 43.

6. William M. Runyan, *Life Histories and Psychobiography: Explorations in Theory and Method* (New York, 1984), pp. 3–6, 123–6, 172. Also see Daniel Bertaux, ed., *Biography and Society: The Life History Approach in the Social Sciences* (Beverly Hills, Calif., 1981), passim.

7. Runyan, *Life Histories*, pp. 8, 191.

8. This assumption is discussed and criticized in Evelyn Fox Keller, *Reflections on Gender and Science* (New Haven, 1985), pp. 95, 115–17.

9. Jean-Paul Sartre, *Search for a Method*, trans. Hazel E. Barnes (New York, 1968), pp. xxi, 79; Runyan, *Life Histories*, pp. 6–9.

10. Elaine Showalter, "The Dark Lady," public lecture at Dartmouth College, July 1986.

11. Keller, *Reflections on Gender and Science*, p. 117.

12. Clifford Geertz, *Local Knowledge: Further Essays in Interpretive Anthropology* (New York, 1983), p. 69.

13. Ibid.

14. Dan Rottenberg, *Finding Our Fathers* (New York, 1977).

15. Among the many autobiographical and biographical excamples depicting a process of assimilation and exclusion, see Hannah Arendt, *Rahel Varnhagen: The Life of a Jewish Woman* (New York, 1974); Francisco de Assis Barbosa, *A Vida de Lima Barreto* (Rio de Janeiro, 1981); George Clare,

199

Last Waltz in Vienna: The Rise and Destruction of a Family, 1842–1942 (New York, 1982); Frantz Fanon, *Black Skin, White Masks: The Experiences of a Black Man in a White World* (New York, 1967); Ludwig Lewisohn, *Up Stream* (New York, 1922); R. Magalhães Júnior, *A Vida Turbulenta de José do Patrocinio* (Rio de Janeiro, 1969); Sigmund Mayer, *Ein jüdischer Kaufmann, 1831–1911: Lebenserinnerungen* (Berlin, 1926); Richard Rodriguez, *Hunger of Memory: The Education of Richard Rodriguez* (New York, 1982); Toni Oelsner, "Three Jewish Families in Modern Germany: A Study of the Process of Emancipation," *Jewish Social Studies*: 4 (3) (July 1942) and (4) (Oct. 1942).

16. Runyan, *Life Histories*, pp. 582–4.

17. Paul Thompson, "Life Histories and the Analysis of Social Change," in Daniel Bertaux, ed., *Biography and Society: The Life History Approach in the Social Sciences* (London, 1981), p. 292.

Chapter 1. The Journey Upward, the Journey Outward

1. See Reinhard Rürup, "Jewish Emancipation and Bourgeois Society," in *Leo Baeck Institute, Year Book XIV*, 1969, p. 67; "Emancipation," in D. Wilhelm Traugott Krug, *Allgemeines Handwörterbuch der Philosophischen Wissenschaften*, Erster Band (Leipzig, 1832), pp. 747–8.

2. Karl Rosenkranz, "Emanzipation des Fleisches," quoted in Karl Martin Grass and Reinhart Koselleck, "Emanzipation," p. 167, in Otto Brunner, Werner Conze, and Reinhart Koselleck, eds., *Geschichtliche Grundbegriffe: Historisches Lexikon zur politisch-sozialen Sprache in Deutschland*, Band 2, E-G (Stuttgart, 1972) [hereafter cited as *Historisches Lexikon*].

3. Leland H. Jenks, "Emancipation," in *Encyclopedia of the Social Sciences*, (New York, 1930) [hereafter cited as ESS], pp. 483–4; "Emanzipation," in *Religion in Geschichte und Gegenwart*, 3d ed., vol. 2 (Tübingen, 1958), pp. 449–54; "Emanzipation," in Joachim Ritter, *Historisches Wörterbuch der Philosophie*, Band 2: D-F (Basel, Stuttgart, 1971–2), pp. 448–9; "Emanzipation," in Krug, *Allgemeines Handwörterbuch*, Erster Band, p. 747; *Historisches Lexikon*, pp. 154–62.

4. *Historisches Lexikon*, pp. 154–7; ESS, "Emanzipation," pp. 483–4; Krug, *Allgemeines Handwörterbuch*, Erster Band, pp. 747–8; Ritter, *Historisches Wörterbuch der Philosophie*, Band 2, p. 448.

5. E. J. Hobsbawm, *The Age of Capital, 1848–1875* (New York, 1975), pp. 1–5.

6. See Eric Foner's discussion of such factors affecting slaveholding societies in *Nothing but Freedom: Emancipation and Its Legacy* (Baton Rouge, 1983), pp. 8–38.

7. ESS, "Emancipation," p. 484.

8. Rürup, "Jewish Emancipation and Bourgeois Society," p. 73. Also see ESS, "Jewish Emancipation," p. 396, and "Emancipation," p. 484; and Serge Daget, "A Model of the French Abolitionist Movement and Its Variations," in Christine Bolt and Seymour Drescher, eds., *Anti-Slavery, Religion, and*

Reform: Essays in Memory of Roger Anstey (Hamden, Conn., 1980), pp. 64–80.

9. For the stages of emancipation leading to the final abolition of slavery in Brazil in 1888, see Robert Brent Toplin, *The Abolition of Slavery in Brazil* (New York, 1971); Robert Conrad, *The Destruction of Brazilian Slavery, 1850–1888* (Berkeley, 1972); Luiz Luna, *O Negro na luta contra a escravidão* (Rio de Janeiro, 1968); and Katia M. de Queirós Mattoso, *To Be a Slave in Brazil, 1550–1888* (New Brunswick, N.J., 1986), pp. 153–76. Also see Robert Brent Toplin, "Upheaval, Violence, and the Abolition of Slavery in Brazil: The Case of São Paulo," *Hispanic American Historical Review* 49 (4) (Nov. 1969); and Thomas Blair, "Mouvements afro-brasiliens de libération, de la période esclavigiste à nos jours," *Présence Africaine* (1965).

10. Roger Bastide and Florestan Fernandes, *Brancos e Negros em São Paulo* (São Paulo, 1959); Florestan Fernandes, *The Negro in Brazilian Society* [original title: *A Integração do Negro na Sociedade de Classes*] (New York, 1971), pp. 1–186; Octavio Ianni, *As Metamorfoses do Escravo* (São Paulo, 1962); Fernando Henrique Cardoso, *Capitalismo e Escravidão no Brasil Meridional* (São Paulo, 1962); Luna, *O Negro na luta contra a escravidão*, pp. 184–93, 202–12; Mattoso, *To Be a Slave in Brazil*, pp. 177–93.

11. Fernandes, *Negro*, p. 48.

12. Ibid., p. 50.

13. William A. Green, *British Slave Emancipation: The Sugar Colonies and the Great Experiment, 1830–1865* (Oxford, 1976), pp. 126, 129–61.

14. Foner, *Nothing but Freedom*, pp. 14, 16, 17; Green, *British Slave Emancipation*, p. 126.

15. See David Roberts, *Paternalism in Early Victorian England* (New Brunswick, N.J., 1979), passim.

16. *Foner, Nothing but Freedom*, pp. 16–25; C. Holt, " 'An Empire over the Mind': Emancipation, Race, and Ideology in the British West Indies and the American South," in J. Morgan Kousser and James M. McPherson, eds., *Region, Race, and Reconstruction: Essays in Honor of C. Vann Woodward* (New York, 1982); Graham Knox, "British Colonial Policy and the Problems of Establishing a Free Society in Jamaica, 1838–1865," *Caribbean Studies* 2 (Jan. 1963); Green, *British Slave Emancipation*, pp. 129–61.

17. Foner, *Nothing but Freedom*, p. 31; Douglas A. Lorimer, *Colour, Class, and the Victorians: English Attitudes to the Negro in the Mid-Nineteenth Century* (New York, 1978); Christine Bolt, *Victorian Attitudes to Race* (London, 1971); Philip D. Curtin, *The Image of Africa: British Ideas and Action, 1780–1850* (Madison, 1964), pp. 384–5.

18. The phrase "the essential oneness of all human nature" is in Jacob Katz, "The Term 'Jewish Emancipation': Its Origin and Historical Impact," in Alexander Altmann, ed., *Studies in Nineteenth-Century Jewish Intellectual History* (Cambridge, Mass., 1964), p. 9. John Toland's ideas about Jewish emancipation and integration are presented in his anonymously published pamphlet *Reasons for Naturalizing the Jews in Great Britain and Ireland, on the Same Foot with All Other Nations* (London, 1714). Lessing's

ideas about Jewish equality are expressed in his play *Der Jude* (1754) and, especially, in *Nathan der Weise* (1779).

19. Christian Wilhelm von Dohm, *Ueber die bürgerliche Verbesserung der Juden* (Berlin, 1781), p. 130.

20. Rürup, "Jewish Emancipation and Bourgeois Society," pp. 12–13, 71.

21. Dohm, *Verbesserung* (trans. as *On the Civil Improvement of the Jews.*). Important sections of this work in English are in Ellis Rivkin, ed., *Readings in Modern Jewish History* (Cincinnati, 1957), pp. 5–7, 9–22, 50–71; Katz, "The Term 'Jewish Emancipation,'" p. 3; and Katz, *Out of the Ghetto: The Social Background of Jewish Emancipation, 1770–1870* (New York, 1978), pp. 57–65.

22. Dohm, *Verbesserung*, p. 28; Katz, "The Term 'Jewish Emancipation,'" p. 13.

23. Dohm, *Verbesserung*, p. 34; Rürup, "Jewish Emancipation and Bourgeois Society," pp. 71–2.

24. Dohm, *Verbesserung*, p. 110; Rürup, "Jewish Emancipation and Bourgeois Society," pp. 60, 72; Katz, *Out of the Ghetto*, pp. 64, 124.

25. Katz, *Out of the Ghetto*, pp. 64–8.

26. For an overview of this legislation, see Rürup, "Jewish Emancipation and Bourgeois Society," pp. 75–80; Kurt Stillschweig, "Jewish Assimilation as an Object of Legislation," *Historia Judaica* 8 (1) (Apr. 1946): 1–18; and Katz, *Out of the Ghetto*, pp. 66, 127–9. In Austria, the Edict of Tolerance obliged Jews in the Emperor's domain to erect schools of their own or to send their children to Christian institutions. The edict is published in Alfred Pribam, *Urkunden und Akten zur Geschichte der Juden in Wien* (Vienna, 1918), vol. 1, pp. 494–500. A translation is in Raphael Mahler, ed., *Jewish Emancipation: A Selection of Documents by R. Mahler*, Pamphlet Series, "Jews and the Post-War World," no. 1 (New York, 1941), pp. 18–20. Translated sections of the edict are also in Paul R. Mendes-Flohr and Jehuda Reinharz, eds., *The Jew in the Modern World* (New York, 1980), pp. 34–6.

27. Katz, *Out of the Ghetto*, p. 128.

28. Ibid., p. 84. Indeed, the call for "dress reform" was a key element of conversionist ideology during the Century of Emancipation. See Chapters 2, 3, 4, and 6 in the present volume for specific illustrations of this phenomenon in Sierra Leone, Brazil, and Austria.

29. See Katz, *Out of the Ghetto*, p. 65, and n. 26, p. 233. Also see Pribam, *Urkunden und Akten*, vol. 1, p. 498.

30. Dohm, *Verbesserung*, p. 110; Rürup, "Jewish Emancipation and Bourgeois Society," p. 72. Also see David S. Landes, "The Jewish Merchant: Typology and Stereotypology in Germany," in *Leo Baeck Institute, Year Book XIX* (London, 1974), pp. 11–30.

31. Landes, "Merchant," pp. 12–14; Monika Richarz, "Jewish Social Mobility in Germany during the Time of Emancipation (1790–1871)," in *Leo Baeck Institute, Year Book XX* (London, 1975), pp. 71–72; Rürup, "Jewish Emancipation and Bourgeois Society," p. 81.

32. Although, as Reinhard Rürup indicates, this access was rarely granted without exceptions, "and frequently under conditions which sub-

sequently impaired the practical value of those concessions." Rürup, "Jewish Emancipation and Bourgeois Society," p. 81.

33. Richarz, "Jewish Social Mobility in Germany during the Time of Emancipation," p. 71; Landes, "Merchant," p. 13.

34. Three twentieth-century works by influential sociologists that refer to assimilation in this sense of complete conformity and merging are indicative of the persistence of this definition of the term: Robert E. Park and E. W. Burgess, *Introduction to the Science of Sociology* (Chicago, 1921), p. 735; J. Gould and W. L. Kolb, eds., *A Dictionary of the Social Sciences* (New York, 1946), p. 38; and G. A. Theodorson and A. G. Theodorson, *A Modern Dictionary of Sociology* (New York, 1969), p. 17. Except where otherwise indicated, all translations in the present volume are by the author.

35. Milton M. Gordon, *Assimilation in American Life: The Role of Race, Religion, and National Origin* (New York, 1964), pp. 60–83.

36. Ibid., p. 79.

37. See Chapters 2 and 6.

38. See Pribam, *Urkunden und Akten*, I, pp. 494–500; Katz, *Out of the Ghetto*, p. 164. See Chapter 3 in the present volume.

39. For additional discussion of this point, see Chapter 3. Also see Sigmund Mayer, *Ein jüdischer Kaufmann, 1831 bis 1911: Lebenserinnerungen* (Berlin, 1926), pp. 175–214; Carl Cohen, "The Road to Conversion," in *Leo Baeck Institute, Year Book VI*, 1961, pp. 259–79. Peter Gay, *Freud, Jews and Other Germans: Masters and Victims in Modernist Culture* (New York, 1978), passim; and Jacob Katz, *From Prejudice to Destruction: Anti-Semitism, 1700–1933* (Cambridge, Mass., 1980), pp. 223–9, 281–91.

40. Gordon, *Assimilation*, pp. 77–8; Jurgen Ruesch, Annemarie Jacobson, and Martin B. Loeb, "Acculturation and Illness," *American Psychological Association, Psychological Monographs: General and Applied*, vol. 62, no. 5 (1948), pp. 1–2, 10–15.

41. For a general discussion of this educational philosophy as developed by Andrew Bell and Joseph Lancaster in the pupil-monitored schools in England and quickly applied throughout most of Western and Central Europe as well as in North America and in areas of British colonial involvement, see Mary Jo Maynes, *Schooling in Western Europe: A Social History* (Albany, 1985), pp. 55, 76–7. Also see C. Kaestle, ed., *Joseph Lancaster and the Monitorial School Movement: A Documentary History* (New York, 1973); and Lawrence Stone, ed., *Schooling and Society: Studies in the History of Education* (Baltimore, 1976), pp. 3–19, 177–91. For a discussion of a specific application of this educational philosophy in Sierra Leone, see Chapter 2 in the present volume.

42. Ruesch, Jacobson, and Loeb, "Acculturation and Illness," p. 22; David Milner, *Children and Race* (London, 1975), pp. 35–60.

43. Ruesch, Jacobson, and Loeb, "Acculturation and Illness," p. 22.

44. Ibid., p. 24.

45. Ibid., p. 23.

46. Katz, *Out of the Ghetto*, p. 84.

47. See Chapter 3.

48. For example, see Julius Fürst, *Henriette Herz, ihr Leben und ihre Erinnerungen* (Berlin, 1858); and Hannah Arendt, *Rahel Varnhagen: The Life of a Jewish Woman* (New York, 1974).

49. Egon Schwarz, "Melting Pot or Witch's Cauldron? Jews and Anti-Semites in Vienna at the Turn of the Century," in David Bronsen, ed., *Jews and Germans from 1860 to 1933: The Problematic Symbiosis* (Heidelberg, 1979), pp. 271–2.

50. The development of sex-role stereotypes in early industrial Europe is discussed in Karin Hausen, "Family and Role-Division: The Polarisation of Sexual Stereotypes in the Nineteenth Century – An Aspect of the Dissociation of Work and Family Life," in R. J. Evans and W. R. Lee, eds., *The German Family* (Totowa, N.J., 1981), pp. 51–83. Also see Martha Vicinus, *Suffer and Be Still: Women in the Victorian Age* (Bloomington, 1972); and Maynes, *Schooling in Western Europe*, pp. 46, 63.

51. Hobsbawm, *The Age of Capital*, pp. 237–41; Joan Kelly, *Women, History, and Theory* (Chicago, 1984), pp. 53, 57, 128–34; Michael Mitteraruer and Reinhard Sieder, *The European Family: Patriarchy to Partnership from the Middle Ages to the Present* (Chicago, 1983), pp. 129–32; Dieter Claessens and Ferdinand W. Menne, "Zur Dynamik der bürgerlichen Familie und ihrer möglichen Alternativen," in Günther Lüschen and Eugen Lupri, eds., *Soziologie der Familie. Kölner Zeitschrift für Soziologie und Soziopsychologie*, vol. 14 (1970), pp. 169 ff.

52. Kelly, *Women, History, and Theory*, pp. 126–34; Barbara Corrado Pope, "Angels in the Devil's Workshop: Leisured and Charitable Women in Nineteenth Century England and France," in Renate Bridenthal and Claudia Koonz, eds., *Becoming Visible: Women in European History* (Boston, 1977), pp. 296–324.

53. See Chapter 2.

54. J. Pinto de Campos, *Carta (que dirigiu) aō Excelentissimo Senhor Ministro dos Negocios Eclesiasticos* (Rio de Janeiro, 1861), p. 20. Also see the chapter "Woman and Man," in Gilberto Freyre, *The Mansions and the Shanties: The Making of Modern Brazil* (Berkeley, 1986), pp. 73–103.

55. For a provocative discussion of the relationship of education and sex-role stereotypes in Western Europe, see Linda L. Clark, *Schooling the Daughters of Marianne: Textbooks and the Socialization of Girls in Modern French Primary Schools* (Albany, 1984). Also see F. Mayeur, *L'éducation des filles en France au XIXe siècle* (Paris, 1979); and L. Strumingher, *What Were Little Girls and Boys Made Of? Primary Education in Rural France* (Albany, 1983).

56. See Chapter 4. Also see Herbert S. Klein, "The Colored Freedmen in Brazilian Slave Society," *Journal of Social History* 3 (1) (1969): 30–52; A. J. R. Russell-Wood, "Colonial Brazil," in David Cohen and Jack P. Greene, eds., *Neither Slave nor Free: The Freedmen of African Descent in the Slave Societies of the New World* (Baltimore, 1972), pp. 98–108; Herbert S. Klein, "Nineteenth-Century Brazil," in Cohen and Greene, eds., *Neither Slave nor Free*, pp. 309–34; and Donald Pierson, "Ascenção Social do Mulato Brasi-

leiro" *Revista do Arquivo Municipal (São Paulo)*, vol. 87 (1942), pp. 107–19.

57. See Chapter 4 for a fuller discussion of "whitening." Also see Thomas E. Skidmore, *Black into White: Race and Nationality in Brazilian Thought* (New York, 1974), pp. 38–78; and Carl N. Degler, *Neither Black nor White: Slavery and Race Relations in Brazil and the United States* (New York, 1971), pp. 153–204.

58. The concept of "primary group" and "secondary group" orientation was first suggested by the American sociologist Charles Horton Cooley. See his *Social Organization* (New York, 1909), Chapter 3. Also see Gordon, *Assimilation*, pp. 31–2, for a discussion of this concept.

59. Marsha L. Rozenblit, *The Jews of Vienna, 1867–1914: Assimilation and Identity* (Albany, 1983), pp. 1–12.

60. Erik H. Erikson uses the term "interwoven with history" in his discussion of psychosocial identity in *Life History and the Historical Moment* (New York, 1975), p. 20.

Chapter 2. Up from Slavery

1. Slaves "recaptured" by British naval squadrons off West Africa and freed in Freetown during the early decades of the nineteenth century were commonly known as "Recaptives" or "Liberated Africans."

2. Methodist Missionary Archives (London), Sierra Leone Boxes [hereafter referred to as MMA:SL], letter from Joseph May, 18 Dec. 1846. Also see MMA:SL, letter from Joseph May, 23 Dec. 1868.

3. For a discussion related to this point – the belief "that mastering the master's tongue was the *sole* path to civilization and to intellectual freedom and social equality for a black person," see Henry Louis Gates, Jr., "Authority, (White) Power and the (Black) Critic: It's All Greek To Me," *Cultural Critique* 7 (Fall 1987): 19–46. Also see his *Figures in Black: Words, Signs, and the 'Racial' Self* (New York, 1987), pp. 3–28, and his "Editor's Introduction: Writing 'Race' and the Difference It Makes," *Critical Inquiry* 12 (1) (Autumn 1985): 7–15.

4. This definition is in Dulcie R. Nicolls, "The Effects of Western Education on the Social Attitudes of the Creoles in Sierra Leone" (thesis for the Diploma in Education, University of Durham through Fourah Bay College, 1960), p. 7.

5. MMA:SL, letter from Joseph May, 8 May 1843.

6. MMA:SL, letter from Joseph May, 18 Dec. 1846.

7. See, for example, MMA:SL, letter from Joseph May, 18 Dec. 1846. In this letter, he provides a fascinating account of an encounter with a fellow Yoruba-speaking "idol" worshiper: "One of them . . . came up to me in a rage and stood in a menacing attitude [and] said: worship your God, and I will worship mine, pointing to the people of other tribes standing by, and said, for these of no intelligible language, allowance might be made for their ignorance, but as for you . . . forsaken [*sic*] the gods of your fathers who bore

you, and pretend to know better than they, by worshipping white man's gods, I don't know what to say of you, he continues cursing, and swearing, and threatening, saying, never, never you come again to disturb and humbug me, with your foolishness, and insolence, if you are out of your sense you had better not come near. In a few days after, it excites my surprise, to see the very same person brought me two children to school, saying 'do daddy [that is, father] take my children in your school though I worship myself the gods who made me, according to the custom of my father who bore me, yet I will not let these worship country gods, like myself, therefore I beg you do teach them good, good, fashion for me'."

8. Eric J. Hobsbawm, *The Age of Capital, 1848–1875* (New York, 1975), p. 274.

9. Although May was not explicit about this connection at this point in his life, he wrote about it to the Reverend W. Boyce in 1868. See MMA:SL, letter from Joseph May, 23 Dec. 1868.

10. Hobsbawm, *Age of Capital*, p. 235.

11. MMA:SL, Joseph May, autobiographical conversion statement, Oct. 1838 [hereafter cited as MMA:SL/J. May, 1838]. Also see J. Claudius May, *A Brief Sketch of the Life of the Rev. Joseph May, Native of the Yoruba Country, and late Wesleyan Minister of the Colony of Sierra Leone, Read at a Service of Song in Zion Church, Freetown, on Sunday, October 25, 1896* ([Freetown], 1896) [hereafter cited as J. Claudius May, *Life of...Joseph May*], p. 18.

12. J. Claudius May, *Life of...Joseph May*, pp. 18–19; MMA:SL, letters from Joseph May, 18 Dec. 1846, 19 Oct. 1857, and 8 Nov. 1873, in which he stresses the advantage of using the vernacular to teach and convert Yoruba-speaking Liberated Africans. The development of Yoruba as a written language gained momentum in the 1840s. This movement was stimulated by British governmental, missionary, and commercial interest in the Niger, and by a small group of Yoruba-speaking Liberated Africans in Sierra Leone who wished to study the language and produce a literature in it. See P. E. H. Hair, *The Early Study of Nigerian Languages: Essays and Bibliographies* (London, 1967), pp. 4–5.

13. J. Claudius May, *Life...of Joseph May*, p. 18.

14. "Creole" came to describe the "colony-born" descendants of all the black groups (Poor Black, Nova Scotian, Maroon, Liberated African) that were settled in Sierra Leone under British sponsorship after 1787. The term, similar to "criollo" in the Spanish-speaking New World, was widely used in the British West Indies, where it also addressed the difference between "native to the colony" and "native to the metropolis." In recent years, J. G. Akintola Wyse and other historians of Sierra Leone have chosen to use "Krio" instead of "Creole" as the term identifying members of the community that emerged during the nineteenth and twentieth centuries. In this way, they wish to highlight the continuous historical identity of this group within Sierra Leone's multiethnic fabric. See Wyse, "Searchlight on the Krios of Sierra Leone" (unpublished paper, Freetown, Sierra Leone), and his *The Krio of Sierra Leone* (Madison, 1989). Also see Murray Last

and Paul Richards, eds., *Sierra Leone, 1787–1987: Two Centuries of Intellectual Life* (Manchester, Eng., 1987), passim. I find this usage anachronistic, and have chosen to use "Creole," the term members of this group applied to themselves throughout most of the period with which the present volume is concerned. For Betsy Ricket and William Wilberforce, see "Family Record of Births & C. of the Rev. Joseph May and Mrs. A. May" and "Genealogical Chart of the May, Stuart, Faulkner families," handwritten manuscripts presented to the author by Mrs. I. Stuart and Mrs. Garnet Smith, Jan. 26, 1976.

15. J. Claudius May, *Life . . . of Joseph May*, p. 19.

16. MMA:SL, letter from Joseph May, 25 Mar. 1861. Also see his letter of 18 Nov. 1858 for his position on the proper relationship of women toward their husbands and fathers. Of course, as E. Frances White has demonstrated, many colony-born women in Sierra Leone escaped the economic restrictions of the domestic sphere and became dominant participants in marketing and trading activities. See her "Creole Women Traders in Sierra Leone: An Economic and Social History, 1792–1945" (Ph.D. dissertation, Boston University, 1978), pp. 56–68, 78–92. Also see her *Sierra Leone's Settler Women Traders: Women on the Afro-European Frontier* (Ann Arbor, 1987).

17. Ann Wilberforce May is mentioned in MMA:SL, letters of 18 Dec. 1846, 16 May 1854, 19 July 1866; in J. Claudius May, *Life . . . of Joseph May*, pp. 18–19; in the "Family Record of Births & C. of the Rev. Joseph May and Mrs. A. May"; and in the "Genealogical Chart of the May, Stuart, Faulkner families."

18. MMA:SL/J. May, 1838.

19. "Iwarreh" is May's spelling of the town's name. Also see Samuel Johnson, *The History of the Yorubas, from the Earliest Times to the Beginning of the British Protectorate* (London, 1921), p. 234; and J. Claudius May, *Life . . . of Joseph May*, p. 7.

20. Ifacayeh = Ifákayé. The name means "Ifá covers the world." I am grateful to Professor Karin Barber for translations and help with Yoruba orthography. For a general discussion of Yoruba names, see Modupe Oduyoye, *Yoruba Names: Their Structure and Meaning* (London, 1982); Johnson, *The History of the Yorubas*, pp. 79–89; and J. Claudius May, *Life . . . of Joseph May*, p. 7.

21. J. Claudius May, *Life . . . of Joseph May*, p. 7.

22. MMA:SL/J. May, 1838; J. Claudius May, *Life . . . of Joseph May*, pp. 7–8; Hugh Clapperton, *Journal of a Second Expedition into the Interior of Africa, from the Bight of Benin to Soccatoo. To which is added, the Journal of Richard Lander from Kano to the Sea-coast, partly by a more eastern route* (London, 1829), pp. 28, 61–5.

23. Robin Law, *The Oyo Empire, c. 1600–c. 1836: A West African Imperialism in the Era of the Atlantic Slave Trade* (Oxford, 1977), p. 90. Law estimates Oyo's size to have been approximately 19,000 square miles.

24. Oyo-Ile was known to the Nupe, Hausa, and first European visitors as Katunga. See Clapperton, *Journal of a Second Expedition into the Interior*

of Africa, pp. 33, 56–8; Peter Morton-Williams, "The Oyo Yoruba and the Atlantic Trade, 1670–1830," *Journal of the Historical Society of Nigeria* 3 (1) (Dec. 1964): 25–45; J. F. A. Ajayi, "The Aftermath of the Fall of Old Oyo," in J. F. A. Ajayi and Michael Crowder, eds., *History of West Africa*, vol. 2, p. 136; and Law, *The Oyo Empire*, pp. 228–33.

25. Law, *The Oyo Empire*, p. 7; Ajayi, "The Aftermath of the Fall of Old Oyo," p. 130.

26. See J. F. Ade Ajayi and Robert Smith, *Yoruba Warfare in the Nineteenth Century* (London, 1964), pp. 9–33; and Ajayi, "The Aftermath of the Fall of Old Oyo," p. 141.

27. For the background of the Hausa-Fulbe Islamic revolutionary movement and its impact on neighboring regions, see: S. J. Hogben and A. H. M. Kirk-Greene, *The Emirates of Northern Nigeria* (London, 1966); H. A. S. Johnston, *The Fulani Empire of Sokoto* (London, 1967); and Mervyn Hiskett, *The Sword of Truth: The Life and Times of the Shehu Usuman Dan Fodio* (New York, 1973).

28. *"Laiye Abiodun l'afi igba won 'wo/ Laiye Awole l'adi adikale."* See Robert S. Smith, *Kingdoms of the Yoruba*, (London, 1969), p. 140.

29. J. Claudius May, *Life ... of Joseph May*, p. 7. Ikotto is probably modern Koto, near Ijaye in the Epo district. See Johnson, *The History of the Yorubas*, p. 234.

30. For an excellent description of Yoruba towns and villages in Old Oyo, see Johnson, *The History of the Yorubas*, pp. 90–4; and Ajayi and Smith, *Yoruba Warfare*, pp. 23–8. For a discussion of Yoruba urbanism in recent times and the layout and morphology of Yoruba towns, see A. Ojo, *Yoruba Culture*, (London and Ife, 1966), pp. 104–57.

31. Johnson, *The History of the Yorubas*, p. 234.

32. Ibid., pp. 234, 386.

33. Ibid; Law, *The Oyo Empire*, p. 194, n. 92, 260, n. 80, 280, 286, 290; Philip D. Curtin, ed., *Africa Remembered: Narratives by West Africans from the Era of the Slave Trade* (Madison, 1968), pp. 299–300, n. 20, for a discussion of slave-revenue use to purchase horses for cavalry.

34. The account in MMA:SL/J. May, 1838, differs from the one in J. Claudius May, *Life ... of Joseph May*. The latter indicates that only one sister was captured.

35. J. Claudius May, *Life ... of Joseph May*, p. 8.

36. "These people that raised up this war they are not another nation," wrote Joseph Wright in an account of his enslavement. "We are all one nation speaking one language." "The Life of Joseph Wright – A Native of Akoo," in MSS:SL, 1835–40. Also see Curtin, ed., *Africa Remembered*, pp. 317–33.

37. "Letter of Mr. Samuel Crowther to the Rev. William Jowett, in 1837, then Secretary of the Church Missionary Society, Detailing the Circumstances Connected with His Being Sold as a Slave," in Curtin, ed., *Africa Remembered*, p. 301.

38. MMA:SL/J. May, 1838; J. Claudius May, *Life ... of Joseph May*, pp. 8, 20. The story of Ifacayeh's sister would provide an interesting comparison

with his own. Unfortunately, little information exists about her. Redeemed by her father at the time of Ifacayeh's captivity, it is not clear when she was again enslaved, where and how she was emancipated, and how she eventually made her way to the Gambia. We do know from J. Claudius May's account (p. 20) that she married "a Mr. Joseph Wright" in Bathurst, and that the couple "had three or four children." For the best study analyzing differences in the enslavement and experiences of women during the era of the slave trade, see Claire Robertson and Martin Klein, eds., *Women and Slavery in Africa* (Madison, 1983).

39. MMA:SL/J. May, 1838; J. Claudius May, *Life . . . of Joseph May*, p. 8.

40. On the nature of Yoruba domestic slavery, see E. A. Oroge, "The Institution of Slavery in Yorubaland with Particular Reference to the Nineteenth Century" (Ph.D. dissertation, University of Birmingham [England], 1971); and Law, *The Oyo Empire*, p. 206; For the best history of slavery within Africa and an analysis of the relationship between domestic slavery and the transatlantic slave trade, see Paul Lovejoy, *Transformations in Slavery: A History of Slavery in Africa* (Cambridge, Eng., 1983).

41. J. Claudius May, *Life . . . of Joseph May*, p. 8.

42. MMA:SL/J. May, 1838.

43. J. Claudius May, *Life . . . of Joseph May*, p. 7; Johnson, *The History of the Yorubas*, p. 81.

44. J. Claudius May, *Life . . . of Joseph May*, p. 9.

45. Badagry was paying tribute to Oyo in the 1820s, which suggests that Ifacayeh's march southward took place along the main Oyo trade route to that coastal entrepôt. That trade route normally went through Egbado territory. See Law, *The Oyo Empire*, p. 180; Morton-Williams, "The Oyo Yoruba and the Atlantic Trade, 1670–1830," p. 40; and Crowther, in Curtin, ed., *Africa Remembered*, p. 297. A barracoon was a fenced or fortified area in which slaves, awaiting resale or shipment, were confined.

46. Adalay is described in J. Claudius May, *Life . . . of Joseph May*, as the "king's chief warrior . . . a relative of Akitoye or Kosoko." But it is likely that Adelay was Adele, the exiled chief of Lagos who ruled Badagry from c. 1821. See R. Lander and J. Lander, *Journal of an Expedition to Explore the Course and Termination of the Niger*, vol. 1 (London, 1832), pp. 47–8; Law, *The Oyo Empire*, p. 180, n. 196.

47. MMA:SL/J. May, 1838; J. Claudius May, *Life . . . of Joseph May*, p. 9. See the accounts of Joseph Wright and Samuel Crowther in Curtin, ed., *Africa Remembered*, pp. 313, 331, for the expression of similar fears.

48. J. Claudius May, *Life . . . of Joseph May*, p. 9.

49. Samuel Ajayi Crowther, *Journal of an Expedition up the Niger and Tshadda Rivers* (London, 1855), Appendix III, pp. 380–1.

50. "Family Record of Births & C. of the Rev. Joseph May and Mrs. A. May" gives December 31, 1826, as the date of embarkation. *Liberated African Register*, in the Sierra Leone Archives at Fourah Bay College, Freetown, Sierra Leone [hereafter cited as SL/LAR], Document #238.

51. J. Claudius May, *Life . . . of Joseph May*, p. 9.

52. MMA:SL/J. May, 1838.

53. See SL/LAR: 97, 113, 196. For the function and duties of the "Anti-Slavery Squadron" in enforcing the British decision to abolish the slave trade, see Christopher Lloyd, *The Navy and the Slave Trade: The Suppression of the African Slave Trade in the Nineteenth Century* (London, 1949).

54. In 1848, when the *Dois Amigos* was again captured, 384 persons were released. SL/LAR: 495.

55. J. Claudius May, *Life... of Joseph May*, p. 10.

56. The best contemporary description of the process of liberation and life in the King's Yard is in [Elizabeth Melville], *A Residence at Sierra Leone, described from a journal kept on the spot, and from letters written to friends at home by Elizabeth Helen Melville; edited by Mrs. Norton* (London, 1849), pp. 208–15. Also see William Hamilton, "Sierra Leone and the Liberated Africans," *The Colonial Magazine and Commercial Maritime Journal* 6 (Sept. 1841): 327–34, 463–9; and John Peterson, *Province of Freedom: A History of Sierra Leone, 1787–1870* (London, 1969), pp. 181–6.

57. Johnson U. J. Asiegbu, *Slavery and the Politics of Liberation, 1787–1861* (London, 1969), p. 25.

58. [Melville], *A Residence at Sierra Leone*, p. 201.

59. The original quote can be found in the Church Missionary Society archives, London, CMS:CA1/079/2, Samuel Crowther to Rev. William Jowett, Fourah Bay, 22 Feb. 1837, pp. 9–10. Also see Crowther, *Journal*, p. 382, for greater detail.

60. See A. Fajana, "Some Aspects of Yoruba Traditional Education," *Odu, Journal of Yoruba and Related Studies* 3 (1) (1966): 16–28; Ojo, *Yoruba Culture*, Chapter 8, pp. 193–235, for a discussion of the content of Yoruba philosophy; Catherine M. U. MacLean, "Yoruba Mothers: A Study of Changing Methods of Child-Rearing in Rural and Urban Nigeria," *Journal of Tropical Medicine and Hygiene* 69 (11) (Nov. 1966): 253–63; and Karin Barber, "How Man Makes God in West Africa: Yoruba Attitudes Towards the *Orisa*," *Africa* 51 (3) (1981): 724–45.

61. See Wande Abimbola, "The Literature of the Ifa Cult," in S. O. Biobaku, ed., *Sources of Yoruba History* (Oxford, 1973), pp. 41–6; Wande Abimbola, *Ifa Divination Poetry* (New York, 1977), pp. 1–15; William Bascom, *The Yoruba of Southwestern Nigeria* (New York, 1969), pp. 70–1; Daryll Forde, *The Yoruba-Speaking Peoples of South-Western Nigeria* (London, 1951), pp. 29–30; E. McClelland, *The Cult of Ifá among the Yoruba: Folk Practice and Art* (London, 1982); and Johnson, *The History of the Yorubas*, pp. 32–4.

62. The literature about Yoruba religion is extensive. An introduction to the subject is in: Johnson, *The History of the Yorubas*, pp. 26–39; J.O. Awolabu, *Yoruba Beliefs and Sacrificial Rites* (London, 1979); William Bascom, *The Yoruba of Southwestern Nigeria*; E. B. Idowu, *Olódùmarè: God in Yoruba Belief* (London, 1962); and E. McClelland, *The Cult of Ifá among the Yoruba: Folk Practice and Art*. Also see Karin Barber, "How Man Makes God in West Africa: Yoruba Attitudes Toward the *Orisa*," *Africa* 51 (3) (1981): 724–44.

63. Johnson, *The History of the Yorubas*, pp. 26–39, 125–6; Bascom, *Yoruba of Southwestern Nigeria*, pp. 20, 65.

64. A copy of the *"Instructions to the Sierra Leone Company Directors"* is in the Sierra Leone Collection, Fourah Bay College Library, Freetown.

65. See Philip D. Curtin, *The Image of Africa: British Ideas and Actions, 1780–1850* (Madison, 1964), pp. 238–40, 414–15; Leo Spitzer, *The Creoles of Sierra Leone: Responses to Colonialism, 1870–1945* (Madison, 1974), p. 45; Edward H. Berman, ed., *African Reactions to Missionary Education* (New York, 1975), pp. 5–6; and [Melville], *A Residence at Sierra Leone*, pp. 252–3. "We perceive," Mrs. Melville wrote in 1846, "that it is not so much *intellect* the negro wants, as a wider field of example and encouragement from others, to teach him to exercise the sense his Creator has given him."

66. The letter is in the *Liberated African Department Letterbook, 1831–1834*, Sierra Leone Government Archives, Freetown.

67. J. Claudius May, *Life ... of Joseph May*, p. 10.

68. He and his companions from the *Dois Amigos* were officially emancipated on April 9, 1827, two months after their arrival in the Sierra Leone colony. See SL/LAR: 238.

69. Peterson, *Province of Freedom*, p. 93.

70. MacCarthy's plan is published in Christopher Fyfe, ed., *Sierra Leone Inheritance* (London, 1964), pp. 131–4. Also see Raymond T. Smith, "Religion in the Formation of West Indian Society: Guyana and Jamaica," in Martin L. Kilson and Robert I. Rotberg, eds., *The African Diaspora: Interpretive Essays* (Cambridge, Mass., 1976) pp. 312–41, for a similar assessment of the role of religious instruction in the British West Indies.

71. Manon Spitzer, "The Settlement of Liberated Africans in the Mountain Villages of the Sierra Leone Colony, 1808–1841" (M.A. thesis, University of Wisconsin, 1969), p. 60; Peterson, *Province of Freedom*, pp. 103–4.

72. Manon Spitzer, "The Settlement of Liberated Africans," pp. 45, 46; M. L. Charlesworth, *Africa's Mountain Valley, or the Church in Regent's Town, West Africa* (London, 1856), p. 37.

73. Charlesworth, *Africa's Mountain Valley*, pp. 40–1; Peterson, *Province of Freedom*, p. 111; Manon Spitzer, "The Settlement of Liberated Africans," pp. 50–1.

74. Peterson, *Province of Freedom*, p. 112; Charlesworth, *Africa's Mountain Valley*, p. 43.

75. See P. D. Curtin, " 'The White Man's Grave': Image and Reality, 1780–1850," *The Journal of British Studies* 1 (1961): 94–5; Peterson, *Province of Freedom*, pp. 139–48; *Church Missionary Society Atlas* (London, 1873), p. 14; and Manon Spitzer, "The Settlement of Liberated Africans," pp. 59–60.

76. See Peterson, *Province of Freedom*, p. 161. Regent had a population of 1300 in 1827 and 30 Liberated Africans worth over $400 (p. 274).

77. Peterson, *Province of Freedom*, p. 64.

78. Although Johnson's description speaks only of boys, girls were also

taught in the schools by means of this method. See Charlesworth, *Africa's Mountain Valley*, pp. 43–4. Also see D. L. Sumner, *Education in Sierra Leone* (Freetown, 1963), p. 21; Peterson, *Province of Freedom*, p. 64; Curtin, *Image of Africa*, p. 262; and Manon Spitzer, "The Settlement of Liberated Africans," p. 44. For a general discussion of the educational philosophy developed by Andrew Bell and Joseph Lancaster in the pupil-monitored schools in England, see Mary Jo Maynes, *Schooling in Western Europe: A Social History* (Albany, 1985), pp. 55, 76–7. Also see C. Kaestle, ed., *Joseph Lancaster and the Monitorial School Movement: A Documentary History* (New York, 1973).

79. Berman, ed., *African Reactions to Missionary Education*, pp. 7–9; Peterson, *Province of Freedom*, pp. 117, 153.

80. See *Liberated African Department Letterbook, 1820–1826*: J. Reffel, chief superintendent, to village superintendents, August 15, 1822; Manon Spitzer, "The Settlement of Liberated Africans," p. 39; and Peterson, *Province of Freedom*, pp. 153–5.

81. Quoted in Manon Spitzer, "The Settlement of Liberated Africans," p. 22. Describing her tuition of one such "protected" child, Mrs. Melville writes: "... I daily give her a lesson in more intelligible language by pointing out each article of furniture, etc., and naming it distinctly, until she slowly pronounces 'chair, table, window, or door,' after me.... She looks about nine years old, and although – as far as reading goes – she knows nothing more than her alphabet, can yet repeat the Prayer-book catechism by rote, and one or two hymns – utterly ignorant all the while of the import of a single word!" *A Residence at Sierra Leone*, p. 74.

82. Peterson, *Province of Freedom*, pp. 101–2.

83. J. Claudius May, *Life ... of Joseph May*, p. 11.

84. Ibid., p. 11.

85. Ibid., p. 12.

86. Ibid., p. 12.

87. For another example, read Mrs. Melville's account of her relationship with her "protected" Liberated African children. *A Residence at Sierra Leone*, pp. 58–9, 73–4, 251–5.

88. For an account of the early history of Fourah Bay College, see Sumner, *Education in Sierra Leone*, pp. 38, 56–67; and Christopher Fyfe, *A History of Sierra Leone* (Oxford, 1962), pp. 236–7, 405 passim.

89. J. Claudius May, *Life ... of Joseph May*, p. 12.

90. Approximately ten years older than Joseph May, Crowther eventually became one of the best known Africans among Christian Britons and North Americans. He acted as a key agent of the "civilizing" process and rose to the position of Anglican bishop, the first African to hold this title. For biographical information on Crowther, see Jesse Page, *The Black Bishop* (London, 1910); J. F. Ade Ajayi, *Christian Missions in Nigeria: The Making of a New Elite, 1841–1891* (London, 1965); and J. F. Ade Ajayi, "Samuel Ajayi Crowther of Oyo," in Curtin, ed., *Africa Remembered*, pp. 289–98.

91. J. Claudius May, *Life ... of Joseph May*, pp. 12–14; MMA:SL/J. May, 1838.

92. J. Claudius May, *Life ... of Joseph May*, p. 13; MMA:SL/J. May, 1838.

93. See Arthur Porter, "Religious Affiliation in Freetown, Sierra Leone," *Africa* 23 (1) (Jan. 1953): 3–14; and Peterson, *Province of Freedom*, p. 231.

94. MMA:SL, letter from Joseph May, 25 March 1861. It is possible that Ifacayeh's negative judgment about Islam may have derived from his association of this religion with the events in Yoruba that led to his initial captivity.

95. Baxter's slur, of course, was without foundation because, by this time, both the Anglicans and dissenting Christian groups included black preachers.

96. MMA:SL/J. May, 1838.

97. J. Claudius May, *Life ... of Joseph May*, pp. 13–14; MMA:SL/J. May, 1838; James W. St. G. Walker, *The Black Loyalists: The Search for a Promised Land in Nova Scotia and Sierra Leone, 1783–1870*, (New York, 1976), pp. 345–6, which has an excellent description of a Methodist service in early colonial Sierra Leone.

98. MMA:SL/J. May, 1838.

99. J. Claudius May, *Life ... of Joseph May*, p. 15.

100. Ibid.; MMA:SL/J. May, 1838.

101. J. Claudius May, *Life ... of Joseph May*, p. 15; MMA:SL/J. May, 1838.

102. MMA:SL/J. May, 1838. Although this description, written to the Methodist Missionary Society's headquarters in London, follows a formulaic style intended to appeal to public supporters of missionary activity, it seems clear that its heartfelt intensity was not posed.

103. J. Claudius May, *Life ... of Joseph May*, p. 15.

104. The "Family Record of Births & C. of the Rev. Joseph May and Mrs. A. May" notes his date of baptism as April 3, 1836, almost nine years after his official "emancipation" in Sierra Leone. The Reverend John May died on October 4, 1828. See Charles Marke, *Origin of Wesleyan Methodism in Sierra Leone and History of Its Missions* (London, 1912), p. 31.

105. Peterson, *Province of Freedom*, p. 128, discusses this demand on the part of CMS missionaries. The phrase "pricked in the heart" is quoted in his book.

106. J. Claudius May, *Life ... of Joseph May*, pp. 15–16; MMA:SL/J. May, 1838.

107. Isaiah: 61; J. Claudius May, *Life ... of Joseph May*, pp. 15–16; MMA:SL/J. May, 1838.

108. MMA:SL/J. May, 1838.

109. J. Claudius May, *Life ... of Joseph May*, pp. 16–17.

110. Ibid., p. 17.

111. MMA:SL, letter from Joseph May, 18 Dec. 1846.

112. Ibid.; other 1840s letters, passim.

113. He died on March 8, 1891.

114. See Spitzer, *Creoles*, pp. 45–69.

115. For May's later difficulties with the missionary establishment, both with its white and black ministers, see MMA:SL, Joseph May letters of 24 Nov. 1873, 27 Mar. 1874, 20 July 1875, 23 July 1875, 11 Aug. 1875, 14

Aug. 1875, 10 Apr. 1876, 30 Jan. 1877, 2 May 1877, 15 May 1877, 14 Oct. 1877, 16 Jan. 1878, 2 Sept. 1878, 19 Apr. 1882, and 29 Apr. 1882.

116. MMA:SL, letter from Joseph May to Rev. John Kilner, 29 Apr. 1882.

117. Peter Gay, *The Bourgeois Experience: Victoria to Freud, Vol. 1: Education of the Senses* (New York, 1984), p. 12.

Chapter 3. Into the Bourgeoisie

1. Prostejov (Prossnitz) is now in Czechoslovakia. In 1713 a total of 319 Jewish families, or 1,393 individuals, were permitted to reside in Prossnitz; in 1793 the number increased slightly to 328 families, or 1,459 persons. In Moravia, only Nikolsburg contained a larger Jewish community than Prossnitz. Hugo Gold, ed., *Gedenkbuch der Untergangenen Judengemeinden Mährens* (Tel Aviv, 1974), p. 104; C. A. Macartney, *The Habsburg Empire, 1790–1918* (London, 1969), p. 77.

2. Gold, ed., *Gedenkbuch . . . Mährens*, pp. 95, 103; Berthold Oppenheim, "Geschichte der Juden in Olmütz," in Hugo Gold, ed., *Die Juden und Judengemeinden Mährens in Vergangenheit und Gegenwart* (Brünn, Austria, 1929), pp. 451–2; H. H. Ben-Sasson, ed., *A History of the Jewish People* (Cambridge, Mass., 1976), pp. 565, 579–80.

3. Gold, ed., *Gedenkbuch . . . Mährens*, p. 104.

4. The Christian population, living in 347 house units, numbered 1,975. See A. Tänzer, *Die Geschichte der Juden in Hohenems und im übrigen Vorarlberg* (Meran, present Italy, 1905), p. 109. For the history of the earliest Jewish settlement in Hohenems, see Tänzer, Chapters 2 and 3.

5. *Die Nachkommen von Moses (Josef) Zweig und Elka (Katti) Chaja Sarah Spitzer: Eine Nachfahrenliste bearbeitet von Julius Röder, Archivar* (Olmütz, present Czechoslovakia, 1932) [hereafter cited as *Nachfahrenliste*], pp. 4, 10.

6. For a comparison, see Toni Oelsner, "Three Jewish Families in Modern Germany," *Jewish Social Studies* 4 (3) (July 1942): 57.

7. For a general discussion of the powers and duties of Jewish community leaders, see Jacob Katz, *Out of the Ghetto: The Social Background of Jewish Emancipation, 1770–1870* (New York, 1978), pp. 19–21.

8. He purchased the 4th division of house #39: two rooms, a kitchen, two chambers [*Kammern*], a small garden, and wood plot. In his deed, he also received permission to erect a *sukkah* (a temporary abode roofed with branches) on the top floor of the house during the Jewish festival of Sukkoth. See *Nachfahrenliste*, pp. 4, 10.

9. The genealogical sources, characteristically neglectful of details about women, do not reveal the name of Josef Petrowitz's spouse, who was Moses Josef Zweig's mother.

10. Because the family enjoyed the hereditary Jewish ritual status of Levites, the name Löwinau most probably derives from this fact.

11. *Nachfahrenliste*, pp. 4, 10, 12. Elka Katti's father was Gabriel Spitzer, from whom Josef Petrowitz purchased a division of house #38 on the *Ju-*

dengasse. No record exists of his occupation, or of Elka Katti's mother's name.

12. Herz Lämle Brettauer was born in Bretten, a town in the German state of Baden. The name Brettauer undoubtedly derives from this fact. For biographical information on Maier Jonathan Uffenheimer and Jonathan Uffenheimer, his father, see Tänzer, *Juden in Hohenems*, pp. 314–15, 417, 779.

13. Although a precise comparison of their wealth is hardly possible, a relative judgment emerges from the fact that Herz Lämle Brettauer's residence in Hohenems (#37 *Judengasse*) was assessed for purposes of taxation in 1806–7 at fl. 3000, and Moses Josef Zweig's house division in the Prossnitz *Judenstadt* was worth less than half that amount at about the same time. See Tänzer, *Juden in Hohenems*, p. 167; *Nachfahrenliste*, pp. 10–11.

14. In Hohenems, the Jews' *Schützbriefe* was revoked for a time in 1676. For the background, see Tänzer, *Juden in Hohenems*, Chapter 2.

15. See Katz, *Out of the Ghetto*, pp. 10, 194.

16. This restriction did not necessarily reflect a particular antagonism against Jews. It was typical of the corporative economic order that permitted no member of one occupational class to transfer to another, or to impinge on another's special activity. For a discussion of this point, see Oelsner, "Three Jewish Families," p. 244.

17. The *Schützbriefe* issued in 1768–69 by Empress Maria Theresa, not long after Hohenems came under Hapsburg rule, is reproduced in Tänzer, *Juden in Hohenems*, pp. 111–26. It provides an excellent example of Jewish rights and restrictions in the years shortly before the promulgation of the Edict of Tolerance.

18. *Nachfahrenliste*; Tänzer, *Juden in Hohenems*, passim.

19. The edict was issued in Lower Austria, including Vienna, Bohemia, Moravia, Silesia, and Hungary, between October 1781 and March 1782. It was not formally promulgated in Vorarlberg until 1784. See Katz, *Out of the Ghetto*, p. 162; Macartney, *Habsburg*, p. 121; and Tänzer, *Juden in Hohenems*, pp. 135–6.

20. Katz, *Out of the Ghetto*, pp. 162–6; Macartney, *Habsburg*, p. 121; William M. Johnston, *The Austrian Mind: An Intellectual and Social History, 1848–1938* (Berkeley, 1972), pp. 16–17; Ben-Sasson, *History*, pp. 755–6.

21. "The records of tradition, viz. Bible and Talmud, were always taught in the national tongue of yore, i.e. Hebrew, or the cognate Aramaic, which had been adopted early in ancient times. Elements of this language including the concepts, mental pictures, and mode of thinking induced by it, penetrated, particularly through the medium of study at all ages, into the respective vernacular of the Jews, in consequence of which the Jewish community developed a particular brand of dialect which was apt to accentuate their segregation linguistically." *Judendeutsch* was one such dialect. Jacob Katz, *Emancipation and Assimilation: Studies in Modern Jewish History* (London, 1972), p. 1.

22. Tänzer, *Juden in Hohenems*, pp. 649, 654, 656; Lothar Rothschild, *Der jüdische Friedhof in Hohenems*, pamphlet, n.p., n.d. (Wiener Library

Archives, London); Katz, *Out of the Ghetto*, pp. 205–6; Leopold Goldschmied, "Geschichte der Juden in Prossnitz," in Gold, ed., *Juden . . . Mährens*, pp. 492, 496.

23. Tänzer, *Juden in Hohenems*, pp. 507, 667; Paula Hyman, "The Other Half: Women in the Jewish Tradition," *Response: A Contemporary Jewish Review*, no. 18 (Summer 1973): 67–75; Charlotte Baum, Paula Hyman, and Sonya Michel, *The Jewish Woman in America* (New York, 1975), pp. 4–15. For accounts of life in Germanic Jewish communities, see Hugo Mandelbaum, *Jewish Life in the Village Communities of Southern Germany* (New York, 1985); and Herman Pollack, *Jewish Folkways in Germanic Lands (1648–1806): Studies in Aspects of Daily Life* (Cambridge, Mass., 1971).

24. Specifically, the prayer asked "für das Wohl des Kaisers und das Gelingen seiner Unternehmungen." See Goldschmied, "Juden in Prossnitz," pp. 492–3.

25. In the Treaty of Pressburg (1805), following the defeat of the combined Austrian and Russian armies by Napoleon, Vorarlberg was ceded to Bavaria. The province remained under Bavarian control until 1813 and was reattached to Austria under the provisions of the Act of the Congress of Vienna in 1815. For a fuller account of Jewish contributions to the Austrian war effort during this period, see Tänzer, *Juden in Hohenems*, pp. 138–59; and Goldschmied, "Juden in Prossnitz," p. 493.

26. Goldschmied, "Juden in Prossnitz," p. 492.

27. Tänzer, *Juden in Hohenems*, pp. 419, 467, 479.

28. Only Raphael Brettauer's first wife, Jeanette Landauer, seems not to have been the child of parents involved in a commercial enterprise. See Tänzer, *Juden in Hohenems*, pp. 327, 429, 430, 468–70, 472–3, 688.

29. Tänzer, *Juden in Hohenems*, pp. 472–3.

30. A. Klima, "Industrial Development in Bohemia, 1648–1781," *Past and Present*, no. 11 (Apr. 1957): 91; Monika Richarz, "Jewish Social Mobility in Germany during the Time of Emancipation (1790–1871)," in *Leo Baeck Institute, Year Book XX*, 1975, pp. 73–4; Ruth Kestenberg-Gladstein, *Neuere Geschichte der Juden in den bömischen Ländern*, vol. 1, (Tübingen, 1969), pp. 96–108.

31. Tänzer, *Juden in Hohenems*, pp. 479, 657; Stefan Zweig, *The World of Yesterday* (Lincoln, 1964), pp. 9–10; Donald Prater, *European of Yesterday: A Biography of Stefan Zweig* (Oxford, 1972), p. 2; Nachum Gross, ed., *Economic History of the Jews* (New York, 1975), pp. 163, 168.

32. Tänzer, *Juden in Hohenems*, pp. 460–1, 480.

33. See Katz, *Out of the Ghetto*, Chapter 11.

34. Tänzer, *Juden in Hohenems*, pp. 460–1. Tavern- and inn-keeping, of course, was a staple of the Jewish economy in the Russian Empire.

35. Tänzer, *Juden in Hohenems*, p. 463. An organization with a similar purpose, the "Verein zur Unterstützung judischer Knaben," was founded at Prossnitz in 1840. See Goldschmied, "Juden in Prossnitz," p. 501.

36. See *Nachfahrenliste*, "Haupttafel," and pp. 13, 20, 24, 28, 32.

37. *Nachfahrenliste*, passim; Kestenberg-Gladstein, *Neuere Geschichte*, p. 106; B. Heilig, "Aufstieg und Verfall des Hauses Ehrenstamm," in *Bul-*

letin für Mitglieder der Gesellschaft der Freunde des Leo Baeck Instituts, no. 10, 1960, pp. 101–22.

38. *Nachfahrenliste*, passim. No information exists about the occupation of the remaining three males.

39. *Nachfahrenliste*, passim.

40. Macartney, *Habsburg*, pp. 39–42; Klima, "Industrial Development," pp. 93–94; Jaroslav Purs, "The Industrial Revolution in the Czech Lands," in *Historica*, vol. 2, Czechoslovakian Academy (Prague, 1960), pp. 183–272.

41. By 1842, about 135 Prossnitz Jews were involved in some aspect of textile production or sale. See Gold, ed., *Gedenkbuch...Mährens*, p. 105.

42. Ruth Kestenberg-Gladstein, "The Jews between Czechs and Germans in the Historic Lands, 1848–1918," in *The Jews of Czechoslovakia*, vol. 1 (New York, 1968), p. 22. In Moravia and Bohemia, a minority of Jews also spoke and wrote in Czech.

43. The concept of the "sojourner," a refinement of Georg Simmel's "stranger," is discussed in Paul C. P. Siu, "The Sojourner," *American Journal of Sociology* 58 (1) (1952): 34–44. Also see Georg Simmel, "The Stranger," in his *On Individuality and Social Forms* (Chicago, 1971).

44. Gold, ed., *Gedenkbuch...Mährens*, p. 105; Goldschmied, "Juden in Prossnitz," p. 501.

45. Tänzer, *Juden in Hohenems*, pp. 341–2, 344, 358, 378, 393–4, 654, 657.

46. Ben-Sasson, ed., *History*, p. 811; Reinhard Rürup, "Jewish Emancipation and Bourgeois Society," in *Leo Baeck Institute, Year Book XIV*, 1969, p. 84; Katz, *Out of the Ghetto*, p. 198; Max Grunwald, *History of the Jews in Vienna* (Philadelphia, 1936), pp. 406–7.

47. For a parallel discussion of generational name-changing among German Jews, see Steven M. Lowenstein, "The Pace of Modernisation of German Jewry in the Nineteenth Century," in *Leo Baeck Institute, Year Book XXI*, 1976, p. 46.

48. 1845 was the birth year of Moritz Zweig, Stefan Zweig's father.

49. *Nachfahrenliste*, passim; Tänzer, *Juden in Hohenems*, pp. 244, 356, 378, 479–81, 542, 699; "Joseph Brettauer," in *Oesterreichisches Biographisches Lexicon, 1815–1950*, vol. 1 (Graz, 1957), p. 113.

50. For a discussion of this trend, see Katz, *Out of the Ghetto*, pp. 176–90.

51. E. J. Hobsbawm, *The Age of Capital: 1848–1875* (New York, 1975), p. 29.

52. See Kestenberg-Gladstein, "The Jews between Czechs and Germans," pp. 27–31.

53. *Nachfahrenliste*, passim.

54. Tänzer, *Juden in Hohenems*, pp. 479–81, 697–700.

55. In the next generation, both Stefan Zweig's marriage to Friderike Maria von Winternitz and his brother Alfred's marriage to Stefanie Duschak are examples of intermarriage.

56. Albert Memmi, *The Liberation of the Jew* (New York, 1973), pp. 71–2.

57. Zweig, *World*, p.6; Jüdische Kultusgemeinde Archives (Vienna): records for 1878, 1879, 1881; Israelitische Allianz zu Wien: *XLI Jahresbericht, erstättet an die XLI ordentliche Generalversammlung am 20 April 1914* (Vienna, 1914).

58. Zweig, *World*, pp. 10–11; Prater, *European*, pp. 2–4.

59. Zweig, *World*, pp. 5–6, 11–12.

60. Ibid., pp. 8, 9–10.

61. Arthur Schnitzler, *Jugend in Wien: Eine Autobiographie* (Frankfurt, 1981), pp. 151–5.

62. Jacob Katz, *From Prejudice to Destruction: Anti-Semitism, 1700–1933* (Cambridge, Mass., 1980), pp. 281–4.

63. Ibid., pp. 5–6, 281–4.

64. Ibid., pp. 5–6, 223–9.

65. Ibid., pp. 265–6.

66. The parallels in timing of emergence and in content between this racist anti-Semitism and the "scientifically" backed European racism directed against "people of color" in Africa and the Americas were significant. See Hannah Arendt, *The Origins of Totalitarianism* (New York, 1973), parts I and II; Curtin, *Image of Africa*, especially Chapter 15; Spitzer, *Creoles of Sierra Leone*, pp. 45–69; and V. G. Kiernan, *The Lords of Human Kind: Black Man, Yellow Man, and White Man in an Age of Empire* (New York, 1986), passim.

Chapter 4. Into the White World

1. Rita Brasilia dos Santos was born in Salvador, Brazil. *Registro do Casamentos*, Arquivo da Curia, Salvador, Bahia, 1740–60, 1760–80 books, passim; *Registro de Batizados, Frequesia de Maragogipe, 1788–1803*, Arquivo da Curia, Salvador, Bahia. Also see "Apontamentos Biographicos de Conselheiro Antônio Pereira Rebouças" and "Nota Biographica do Conselheiro Antônio Pereira Rebouças," *Coleção A. P. Rebouças*, Biblioteca Nacional (Rio de Janeiro): I–3, 24, 60, I–3, 24, 63; and I–3, 24, 61.

2. Carl Degler, *Neither Black nor White: Slavery and Race Relations in Brazil and the United States* (New York, 1971), pp. 107–9, 219–32.

3. Ibid., passim; A. J. R. Russell-Wood, "Colonial Brazil," in David Cohen and Jack P. Greene, eds., *Neither Slave nor Free: The Freedmen of African Descent in the Slave Societies of the New World* (Baltimore, 1972), pp. 98–108.

4. Thomas E. Skidmore, *Black into White: Race and Nationality in Brazilian Thought* (New York, 1974), pp. 64–78.

5. *Registro do Casamentos*, Arquivo da Curia, Salvador, Bahia, 18th-century books, passim. Both marriage and baptismal records included racial identification of nonwhites. Also see Russell-Wood in Cohen and Greene, eds., *Neither Slave nor Free*, p. 84: "... the term *mulato* generally possessed a pejorative connotation and was replaced in contemporary documents by the more common *pardo*."

6. Although no national census was taken for Brazil until 1872, the imbalance between the number of white males and white women during the colonial era is often mentioned in contemporary as well as modern literature. According to A. J. R. Russell-Wood: "From the outset the Crown was acutely conscious of social and demographic problems caused by a shortage of white women of marriageable age in Brazil. Furthermore, the Crown was sensitive to the moral evils and adverse repercussions on colonial society resulting from the solution chosen by the colonists, namely, concubinage with Amerindian or black women and an apparent preference for them even if white were available." See his "Female and Family in the Economy and Society of Colonial Brazil," in Asunción Lavrin, ed., *Latin American Women: Historical Perspectives* (Westport, Conn., 1978), p. 62. Also see Dauril Alden, "The Population of Brazil in the Late Eighteenth Century: A Preliminary Study," *Hispanic American Historical Review* 43 (1963): 173–205; Herbert S. Klein, "The Colored Freedmen in Brazilian Slave Society," *Journal of Social History*, 3 (1) (1969): 30–52; and Joaquim Norberto de Souza e Silva, *Investigações sôbre os recenseamentos da população geral do império* (Documentos Censitários, Serie B, No. 1, Serviço Nacional de Recenseamento, Rio de Janeiro, 1951; this is a reprint of a work originally published in 1871).

7. See A. J. R. Russell-Wood, "Class, Creed, and Colour in Colonial Bahia: A Study in Prejudice," *Race* 9 (2) (1967): 133–57, and his "Colonial Brazil," in Cohen and Greene, eds., *Neither Slave nor Free*, pp. 84–133. Also see C. R. Boxer, *Race Relations in the Portuguese Colonial Empire, 1414–1825* (Oxford, 1963), his *The Portuguese Seaborne Empire* (Oxford, 1963), and his "The Colour Question in the Portuguese Empire, 1415–1825," *Proceedings of the British Academy*, vol. 47 (London, 1961); Roger Bastide and Florestan Fernandes, *Brancos e Negros em São Paulo*, 2d ed. (São Paulo, 1959); Emilia Viotti da Costa, *Da Senzala à Colonia* (São Paulo, 1966); Florestan Fernandes, *A Integração do Negro à Sociedade de Classes* (São Paulo, 1964), and *O Negro no Mundo dos Brancos* (São Paulo, 1972); and Octavio Ianni, *As Metamorfoses do Escravo* (São Paulo, 1962).

8. Alden, "The Population of Brazil in the Late Eighteenth Century," pp. 173–205; Russell-Wood, "Colonial Brazil," pp. 85, 97–8; Emilia Viotti da Costa, *The Brazilian Empire* (Chicago, 1985), pp. 90, 173, 199. According to Russell-Wood, "the census taken in Salvador in 1775 revealed that the urban population of 35,253 was composed of 12,720 whites, 4,207 free mulattoes, 3,630 free blacks, and 14,696 slaves. By 1807 the total population had increased to 51,000" – with the percentage of persons of color growing from 64% to 72% (20% mulattoes, 52% blacks).

9. Boxer, *Race Relations*, p. 116; Russell-Wood, "Colonial Brazil," pp. 110–12, 117.

10. Russell-Wood, "Colonial Brazil," pp. 113–17. Also see his "Class, Creed, and Colour in Colonial Bahia: A Study in Prejudice," pp. 151–5; and Klein, "The Colored Freedmen in Brazilian Slave Society," pp. 42–51.

11. Russell-Wood, "Colonial Brazil," passim; Viotti da Costa, *The Brazilian Empire* p. 186.

12. Skidmore, *Black into White*, pp. 64–69 ff.; Degler, *Neither Black nor White*, pp. 191–5.

13. For a discussion of the "somatic norm image and marriage in multiracial societies," see Harmannus Hoetink, *Slavery and Race Relations in the Americas: Comparative Notes on Their Nature and Nexus* (New York, 1973), especially pp. 192–210. Also see Sidney W. Mintz, "Groups, Group Boundaries, and the Perception of 'Race,' " in *Comparative Studies in Society and History*, 13 (4) (Oct. 1971): 442 ff.

14. Skidmore, *Black into White*, p. 77; Viotti da Costa, *The Brazilian Empire*, p. 239.

15. Brazilian immigration policy in the latter part of the nineteenth century, which favored Europeans and discriminated against Africans and, to a lesser extent, Asians, was clearly linked to this "whitening" ideology. "Whitening," it should be noted, was advocated elsewhere besides Brazil. In Sierra Leone, for example, Joseph Renner-Maxwell, a British-educated Creole who had married an Englishwoman, wrote a book in which he urged his fellow black Africans to consider intermarriage and "lightening" of their family line as a solution to race prejudice. See his *The Negro Question, or Hints for the Physical Improvement of the Negro Race, with Special Reference to West Africa* (London, 1892). Also see Leo Spitzer, *The Creoles of Sierra Leone: Responses to Colonialism, 1870–1945* (Madison, 1974), pp. 133–5.

16. See Stuart B. Schwartz, *Sugar Plantations in the Formation of Brazilian Society*, (New York, 1985), pp. 331–2; Schwartz, "The Manumission of Slaves in Colonial Brazil, Bahia, 1648–1745," *Hispanic American Historical Review* 54 (4) (Nov. 1974): 603–35. Degler, *Neither Black nor White*, pp. 40–42; Russell-Wood, "Colonial Brazil," pp. 85–98; and Klein, "The Colored Freedmen in Brazilian Slave Society," pp. 36–42. On the other hand, Kathleen J. Higgins argues that manumission in Minas Gerais (where the majority of Brazilian slaves lived in the eighteenth century), did *not* accelerate significantly during this period. See her "The Slave Society in Eighteenth-Century Sabara: A Community Study in Colonial Brazil" (Ph.D. dissertation, Yale University, 1987).

17. It is estimated that the total population of the captaincy-general of Bahia de Todos os Santos in 1780 was 289,000; and, according to a census taken in the city of Salvador in 1775, the population of this urban center was over 35,000. See Alden, "The Population of Brazil in the Late Eighteenth Century," pp. 186, 191; Russell-Wood, "Colonial Brazil," p. 97; and Klein, "The Colored Freedmen in Brazilian Slave Society," p. 313.

18. Russell-Wood, "Colonial Brazil," pp. 86–91.

19. See Higgins, "The Slave Society in Eighteenth-Century Sabara," passim; interview with Dr. Carlos Souza Rebouças in Rio de Janeiro, Dec. 1974.

20. Quoted in Pedro Calmon, *História do Brasil na Poesia do Povo* (Rio de Janeiro, 1943), p. 76.

21. Boxer, *Race Relations*, pp. 114–15; *Trovador: Collecção de Modinhas, Recitativos, Arias, Lundús, etc.* (Rio de Janeiro, 1876), vol. 1, p. 148. Also

see Gilberto Freyre, *The Mansions and the Shanties: The Making of Modern Brazil* (Berkeley, 1986), pp. 380–2. Many variants exist in folk poetry alluding to the "gustatory" sexuality of *mulatas*. For example:

> *Mulatinha bohitinha*
> *Não devia de nascer:*
> *É como a fructa madura*
> *Que todos querem comer.*

> Pretty Mulatinha
> Should not have been created:
> She is like a ripe fruit
> That everyone wants to eat.

22. Hoetink, *Slavery and Race Relations in the Americas*, p. 202 n. 14, ff.; A. J. R. Russell-Wood, "Female and Family in the Economy and Society of Colonial Brazil," pp. 68–70; Russell-Wood, "Women and Society in Colonial Brazil," *Journal of Latin American Studies* 9 (1): 3–11; Viotti da Costa, *The Brazilian Empire*, pp. 136, 180.

23. See "Reboussa, Rebouça, Rebossa, Reboça, Reborsa, Reborça, Rebouças," mimeographed genealogical sheet drawn up by Carlos da Silveira in the Dr. Carlos Souza Rebouças collection [hereafter cited as CSR], formerly in Rio de Janeiro, now housed at the Instituto Gilberto Freyre, in Recife. Also see Carlos da Silveira, "Notas genealógicas sôbre a familia Rebouças da Palma, Oriundo do Vale do Paraíba do Sul, Estado de São Paulo," in *Revista do Arquivo Municipal de São Paulo*, vol. 27 (Sept. 1936); and Miguel Roque dos Reys Lemos, *Anais Municipais de Ponte de Lima*, 2d ed. (Ponte de Lima, Portugal, 1977), passim.

24. André Rebouças, *Diario e Notas Autobiográficas* (Rio de Janeiro, 1938), p. 12; Antônio Pereira Rebouças, *Recordaçoes da Vida Patriotica: Comprehendida nos Acontecimentos Politicos de Fevereiro de 1821 a Setembro de 1822; de Abril a Outubro de 1831; de Fevereiro de 1832 e de Novembro de 1837 a Março de 1838* (Rio de Janeiro, 1879), p. 31, n. 2; André Rebouças, "Apontamentos Biographicos de Conselheiro Antônio Pereira Rebouças," *Coleção A. P. Rebouças*, Biblioteca Nacional (Rio de Janeiro), I–3, 24, 60, p. 1; I–3, 24, 61. For the "Bahian Conspiracy of the Tailors [or artisans]," see Kenneth R. Maxwell, *Conflicts and Conspiracies: Brazil and Portugal, 1750–1808* (Cambridge, Eng., 1973), pp. 218–23.

25. *Registro do Casamentos*, Arquivo da Curia, Salvador, Bahia, 1820–40 book; André Rebouças, *Diario e Notas Autobiográficas*, p. 12; A. P. Rebouças, *Recordaçoes da Vida Patriotica*, p. 31, n. 2; conversation with Dr. Carlos Souza Rebouças in Rio de Janeiro, Dec. 1974.

26. Fernando de Azevedo, *Brazilian Culture: An Introduction to the Study of Culture in Brazil* (New York, 1950), pp. 361–3, 365–81.

27. The educational approach of the Jesuits survived their expulsion from Brazil in 1759. See Azevedo, *Brazilian Culture*, p. 362.

28. Quoted in Degler, *Neither Black nor White*, pp. 234.

29. Viotti da Costa, *The Brazilian Empire*, pp. 185–6; Russell-Wood, "Fe-

male and Family in Colonial Brazil," p. 93. As late as 1832, there were no more than twenty grade schools in all of Brazil catering to girls. See Azevedo, *Brazilian Culture*, pp. 334–5, 374.

30. A. P. Rebouças, *Recordaçoes da Vida Patriotica*, p. 31, n. 2.

31. For a study of the devastating effects of this cholera epidemic, see Donald B. Cooper, "The New 'Black Death': Cholera in Brazil, 1855–1856," in Kenneth F. Kiple, ed., *The African Exchange: Toward a Biological History of Black People* (Durham, N.C., 1987), pp. 235–56. According to Cooper, "the cholera epidemic of 1855–1856, which invaded thirteen provinces of Brazil from north to south and killed upwards of 200,000 persons, was the single worst medical crisis ever to confront Brazil.... It was a nineteenth-century, South American holocaust, a new 'black death' that ranks as Brazil's greatest and most dramatic demographic disaster" (p. 254).

32. See Lafayette de Toledo, "Os Rebouças" in *Almanach da Companhia Mogyana, 1908–1909*, p. 104 (CSR Collection); A.P. Rebouças, *Recordaçoes da Vida Patriotica*, p. 73, n. 3.; Herbert S. Klein, "Nineteenth-Century Brazil," in Cohen and Greene, eds., *Neither Slave nor Free*, p. 328.

33. André Rebouças, *Diario e Notas Autobiográficas*, 15 Dec. 1872, p. 218; A. P. Rebouças, *Recordaçoes da Vida Patriotica*, pp. 31–2.

34. No law school existed in Brazil until 1827, when one was organized in São Paulo and a second in Olinda. See E. Bradford Burns, *History of Brazil* (New York, 1980), p. 104.

35. *Coleção A. P. Rebouças*, Biblioteca Nacional (Rio de Janeiro): I–3, 21, 61, pp. 1, 3; "Apontamentos Biographicos do Conselheiro Antônio Pereira Rebouças," I–3, 24, 60; "Nota Biographica do Conselheiro Antônio Pereira Rebouças," I–3, 24, 63, pp. 1–2; Enéas Pereira Dourado, "O Velho Rebouças," *Diario de Noticias* (Rio de Janeiro), 26 Aug. 1962.

36. *Coleção A. P. Rebouças*, Biblioteca Nacional (Rio de Janeiro): I–3, 21, 61; "Apontamentos Biographicos do Conselheiro Antônio Pereira Rebouças," I–3, 24, 60; "Nota Biographica do Conselheiro Antônio Pereira Rebouças," I–3, 24, 63; Enéas Pereira Dourado, "O Velho Rebouças," *Diario de Noticias* (Rio de Janeiro), 26 Aug. 1962.

37. The literature on Brazilian independence is voluminous. Emilia Viotti da Costa provides an excellent overview in her "The Political Emancipation of Brazil," in A. J. R. Russell-Wood, ed., *From Colony to Nation: Essays on the Independence of Brazil* (Baltimore, 1975), pp. 43–8. The fundamental works in Portuguese are Oliveira Lima, *O Movimento da Independência 1821–1822* (São Paulo, 1922); F. Adolfo de Varnhagen, *História da Independência do Brazil*, vol. 173, *Revista do Instituto Histórico e Geográphico Brasileiro*, 1938; and Tobias Monteiro, *História do Império*, 2 vols. (Rio de Janeiro, 1939). Also see the essays and bibliographic study in Carlos Guilherme Mota, ed., *1822: Dimensões* (São Paulo, 1972). For English surveys of political developments leading to the empire, see C. H. Haring, *Empire in Brazil: A New World Experiment with Monarchy* (Cambridge, Mass., 1958), passim; and R. A. Humphreys, "Monarchy and Empire," in H. V. Livermore, ed., *Portugal and Brazil: An Introduction* (Oxford, 1963), pp. 301–19.

38. A. P. Rebouças, *Recordaçoes da Vida Patriotica*, pp. 33–4. For back-

ground and general context of the independence movement in Bahia, see Braz do Amaral, *Historia da Independencia na Bahia*, 2d. ed. (Salvador, Bahia, 1957), Chapters 1 and 2. Also see F. W. O. Morton, "The Conservative Revolution of Independence: Economy, Society, and Politics in Bahia, 1790–1840" (Ph.D. dissertation, Oxford University, 1974).

39. *Coleção A. P. Rebouças*, Biblioteca Nacional (Rio de Janeiro): I–3, 24, 64; "O bem que fez e o mal que evitou" I–3, 24, 59; A. P. Rebouças, *Recordaçoes da Vida Patriotica*, pp. 53–6; "A Independência dia a dia: A aclamação em Cachoeira," *O Globo* (Rio de Janeiro), 27 June 1972, p. 11.

40. A. P. Rebouças, *Recordaçoes da Vida Patriotica*, p. 43.

41. "Nota Biographica do Conselheiro Antônio Pereira Rebouças," *Coleção A. P. Rebouças*, Biblioteca Nacional (Rio de Janeiro): I–3, 24, 63; E. P. Dourado, "O Velho Rebouças," *Diario de Noticias*, 26 Aug. 1962.

42. See Emilia Viotti da Costa, *The Brazilian Empire*, pp. 75–7, 186, 190, 243.

43. Within a few years, he became an officer of this order. See "Nota Biographica do Conselheiro Antônio Pereira Rebouças," *Coleção A. P. Rebouças*, Biblioteca Nacional (Rio de Janeiro): I–3, 24, 57; I–3, 24, 60; I–3, 24, 63.

44. *Deputado Conselheiro a Assemblea Geral do Governo, e Conselheiro Geral da Provincia*. See "Nota Biographica do Conselheiro Antônio Pereira Rebouças," *Coleção A. P. Rebouças*, Biblioteca Nacional (Rio de Janeiro): I–3, 24, 63; I–3, 24, 56; and Dourado, "O Velho Rebouças," *Diario de Noticias*, 26 Aug. 1962.

45. *Coleção A. P. Rebouças*, Biblioteca Nacional (Rio de Janeiro): mss 31, 13, 13; "Apontamentos Biographicos do Conselheiro Antônio Pereira Rebouças," I–3, 24, 60. An account of this episode is in Felisbelo Freire, *História de Sergipe* (Petrópolis, 1977), pp. 256–71.

46. See João José Reis, "Restless Times: Slave Revolts and Free People's Movements up to 1835," in his "Slave Rebellion in Brazil: The African Muslim Uprising in Bahia, 1835" (Ph.D. dissertation, University of Minnesota, 1982), pp. 57–123; "A Elite Baiana Face os Movimentos Sociais, Bahia: 1824–1840," *Revista de História*, no. 108 (São Paulo, 1976), pp. 341–84. Luiz Luna, *O Negro Na Luta Contra a Escravidão* (Rio de Janeiro, 1968), pp. 129–49.

47. For a discussion of such fears of rebellion and the imposition of deterrent measures in the late colonial era, see Russell-Wood, "Colonial Brazil," p. 95; Norman Holub, "The Brazilian Sabinada (1837–38): Revolt of the Negro Masses," *Journal of Negro History* 54 (3) (July 1969): 278.

48. André Rebouças, "Registro de Correspondencia": letters to Visconde de Taunay, 8 May 1892, 10 Aug. 1897, CSR; "Emigra a Familia Rebouças da Bahia," note written by André Rebouças in Capetown, South Africa, 2 Jan. 1893.

49. Daniel Goleman, *Vital Lies, Simple Truths: The Psychology of Self-Deception* (New York, 1985), pp. 21–5.

50. See Alfred Adler on the role of the "inferiority complex" as positive driving force and on "striving as ultimate adaptation." Heinz L. Ansbacher and Rowena R. Ansbacher, eds., *The Individual Psychology of Alfred Adler:*

A Systematic Presentation in Selections from His Writings (New York, 1956), pp. 101–19, 256–62. Also see Chapter 5 in the present volume for additional discussion of this point.

51. Holub, "The Brazilian Sabinada (1837–38): Revolt of the Negro Masses," pp. 276–9; A. K. Manchester, *British Preeminence in Brazil: Its Rise and Decline* (Chapel Hill, 1933), passim.

52. Antônio Pereira Rebouçõas, *Recordaçoes da Vida Parlamentar*, vol. 1 (Rio de Janeiro, 1870), pp. 523–5; Holub, "The Brazilian Sabinada (1837–38): Revolt of the Negro Masses," p. 278, n. 14; André Rebouças, *Diário e Notas Autobiográficas*, ed. Ana Flora and Ignacio José Verissimo (Rio de Janeiro, 1938), pp. 12, 284, 286.

53. See "Apontamentos Biographicos" and "Nota Biographica do Conselheiro Antônio Pereira Rebouças," *Coleção A. P. Rebouças*, Biblioteca Nacional (Rio de Janeiro): I–3, 24, 60, I–3, 24, 63, also see I–3, 24, 61, and *Recordaçoes da Vida Patriotica*, pp. 101–5. For the Sabinada, see Publicaçoes do Estado da Bahia, *A revolução de 7 de novembro de 1837 (Sabinada)*, 3 vols. (Bahia, 1937–45); José Wanderley de Araujo Pinho, "A Sabinada," *Revista do Instituto Histórico da Bahia*, vol. 106 (1930), pp. 635–793; Luiz Vianna Filho, *A Sabinada: A Republica bahiana de 1837* (Rio de Janeiro, 1938); Braz do Amaral, "A Sabinada: Historia da Revolta da Cidade da Bahia em 1837," *Revista do Instituto Geographico e Historico da Bahia*, Numero Especial (Salvador, Bahia, 1909); João José Reis, "A Elite Bahiana Face os Movimentos Sociais, Bahia: 1824–1840," *Revista de História*, no. 108 (São Paulo, 1976), pp. 341–84; and Holub, "The Brazilian Sabinada (1837–38): Revolt of the Negro Masses."

54. For additional information on Rebouças's role in the Sabinada, see *Coleção A. P. Rebouças*, Biblioteca Nacional (Rio de Janeiro): I–3, 23, 10, I–3, 23, 68–75, 78–80. Also see André Rebouças, *Diário e Notas Autobiográficas*, letter of 24 Apr. 1894 to Visconde Taunay, pp. 410–11.

55. Holub, "The Brazilian Sabinada (1837–38): Revolt of the Negro Masses," p. 279.

56. Important works by these revisionist social scientists include: Florestan Fernandes and Roger Bastide, *Brancos e Negros em São Paulo* (São Paulo, 1955); Fernandes, *A Integração do Negro na Sociedade de Classes* (São Paulo, 1964); *O Negro No Mundo dos Brancos* (São Paulo, 1972); and Octavio Ianni, *As Metamorfoses do Escravo* (São Paulo, 1962), and *Raças e Classes Sociais no Brasil* (Rio de Janeiro, 1966). For a discussion of this revisionist "São Paulo School," see Skidmore, *Black into White*, pp. 214–18.

57. Fernandes, *The Negro in Brazilian Society*, p. 137.

58. Ibid., pp. 187–233.

59. Viotti da Costa, *The Brazilian Empire*, p. 240, arrives at a similar conclusion regarding approaches postulating the manipulative character of the myth of "racial democracy."

60. Louis Althusser, "Ideology and Ideological State Apparatuses," in *Lenin and Philosophy and Other Essays*, trans. Ben Brewster (London, 1971), p. 155. My italics.

Chapter 5. The Marginal Situation, Individual Psychology, and Ideology

1. See H. F. Dickie-Clark, "The Marginal Situation: A Contribution to Marginality Theory," *Social Forces* 44 (3) (Mar. 1966):363–70; and, especially, his *The Marginal Situation* (London, 1966).

2. Dickie-Clark, *Marginal Situation*, pp. 27–48, 185–6.

3. Heinz L. Ansbacher and Rowena R. Ansbacher, "Introduction" to *The Individual Psychology of Alfred Adler: A Systematic Presentation in Selections from His Writings* (New York, 1956), p. 1. Also see Alfred Adler, "On the Origin of the Striving for Superiority and of Social Interest (1933)," in his *Superiority and Social Interest: A Collection of Later Writings*, ed. H. L. Ansbacher and R. R. Ansbacher (New York, 1979), pp. 29–40.

4. "When Adler combined the concept of the fiction with that of the goal, as in the fictional goal or the fictional final goal or the guiding fiction, he implied that his view of causality was subjectivistic, that it was determined only in a restricted sense, and that it took unconscious processes into account.... The term fictional goal also expressed Adler's conviction that the origin of the goal is, in the last analysis, not reducible to objective determiners. Although the objective factors of heredity and environment, organ inferiorities, and past experiences are utilized by the individual in the process of forming his final goal, the latter is still a fiction, a fabrication, the individual's own creation. Such causality corresponds to 'soft' determinism, that is, 'determinism from the inner nature of life,' as contrasted to 'hard' determinism 'from external pressures alone'." See Ansbacher and Ansbacher, eds., *The Individual Psychology of Alfred Adler*, pp. 88, 89, 90–95.

5. On the differences, for example, between "objectivistic" Freudian and "subjectivistic" Adlerian theoretical propositions regarding basic human drives, see Ansbacher and Ansbacher, eds., *The Individual Psychology of Alfred Adler*, pp. 3–10, 56–60, 159–61, 285–6.

6. See Bertha Orgler, *Alfred Adler: The Man and His Work* (New York, 1963), pp. 15–23. Although the pattern of social mobility in his own life history and that of members of his family greatly resembled that of the Zweigs, Brettauers, and of numerous other Jews in Central Europe, one wonders how conscious Adler himself was about the role that his personal assimilationist background played in influencing the development and evolution of his psychological theories.

7. "Freud criticized Adler for introducing the term 'fiction' into his writings... [because] he thought of fiction as merely another word for fantasy. ... The difference here is that Freud had defined fantasy as a 'mode of thought-activity...free from reality-testing and...subordinated to the pleasure principle alone' [*Collected Papers*, vol. 4, (London, 1924–50), pp. 16–17)], whereas for Adler fiction, far from being a mere subjective fancy, was an indispensable device for problem-solving in real life." See Ansbacher and Ansbacher, *The Individual Psychology of Alfred Adler*, p. 97.

8. For the "classic" theoretical exposition of the concept of cultural hegemony and the relation between culture and power under capitalism, see Antonio Gramsci, *Selections from the Prison Notebooks*, ed. and trans. Quentin Hoare and Geoffrey Nowell Smith (New York, 1971), passim. Alternatively, for an excellent selection of Gramsci's writings on this topic, see David Forgacs, ed., *A Gramsci Reader: Selected Writings 1916–1935* (London, 1988), pp. 189–221. Also see T. J. Jackson Lears, "The Problem of Cultural Hegemony: Problems and Possibilities," *American Historical Review*, 9 (3) (June 1985):567–93.

9. Louis Althusser, "Ideology and Ideological State Apparatuses (Notes towards an Investigation)," in *Lenin and Philosophy and Other Essays*, trans. Ben Brewster (New York, 1971), p. 143. Also see Catherine Belsey, "Constructing the Subject: Deconstructing the Text," in Judith Newton and Deborah Rosenfelt, eds., *Feminist Criticism and Social Change: Sex, Class, and Race in Literature and Culture* (New York, 1985), p. 46; and P. Q. Hirst, "Althusser and the Theory of Ideology," *Economy and Society* 5 (4) (1976).

10. For a discussion of the notion that "every language contains the elements of a conception of the world and of a culture," see Gramsci, *Selections from the Prison Notebooks*, pp. 324–5. Also see Lears, "The Problem of Cultural Hegemony: Problems and Possibilities," p. 569; and Tony Bennett, et al. eds., *Culture, Ideology, and Social Process* (London, 1981), pp. 200–2.

11. Althusser, "Ideology and Ideological State Apparatuses," pp. 154–6; Belsey, "Constructing the Subject: Deconstructing the Text," p. 46. Althusser identified the following as Ideological State Apparatuses (ISA):

- the religious ISA (the system of the different Churches),
- the educational ISA (the system of the different public and private 'Schools'),
- the family ISA,
- the legal ISA,
- the political ISA (the political system, including the different Parties),
- the trade-union ISA,
- the communications ISA (press, radio and television, etc.)
- the cultural ISA (Literature, the Arts, sports, etc.)

12. Belsey, "Constructing the Subject: Deconstructing the Text," p. 46.

13. Althusser, "Ideology and Ideological State Apparatuses," pp. 158–62.

14. Gramsci, *Selections from the Prison Notebooks*, p. 12. Gramsci defines hegemony as "the 'spontaneous' consent given by the great masses of the population to the general direction imposed on social life by the dominant fundamental group; this consent is 'historically' caused by the prestige (and consequent confidence) which the dominant group enjoys because of its position and function in the world of production."

15. For examples, see Lears, "The Problem of Cultural Hegemony," p. 573.

16. Althusser, "Ideology and Ideological State Apparatuses," p. 171. The italics are his.

17. It does this, as Althusser indicates, by addressing individuals as if

they were "a free subjectivity, a centre of initiatives," as persons initiating and responsible for their actions. This recognition of autonomy encourages individuals "willingly" to adopt the *position of subject* that their participation in the social formation demands. "Ideology and Ideological State Apparatuses," p. 182.

18. Gramsci, *Selections from the Prison Notebooks*, p. 195; Lears, "The Problem of Cultural Hegemony," p. 574; Chantal Mouffe, "Hegemony and Ideology in Gramsci," in Bennett et al., eds., *Culture, Ideology, and Social Process*, pp. 228–9.

19. For a fascinating study of Central European folk life, see Herman Pollack, *Jewish Folkways in Germanic Lands, 1648–1806* (Cambridge, Mass., 1971).

20. Leo Spitzer, *The Creoles of Sierra Leone: Responses to Colonialism, 1870–1945* (Madison, 1974), pp. 26–36.

21. See Robert E. Park, "Human Migration and the Marginal Man," *American Journal of Sociology* 33 (6) (May 1928): 881–93; and Everett V. Stonequist, *The Marginal Man* (New York, 1937), p. 8. Also see his "The Problem of the Marginal Man," *American Journal of Sociology* 41 (1) (July 1935): 1–12, and "The Marginal Character of the Jews," in I. Graeber and S. H. Britt, eds., *Jews in a Gentile World* (New York, 1942). Many refinements of Park and Stonequist's "Marginal Man" theory exist. For examples, see Milton M. Goldberg, "A Qualification of the Marginal Man Theory," *American Sociological Review* 6 (1) (1941): 52–8; S. Slotkin, "The Status of the Marginal Man," *Sociology and Social Research* 28 (1) (Sept. 1943): 47–54; A. W. Green, "A Re-Examination of the Marginal Man Concept," *Social Forces* 26 (2) (1947): 167–71; Everett C. Hughes, "Social Change and Status Protest: An Essay on the Marginal Man," *Phylon* 10 (1949): 58–65; D. I. Golovensky, "The Marginal Man Concept: An Analysis and Critique," *Social Forces* 30 (2) (1952): 333–9; A. C. Kerchoff, "An Investigation of Factors Operative in the Development of the Personality Characteristics of Marginality" (Ph.D. dissertation, University of Wisconsin, 1953); David Riesman, "Some Observations Concerning Marginality," in his *Individualism Reconsidered* (Glencoe, Ill., 1954), pp. 153–78; A. C. Kerchoff and T. C. McCormick, "Marginal Status and Marginal Personality," *Social Forces* 34 (1) (1955): 48–55; A. Antonovsky, "Toward a Refinement of the 'Marginal Man' Concept," *Social Forces* 35 (1) (1956): 57–62; J. W. Mann, "Group Relations and the Marginal Personality," *Human Relations* 11 (1) (1958): 77–92; Allan Mazur, "The Accuracy of Classic Types of Ethnic Personalities," *Jewish Social Studies* (April 1971): 187–211; Ruth Johnston, "The Concept of the 'Marginal Man': A Refinement of the Term," *Australia and New Zealand Journal of Sociology* 12 (2) (June 1976): 145–7. Also see Deborah Pellow, "Marginality and individual consciousness: women in modernizing Africa", Working paper #28, Michigan State University (East Lansing, 1983).

22. The term "barrier" was first employed in this light by Kurt Lewin in *Resolving Social Conflicts* (New York, 1948), pp. 145–58. See discussion of "barrier" in Dickie-Clark, *Marginal Situation*, pp. 12, 31–4.

23. Dickie-Clark, *Marginal Situation*, p. 12, n. 1., 32–4; Lewin, *Resolving Social Conflicts*, pp. 145–7.

24. According to Dickie-Clark, "permeability, as distinct from transcendence, can mean that the cultural characteristics of the dominant stratum in the hierarchy seep through the barrier and are taken over by subordinate strata. This happens to some extent in all 'real-life' hierarchies of any complexity. Even in slave societies – if only amongst the more favoured house slaves – and in the Indian caste system, this kind of cultural seepage takes place. This is even more likely to happen in hierarchical situations of a restricted kind within a single, common culture. So, in this sense, all hierarchical situations have permeable barriers." See his *Marginal Situation*, p. 33.

Chapter 6. "I belong nowhere, and everywhere am a stranger"

1. André Rebouças, *Diário e Notas Autobiográficas*, ed. Ana Flora and Ignacio José Verissimo (Rio de Janeiro, 1938) [hereafter cited as *Diario*], pp. 15–17.

2. *Sierra Leone Weekly News* [hereafter cited as *Weekly News*] "Obituary for Cornelius May," 18 May 1929; interview with Mrs. Tungi Stuart and Mrs. Isa Smith, granddaughters of Cornelius May, in Freetown, Jan. 1976.

3. Zweig, *The World of Yesterday* (Lincoln, Nebraska, 1943), pp. 95–6, 110, 125. On Taine and Zweig, see Robert Dumont, *Stefan Zweig et la France* (Paris, 1967), pp. 28–9.

4. Zweig, *World*, pp. 11–12; Donald A. Prater, *European of Yesterday: A Biography of Stefan Zweig* (Oxford, 1972), p. 4. A revised version of Prater's work has been published in German: *Stefan Zweig, Das Leben eines Ungeduldigen* (Frankfurt am Main, 1984).

5. Zweig, *World*, p. 12.

6. Ibid., pp. 198–9; Prater, *European*, vii; Harry Zohn, "Stefan Zweig als Mittler in der europäischen Literatur," *Das Jüdische Echo* (Wien) 27 (1) (Sept. 1978): 47–52.

7. See Zweig, *World*, passim. Also see "An Inventory: Stefan Zweig Archives," mimeographed *Catalogue of the Stefan Zweig Collection* at Reed Library, State University College at Fredonia, N.Y., passim; Friderike Zweig, *Greatness Revisited* (Boston, 1971), pp. 70–88; Helene Kastinger Riley, "The Quest for Reason: Stefan Zweig's and Romain Rolland's Struggle for Pan-European Unity," and Clair Hoch, "Friendship and Kinship between Georges Duhamel and Stefan Zweig," in Marion Sonnenfeld, ed., *The World of Yesterday's Humanist Today: Proceedings of the Stefan Zweig Symposium* (Albany, 1983), pp. 20–31, 40–63.

8. Rebouças, *Diario*, pp. 185, 190, 290. Gomes dedicated his opera *Salvador Rosa* to Rebouças, who, in turn, presented Gomes with a collection of Walter Scott romances – to inspire future operas.

9. Leo Spitzer, *The Creoles of Sierra Leone: Responses to Colonialism, 1870–1945* (Madison, 1974), pp. 24–6.

10. See *Weekly News*, 15 Apr. 1883, 6 June 1885: "The Social and Political

Relations of Sierra Leone Natives to the English People" and "Life and Experiences of Joseph Boston May," by Joseph B. May; *Weekly News*, editorial and letters to editor 13 and 20 Sept. 1884; "My View of Things," 5 Mar. 1887; "Superstition in Freetown," 23 Nov. 1889; "Passing Topics," 27 Sept. 1890.

11. Zweig letter to Rabbi Dr. Lemle (? Sept. 1941), quoted in Prater, *European*, p. 316. Also see Alberto Dines, *Morte No Paraîso: A Tragédia de Stefan Zweig* (Rio de Janeiro, 1981), p. 312.

12. Quoted in Prater, *European*, p. 88.

13. Zweig, *World*, pp. 101–9.

14. Rebouças, *Diario*, pp. 138, 238, 284, 286.

15. For example, see ibid., p. 54.

16. See David Milner, *Children and Race* (Middlesex, 1975), pp. 35–60, for a discussion of the role played by direct and indirect tuition in the socialization of attitudes and identity.

17. Rebouças, *Diario*, p. 15 (2 Dec. 1857), p. 17 (Nov.–Dec. 1862), p. 126 (27 July 1866), p. 130 (11 Aug. 1866), p. 166 (7 May 1868).

18. Ibid., p. 138.

19. André Rebouças, *Registro da Correspondencia*, letter to Rangel da Costa (11 Aug. 1895), in the Dr. Carlos Souza Rebouças collection [hereafter cited as RC/CSR], formerly in Rio de Janeiro, now housed at the Instituto Gilberto Freyre, in Recife; *Diario*, pp. 91, 181, 196; Ignacio José Verissimo, *André Rebouças atraves de sua autobiografia* (Rio de Janeiro, 1939), pp. 71–4.

20. Rebouças, *Diario*, pp. 198, 245–53; Verissimo, *Rebouças... autobiografia*, pp. 87, 172–3. Rebouças identified the hall as the "Grand Opera House," but it probably was the Academy of Music Opera Hall, predecessor of the Metropolitan Opera, which contained the largest stage in the world and seated 4,600. *The New Grove Dictionary of American Music*, vol. 3 (New York, 1986), pp. 352–3.

21. Rebouças, *Diario*, pp. 190, 194; Verissimo, *Rebouças... autobiografia*, pp. 73–4.

22. Rebouças, RC/CSR, letter to Taunay (27 Jan. 1897); *Diario*, pp. 169, 195 (28 Aug. 1871), 269 (8 Nov. 1874), 289 (8 July 1880).

23. Rebouças, RC/CSR; miscellaneous file: "Saudação a S.M.O Imperador D. Pedro II Pelo seu 64° Anniversario." Written aboard the *Alagoas* en route to exile in Europe on 30 December 1892, this gives an account of the early history of this relationship.

24. André Pinto Rebouças, *A questão do Brazil; cunho escravocrata do attentado contra a familia imperial* (Lisbon, 1889–90), p. 27; RC/CSR, letters to Taunay (13 May 1891 and 17 Jan. 1893); *Diario*, 4 Jan., 2 Apr. 1864, 11, 12 Sept. 1865, 21 July 1866, 9 May 1869.

25. For Rebouças's role in the abolitionist campaign, see Joaquim Nabuco, *Minha Formação* (Rio de Janeiro, 1900), pp. 234–40; Carolina Nabuco, *The Life of Joaquim Nabuco* (Stanford, Calif., 1950), pp. 71–4, 102–5; and Rebecca Baird Bergstresser, "The Movement for the Abolition of Slavery in Rio de Janeiro, Brazil, 1880–1889" (Ph.D. dissertation, Stanford University, 1973) (University Microfilms #73-20462), pp. 79–83, 106–7, 126–

38, 150–5, 174–88. For his own perceptions, see his diaries for the period in the Instituto Historico e Geografico Brasileiro (Rio de Janeiro) [hereafter cited as IHGB]. Also see RC/CSR, miscellaneous file: *"Apotheose Abolicionista, Escripta no Album offerecido ao Imperador D. Pedro II em sua chegada no Rio de Janeiro em 22 Agosto 1888"* and *"O Idylio Abolicionista,"* written in Capetown, 7 Jan. 1893, *"D. Isabel I: Mensagem da British and Foreign Anti-Slavery Society,"* written in Capetown, 7 Jan. 1893; *Confederação abolicionista: Abolição imediata e sem indemnição* (Rio de Janeiro, 1883).

26. His abolitionist and reformist ideas are spelled out in part in André Rebouças, *A Democracia Rural Brasileira: Propaganda Abolicionista e Democratica* (Rio de Janeiro, 1883). Also see *Diario*, p. 313 (14 May 1888).

27. Rebouças, *A questão*, p. 1.

28. Ibid., p. 7.

29. See Rebouças, 1888 and 1889 diaries, IHGB, passim.

30. Rebouças, *A questão*, p. 4.

31. Ibid., p. 7.

32. Rebouças, 1889 diary, IHGB, 15 and 16 Nov. 1889.

33. Rebouças was included on the passenger list as "tutor of the princess" and, with others in the royal entourage, took up residence in the Hotel Braganza, Lisbon. See *Diario*, pp. 351–4 (18 Nov.–7 Dec. 1889).

34. Rebouças, *A questão*, pp. 2, 8; R. Magalhães Junior, *A Vida Turbulenta de José do Patrocinio* (Rio de Janeiro, 1969), passim.

35. Rebouças, RC/CSR, letter to Taunay, 31 Oct. 1891.

36. Rebouças, RC/CSR, letter to Taunay, 13 Oct. 1891, and to José Americo dos Santos, 17 Oct. 1891; *Diario*, p. 357 (29 Dec. 1889).

37. Rebouças, RC/CSR, letter to Dr. José Grey, 13 July 1895.

38. He intended to work gratis for Antonio Julio Machado as an engineer on the Loanda–Ambacca railroad construction, in what is now Angola. This project fell through while Rebouças was still in transit down the east coast of Africa. When he heard the news, he interrupted his journey in Lourenço Marques (present Maputo, Mozambique). See Rebouças, RC/CSR, letter to Taunay, 3 Jan. 1892, to Rangel da Costa, 5 Jan. and 12 Mar. 1892, to Sassetti, 30 Jan. 1892. Despite some minor factual inaccuracies, Taunay's recollections of Rebouças during this period are interesting. See his "André Rebouças," *Revista do Instituto Historico e Geografico Brasileiro*, vol. 57, part 2 (1914), pp. 115–24.

39. Rebouças, RC/CSR, letter to Rangel da Costa, 5 Jan. 1892, to Taunay, 11 Jan. 1892, to Stanley Youle, 23 Jan. 1892, to Machado, 28 Feb. 1892.

40. Rebouças, RC/CSR, letter to Taunay, 8 May 1892.

41. Ibid. Also see letter to Taunay, 14 May 1892, for similar sentiment.

42. Rebouças, RC/CSR, letter to Taunay, 3 Jan. 1892, to Haupt, 3 Mar. 1892, to Taunay, 3 Mar. 1892.

43. Rebouças, RC/CSR, miscellaneous file: *"Nova Propaganda Abolicionista"* (13 May 1892).

44. Rebouças, RC/CSR, miscellaneous file: *"Escravidão n'Africa Oriental"* (27 May 1892); also in 1892 letterbook (*Registro da Correspondencia*) as letter to Machado.

45. Rebouças, RC/CSR, miscellaneous file: *"Nova Propaganda Abolicionista: Vestir 300,000,000 de Negros Africanos."* This was written in Lourenço Marques on 13 May 1892 (fourth anniversary of abolition) and copied in Capetown on stationery of the *"Sociedade Brazileira contra a escravidão"* on 15 Jan. 1893. He had taken this stationery with him into exile. Also see RC/CSR, letters to Taunay, 26 May and 17 June 1892.

46. Rebouças, 1893 *Diario*, IHGB, 2, 8, 14, 15, Jan., 2, 7 Feb. *Ydillios Africanos VI* was written in Barbeton on 30 May 1892, and published by José do Patrocinio in the *Cidade de Rio* (Rio de Janeiro), 4 Feb. 1893.

47. Rebouças, RC/CSR, miscellaneous file: *"Escravidão n'Africa Oriental."* Also RC/CSR, letter to Rangel da Costa, 14 June 1892, to Machado, 21 June 1892, to the Barão de Pacô-Vieira, 23 July 1894; *Diario*, p. 413.

48. Petrópolis, a town in the mountains near Rio de Janeiro, was the imperial retreat from the heat and hustle-bustle of the capital city. Rebouças, RC/CSR, letter to Rangel da Costa, 14 June 1892, to Taunay, 26 May 1892.

49. Rebouças, RC/CSR, letter to W. C. Gowie, Grahamstown, 8 July 1892; letter to Taunay, 14 July 1892, in Taunay family archives, São Paulo.

50. Rebouças, RC/CSR, letter to Machado, 11 Dec. 1892, to Taunay and Nabuco, 12 and 21 Dec. 1892.

51. "Overdetermined from without" is Frantz Fanon's phrase. See his *Black Skin, White Masks* (New York, 1967), pp. 116, 117. Also see Rebouças, RC/CSR, letter to Taunay, 20 June 1893.

52. Rebouças, RC/CSR, letter to Taunay, 19 Dec. 1895. Also see letter to manager of British Bank of South America, 27 Feb. 1895, to Taunay, 26 Nov. 1894, 10 Mar., 3 Oct., 16 Oct., 23 Nov., 10 Dec., 19 Dec. 1897; 24 Mar., 10 Apr., 27 Apr. 1898, in Taunay family archives, São Paulo.

53. Rebouças, *Diario*, pp. 451–2; Alfredo d'Escragnolle, Visconde de Taunay, "André Rebouças," *Revista do Instituto Historico e Geografico Brasileiro*, vol. 67 (1914) part 2a, p. 124; interview with Dr. Carlos de Souza Rebouças in Rio de Janeiro, Dec. 1974.

54. See Chapter 2. Also see Philip D. Curtin, *The Image of Africa: British Ideas and Action, 1780–1850* (Madison, 1964), pp. 238–40, 414–15, 425–6; Spitzer, *Creoles*, p. 45; Michael Banton, *The Idea of Race* (London, 1974), pp. 1–62; Christine Bolt, *Victorian Attitudes to Race* (London, 1971), passim; Douglas A. Lorimer, *Colour, Class, and the Victorians: English Attitudes to the Negro in the Mid-Nineteenth Century* (Leicester, 1978), passim.

55. See, for example, Richard F. Burton, *Wanderings in West Africa, from Liverpool to Fernando Po, By a F.R.G.S.* (London, 1863), vol. 1; R. F. Burton and J. L. Cameron, *To the Gold Coast for Gold* (London, 1883); G. A. L. Banbury, *Sierra Leone, or The White Man's Grave* (London, 1881); and A. B. Ellis, *West African Sketches* (London, 1881).

56. Spitzer, *Creoles*, pp. 45–50.

57. *Weekly News*, 26 Feb. 1887.

58. E. W. Blyden, *Christianity, Islam, and the Negro Race*, 2d ed. (London, 1889), pp. 317–18, 398–9, 433–44; *Weekly News*, 11 Apr. 1891.

59. Blyden was of Ibo ancestry, born on St. Thomas in the Virgin Islands

in 1832. When, because of his race, he was refused admission to colleges in the United States, he accepted an offer by the New York Colonization Society to emigrate to and study in Liberia. Landing there in 1851, he began his long and active connection with West Africa. He spent the next twenty years of his life in that country practically without interruption. During this time, he became an ordained and licensed Presbyterian minister, editor of the *Liberia Herald*, and principal of Alexander High School in Monrovia, a professor, and later, vice-principal of Liberia College, secretary of state, minister plenipotentiary to the Court of St. James, and a three-time unsuccessful candidate for the presidency of the republic. Largely through self-teaching, he claimed to have mastered Latin, Greek, Hebrew, Arabic, Spanish, Dutch, French, and German. In the late 1870s, after acquiring powerful political enemies in Liberia, he spent more and more time in Sierra Leone. Eventually, although absent for extended stays in Europe, America, and other parts of Africa, Freetown and not Monrovia became his home until his death in 1912. For additional biographical information, see Hollis R. Lynch, *Edward Wilmot Blyden, Pan-Negro Patriot, 1832–1912* (London, 1967); Edith Holden, *Blyden of Liberia, An Account of the Life and Labors of Edward Wilmot Blyden, LL.D., As Recorded in Letters and in Print* (New York, 1967). A version of this discussion has appeared in Spitzer, *Creoles*, pp. 111–15.

60. E. W. Blyden, *Christianity, Islam, and the Negro Race*, pp. 317–18.

61. E. W. Blyden, *Proceedings at the Banquet in Honour of Edward Wilmot Blyden, LL.D., on the Occasion of his Retirement From His Official Labours in the Colony of Sierra Leone, January 24th, 1907* (London, 1907), pp. 40–1; *Weekly News*, "Banquet in Honor of C. E. Wright," 28 Nov. 1903.

62. Blyden used "Negro personality," a concept that Ghana's Kwame Nkrumah later adopted and renamed the "African personality."

63. E. W. Blyden, *Africa and the Africans, Proceedings on the Occasion of a Banquet Given to E. W. Blyden by West Africans in London, August 15, 1903* (London, 1903), p. 44; Blyden, *African Life and Customs* (London, 1908), pp. 9–36; *Sierra Leone Guardian and Foreign Mail* (Freetown), "Obituary," 16 Feb. 1912.

64. *Weekly News*, "Banquet in Honor of C. E. Wright," 28 Nov. 1903. Also see Great Britain, Public Records Office, CO 267/324, Blyden to Earl Kimberley, 1873; Blyden, *Christianity, Islam, and the Negro Race*, pp. 76–7, 254, 317–18; and Blyden, *Aims and Methods of a Liberal Education for Africans, Inaugural Address delivered by E. W. Blyden, LL.D., President of Liberia College, January 5, 1881* (Cambridge, Mass., 1882), pp. 6–11.

65. *Weekly News*, 20 June 1891.

66. *Methodist Herald* (Freetown), 21 Dec. 1887.

67. *Weekly News*, "Obituary," May 18, 1929; Great Britain, Public Records Office, CO 267/590, 8 Feb. 1921; interview with Mrs. Tungi Stuart and Mrs. Isa Smith in Freetown, Jan. 1976.

68. Great Britain, Public Records Office, CO 267/590, 8 Feb. 1921. For May's participation in the National Congress of British West Africa, see sources cited in Spitzer, *Creoles*, pp. 171–8.

69. May, the mayor, as well as the foreman of works, the town clerk, and

the city treasurer were convicted of "defrauding the Freetown Corporation by obtaining by false pretences [and, presumably, for their own profit] corrugated iron to the value of some £25." For the Freetown municipality scandals, see Great Britain, Public Records Office, CO 267/616, files 5148 and 6906 (Report of the Commission of Inquiry) [the O'Brien Commission Report]; and Sierra Leone Colony, Legislative Council Debates, 24 Nov. 1925, 28 Dec. 1926. For background on the Freetown Municipal [City] Council, see Sierra Leone, Legislative Council: Appendix to the Governor's Annual Address, 24 November, 1925. Also see S. A. J. Pratt, "The Government of Freetown," in Christopher Fyfe and Eldred Jones, eds., *Freetown: A Symposium* (Freetown, 1968), pp. 154–65; Akintola J. G. Wyse, "The Dissolution of Freetown City Council in 1926: A Negative Example of Political Apprenticeship in colonial Sierra Leone," in Murray Last and Paul Richards, eds., *Sierra Leone, 1787–1987: Two Centuries of Intellectual Life* (Manchester, Eng., 1987), pp. 422–38.

70. *West Africa* [weekly London newspaper], 29, 30 Oct. 1926, pp. 653, 1444; *Weekly News*, "Letter by Cornelius May," 22 Oct. 1927; *Weekly News*, "Obituary for Cornelius May," 18 May 1929.

71. Zweig, *World*, p. 196.

72. Ibid., p. 194.

73. Prater, *European*, p. 348; Erwin Rieger, *Stefan Zweig, Der Mann und das Werk* (Berlin, 1928), pp. 9–14; Walter Bauer, "Stefan Zweig der Europäer," in Hans Arens, ed., *Stefan Zweig, Sein Leben-Sein Werk* (Esslingen, Germany, 1949), pp. 130–45.

74. Zweig, *World*, pp. 7–9, 25, 63, 102–5. Also see Jacob Katz, *From Prejudice to Destruction: Anti-Semitism, 1700–1933* (Cambridge, Mass., 1980), pp. 223–9, 281–91; Peter G. J. Pulzer, *Rise of Political Anti-Semitism in Germany and Austria* (New York, 1964), pp. 293–333; F. L. Carsten, *Fascist Movements in Austria* (London, 1977), pp. 9–29; William M. Johnston, *The Austrian Mind: An Intellectual and Social History, 1848–1938* (Berkeley, 1972), pp. 63–6; Anna Drabek, Wolfgang Häusler, Kurt Schubert, Karl Stuhlpfarrer, and Nikolaus Vielmetti, *Das oesterreichische Judentum* (Vienna, 1974), pp. 108–21; and Hannah Arendt, *The Origins of Totalitarianism: Part I: Antisemitism* (New York, 1973), pp. 3–120.

75. Zweig, *World*, pp. 316–23; Robert Dumont, *Stefan Zweig et la France* (Paris, 1967), passim; Zohn, "Stefan Zweig als Mittler in der europäischen Literatur," pp. 47–52. For the most complete bibliography of works by and about Zweig, see Randolph J. Klawiter, *Stefan Zweig: A Bibliography* (Chapel Hill, 1965).

76. Hannah Arendt, *The Jew as Pariah* (New York, 1978), pp. 112–21; Zweig, *World*, p. 316.

77. Quoted in David Ewen, "Stefan Zweig Calls Anti-Semitism a Moldering Evil," *The American Hebrew* (New York) 80 (22) (15 Apr. 1932): 551, 572. Also see Werner J. Cahnman, "Stefan Zweig in Salzburg," *The Menorah Journal* 30 (2) (July-Sept. 1942): 195–8, for an account of an interview with Zweig in 1931 that reveals much about his feelings at that time toward Judaism and anti-Semitism.

78. Zweig, *World*, pp. 358–89; Prater, *European*, pp. 210–11, 233, 234;

Drabek et al., *Oesterreichische Judentum,* pp. 141–64; Carsten, *Fascist Movements,* pp. 189–210.

79. Zweig letter to Ebermayer, 11 May 1933, in Erich Ebermayer, *Buch der Freunde* (Lohhof bein München, 1960), p. 53; letter to Friderike, June 1933, in *Stefan and Friderike Zweig, Their Correspondence, 1912–1942* (New York, 1954), p. 256.

80. Zweig letter to Franz Karl Ginzky, 4 May 1934, in the manuscript collection of the Wiener Stadt- und Landesbibliothek [hereafter cited as W/SB], I.N. 157, 438.

81. Stefan Zweig, "Their Souls a Mass of Wounds – an address on the Jewish Children in Germany," given at the home of Mrs. Anthony de Rothschild, London, 30 Nov. 1933. A copy of this speech is in the archives of the Wiener Library, London.

82. See Stefan Zweig, *Triumph und Tragik des Erasmus von Rotterdam* (Vienna, 1934); letter to Richard Strauss, 17 May 1934, in *A Confidential Matter: The Letters of Richard Strauss and Stefan Zweig, 1931–1935* (Berkeley, 1977), pp. 43–4; letters to Friderike, 21 Sept., 8 Oct. 1935, in *Correspondence,* pp. 274, 279.

83. Zweig, *World,* pp. 408, 409, 412.

84. A stimulating discussion of this point is in Josef Kastein, *Wege und Irrwege, Drei Essays zur Kultur der Gegenwart* (Tel Aviv, n.d.), pp. 39–42; W/SB, Zweig letter to Felix Braun, 29 Mar. 1938 (I.N. 198.080); Prater, *European,* pp. 267, 280.

85. W/SB, Zweig letter to Felix Braun, 16 Oct. 1939 (I.N. 198.102).

86. Zweig, *World,* pp. 427–8.

87. A controversial discussion of the character of Zweig's Jewishness is in Leon Botstein, "Stefan Zweig and the Illusion of the Jewish European," in Marion Sonnenfeld, ed., *The World of Yesterday's Humanist Today: Proceedings of the Stefan Zweig Symposium* (Albany, 1983), pp. 82–110. Also see Mark H. Gelber, "Stefan Zweig's verspätete bekehrung zum Judentum? Ein überblick zum Zentenarium in Beer Scheva und eine fortsetzung der debatte," in *Leo Baeck Institute Bulletin,* No. 63 (1982), pp. 1–11.

88. Stefan Zweig, *Jeremias. Eine dramatische Dichtung in neun Bildern* (Leipzig, 1917); Zweig letter to Friderike, 28 May 1936, *Correspondence,* p. 284.

89. W/SB, Zweig letter to Felix Braun, 20 June 1939 (I.N. 198.094); Zweig, *World,* pp. 20–4.

90. See, for example, W/SB, Zweig letter to Felix Braun, 7 Apr. 1938 (I.N. 198.081), 27 Apr. 1939 (I.N. 198.094); to Gisella Selden-Goth, 22 Apr. 1938, in "Stefan Zweig: Briefe aus der Emigration" (archives of the Wiener Library, London); to Friderike Zweig, 16, 30 Nov. 1940, *Correspondence,* pp. 320, 321; Prater, *European,* pp. 274–5. Also see "Diary of the second war [1 Sept.–17 Dec. 1939]" (written in English) and "Notebook war 1940 [22 May–19 June 1940], in Stefan Zweig, *Tagebücher* (Frankfurt am Main, 1984), pp. 415–73.

91. W/SB, Zweig letter to Felix Braun, 16 Oct. 1939 (I.N. 19.102).

92. For criticisms of Zweig's position toward Zionism and his personal

political engagement, see Kastein, *Wege und Irrwege*, passim; Alfred Werner, "Stefan Zweig's Tragedy" in *Jewish Affairs* (London), Feb. 1952, pp. 21–5; and Arendt, *Jew as Pariah*, pp. 112–21.

93. Zweig letter to Heinrich Eisemann, 22 July 1941 (archives of the Leo Baeck Institute, New York); W/SB, Zweig letters to Felix Braun, 25 July 1938 (I.N. 198.085), 4 Aug. 1938 (I.N. 198.086), 20 June 1939 (I.N.198.094).

94. Prater, *European*, p. 321; Zweig, *Tagebücher*, pp. 453–73.

95. Letter to Friderike Zweig, 26 Aug. 1936, *Correspondence*, p. 290.

96. According to the Zweigs' neighbor in Petrópolis, the Chilean poet Gabriela Mistrál. See her "Croce, Valéry und Stefan Zweig," in *Frankfurter Allgemeine Zeitung*, 6 Apr. 1954.

97. John Fowles, "Introduction" to *The Royal Game and Other Stories* (New York, 1981), p. xvii.

98. Zweig letter to Robert Faesi, 1939, quoted in Prater, *European*, p. 320.

99. Letter to Friderike Zweig, undated [Nov. 1940], *Correspondence*, p. 319.

100. Zweig, *World*, "Preface," p. xviii. Also see W/SB, Zweig letter to Felix Braun, undated [summer], 1941 (I.N. 198.120), to Heinrich Eisemann, 22 July 1941, and to Eisenmann from Brazil, undated [early 1942] (archives of the Leo Baeck Institute, New York).

101. Zweig, *World*, "Publisher's Postcript," p. 437.

102. Zweig, of course, had employed the phrase "the silent woman" himself. Early in the 1930s, he wrote the libretto for Richard Strauss's opera *Die schweigsame Frau (The Silent Woman)*, based on Ben Jonson's comedy *Epicoene, or The Silent Woman*. Even though Strauss was president of Hitler's State Music Council at the time, the opera was performed only three times in Dresden in June 1935 and then, because of the appearance of Zweig's name on the program, was suppressed. The story of the brief collaboration of Zweig and Strauss is a fascinating one and is described in *A Confidential Matter: The Letters of Richard Strauss and Stefan Zweig, 1931–1935*, passim.

Chapter 7. The Way Out:
From the "Savage God" to "Holy Violence"

1. See Henry Louis Gates, Jr., "Editor's Introduction: Writing 'Race' and the Difference It Makes," *Critical Inquiry* 12 (1) (Autumn 1985): 13. I am also grateful to Professor Keith Walker for making me aware of this incident.

2. Joseph Roth, author of *Radetzkymarsch* and one of Zweig's most intimate friends, might also be included in this group. Zweig "was convinced that Roth's drinking was a form of suicide." See Donald A. Prater, *European of Yesterday: A Biography of Stefan Zweig* (Oxford, 1972), p. 298; and David Bronsen, *Joseph Roth: Eine Biographie* (Köln, 1974), pp. 588–608. Also see Zweig letters to Friderike, in *Stefan and Friderike Zweig: Their Corre-*

spondence, 1912–1942 (New York, 1954): 25 Sept. 1935 (p. 224), undated 1940 (p. 311), 13 Mar. 1941 (pp. 325–26); William M. Johnston, *The Austrian Mind: An Intellectual and Social History, 1848–1938* (Berkeley, 1972), pp. 174–80; and Wolfram Kurth, *Genie, Irsinn und Ruhm: Genie-Mythos und Pathographie des Genies* (Munich, 1967).

3. According to Lucy S. Dawidowicz: "Among some Jews who had staked their whole existence on identity with Germany, despair led to suicide. Between 1932 and 1934, nearly 350 Jews committed suicide, a rate 50 percent higher than in the rest of the population." For months after *Kristallnacht* in 1938, "suicides accounted for more than half the Jewish burials." See her *The War Against the Jews, 1933–1945* (New York, 1975), pp. 232, 264, 292. Also see Hannah Arendt, *The Jew as Pariah* (New York, 1978), pp. 58–9.

4. Bruno Frank in *Aufbau* (New York) 27 Feb. 1942, quoted in Prater, *European*, p. 344.

5. Thomas Mann, quoted in Anthony Heilbut, *Exiled in Paradise: German Refugee Artists and Intellectuals in America, from the 1930s to the Present* (New York, 1983), p. 404.

6. Hannah Arendt, "We Refugees" (1944) in her *The Jew as Pariah*, pp. 58–60. Also see her "Portrait of a Period" (1943) in the same collection, pp. 112–21; and Elizabeth Young-Bruehl, *Hannah Arendt: For Love of the World* (New Haven, 1984), p. 193.

7. Arendt, *The Jew as Pariah*, p. 59.

8. Alfred Alvarez, *The Savage God: A Study of Suicide* (New York, 1972), p. 272.

9. Jean Baechler, *Suicides*, trans. Barry Cooper (New York, 1979), pp. 42–55.

10. Alan Janik and Stephen Toulmin, *Wittgenstein's Vienna* (New York, 1973), pp. 172–3; Johnston, *Austrian Mind*, pp. 137–40, 158–61; Harry Zohn, "Karl Kraus: 'Jüdischer Selbsthasser' oder 'Erzjude'?" in *Modern Austrian Literature*, vol. 8, no. 1/2 (1975), p. 1. Schönberg returned to Judaism later in life. For an insightful analysis of the phenomenon of Jewish self-hatred and brief life accounts of Weininger, Trebitsch, and the Jewish anti-Semites Paul Reé, Max Steiner, Walter Calé, and Maximilian Harden, see Theodor Lessing, *Der jüdische Selbsthass* (Berlin, 1930). Also see Abraham I. Golomb, "Jewish Self-Hatred," in *YIVO Annual of Jewish Social Science*, vol. 1 (New York, 1946), pp. 250–9; and "Hermann Levi: A Study in Service and Self-Hatred," in Peter Gay, *Freud, Jews, and other Germans* (New York, 1978), pp. 189–230.

11. Marsha L. Rozenblit, *The Jews of Vienna, 1867–1914: Assimilation and Identity* (Albany, 1983), pp. 7, 132. Also see George E. Berkley, *Vienna and Its Jews: The Tragedy of Success* (Cambridge, Mass., 1988), pp. 53–5, 324–8. For a discussion of Jewish conversion in nineteenth- and twentieth-century Germany, see Carl Cohen, "The Road to Conversion," *Leo Baeck Institute, Year Book VI*, 1961, pp. 259–79; and Gay, *Freud, Jews*, pp. 97–8.

12. In the original German: "Der Taufzettel ist das Entreebillet zur eu-

ropäischen Kultur." See Heinrich Heine, "Gedanken und Einfelle," in *Heines Werke*, vol. 7 (Leipzig, 1922), p. 407.

13. Rozenblit, *The Jews of Vienna*, p. 137. "... most Jewish women who converted [in Vienna between 1870 and 1910] came from the lower classes and probably accepted baptism in order to marry fellow gentile workers. ... Middle-class Jewish women, those who did not list occupations in the conversion records, also embraced Christianity or *Konfessionslosigkeit* at the end of the nineteenth century. Women who had no careers obviously did not convert to smooth their career paths. Rather they converted either for genuine religious reasons or to marry gentiles" (p. 139).

14. Alma Mahler Werfel, *Gustav Mahler: Memories and Letters* (New York, 1946; reprinted 1968), p. 101. Quoted in Rozenblit, *The Jews of Vienna*, p. 134.

15. Albert Memmi, *The Liberation of the Jew* (New York, 1966), pp. 70, 71; Gay, *Freud, Jews*, p. 97.

16. Gay, *Freud, Jews*, p. 98.

17. Talcott Parsons, "The Problem of Polarization on the Axis of Color," in John Hope Franklin, ed., *Color and Race*, (Boston, 1968), p. 365. Also see H. Hoetink, *Slavery and Race Relations in the Americas: An Inquiry into Their Nature and Nexus*, (New York, 1973), pp. 142–4.

18. For a general comparative discussion of "whitening" as a factor for social mobility among persons of color in the Americas, see Hoetink, *Slavery and Race Relations in the Americas*, pp. 89–106, 192–210. For a discussion of Brazilian "whitening," see Thomas Skidmore, *Black into White: Race and Nationality in Brazilian Thought* (New York, 1974), passim.

19. For Joseph Renner-Maxwell's ideas, see his *The Negro Question, or Hints for the Physical Improvement of the Negro Race, with Special Reference to West Africa* (London, 1892), pp. 65, 85–6; and Leo Spitzer, *The Creoles of Sierra Leone: Responses to Colonialism, 1870–1945* (Madison, 1974), pp. 134–5.

20. Quoted in Magnus Mörner, *Race Mixture in the History of Latin America*, (Boston, 1967), p. 73.

21. For example, see Nella Larsen, *Quicksand* (New York, 1928), and *Passing* (New York, 1929); Jessie Fauset, *Plum Bun* (New York, 1929); and Walter White, *Flight* (New York, 1926).

22. Hoyt Fuller, "Introduction" to Nella Larsen, *Passing* (New York, 1971), p. 14. Also see Mary Helen Washington, "The Mulatta Trap: Nella Larsen's Women of the 1920's," in her *Invented Lives: Narratives of Black Women, 1860–1960* (New York, 1987), pp. 159–67.

23. See Rozenblit, *The Jews of Vienna*, pp. 23–4, 34–43.

24. Herbert A. Strauss, "The Movement of People in a Time of Crisis," in Jarrell C. Jackman and Carla M. Borden, eds., *The Muses Flee Hitler: Cultural Transfer and Adaptation, 1930–1945* (Washington, D.C., 1983), pp. 49–51. Also see Ronald Sanders, *Shores of Refuge: A Hundred Years of Jewish Emigration* (New York, 1988), passim.

25. See Laura Fermi, *Illustrious Immigrants: The Intellectual Migration*

from Europe, 1930–1941, 2d. ed. (Chicago, 1971); Donald Fleming and Bernard Baylin, eds., *The Intellectual Migration: Europe and America, 1930–1960* (Cambridge, Mass., 1969); and Jackman and Borden, eds., *The Muses Flee Hitler*, passim.

26. For Blyden and late nineteenth-century Creole responses in Sierra Leone, see Chapter 6, especially note #59. Also see my *Creoles*, pp. 108–38. For a general introduction to *négritude* literature and criticism, see Léopold Sédar Senghor, *Anthologie de la nouvelle poésie nègre et malagache* (Paris, 1940); Claude Wauthier, *The Literature and Thought of Modern Africa: A Survey* (London, 1966); and Lilyan Kesteloot, *Black Writers in French: A Literary History of Negritude*, trans. E. C. Kennedy (Philadelphia, 1974).

27. Abiola Irele, "Négritude-Literature and Ideology," *Journal of Modern African Studies* 3 (4) (1965), p. 511.

28. Aimé Césaire, *Cahier d'un retour au pays natal* (Paris, 1956, 1971), pp. 117, 119–21. Translation by Marianne Hirsch. The original reads:

> Écoutez le monde blanc
> horriblement las de son effort immense
> ses articulations rebelles craquer sous les étoiles
> dures
> ses raideurs d'acier bleu transperçant la chair
> mystique
> écoute ses victoires proditoires trompeter ses
> défaites
> écoute aux alibis grandioses son piètre
> trébuchement
>
> Pitié pour nos vainqueurs omniscients et naifs!...
>
> *Eia* pour ceux qui n'ont jamais rien inventé
> pour ceux qui n'ont jamais rien exploré
> pour ceux qui n'ont jamais rien dompté
>
> mais ils s'abandonnent, saisis, à l'essence de tout
> chose
> ignorant des surfaces mais saisis par le mouvement
> de toute chose
> insoucieux de dompter, mais jouant le jeu du
> monde.

29. Césaire, *Cahier*, p. 117. Translation by Emile Snyder.

30. L. Damas, *Black Label* (Paris, 1956), p. 52. Translated by Gerald Moore in *Seven African Writers* (London, 1962), p. xx.

31. Léopold Sédar Senghor, "The Spirit of Civilisation, or the Laws of African Negro Culture," in *The First Conference of Negro Writers and Artists* (Paris, 1956), pp. 51–64. Also see Harold Scheub, "Soukeîna and Isabelle: Senghor and the West," in P. D. Curtin, ed., *Africa and the West* (Madison, 1972), pp. 189–230.

32. Senghor, "For Koras and Balafongs," in *Selected Poems*, trans. John Reed and Clive Wake (New York, 1964), pp. 13–14.

33. See Spitzer, *Creoles*, pp. 120–31, for a discussion of these types of responses by the Creoles of Sierra Leone.

34. James Africanus Beale Horton, *West African Countries and Peoples, British and Native. With the requirements necessary for establishing that self government recommended by the Committee of the House of Commons, 1865; and a Vindication of the African Race* (London, 1868), p. 67. Also see the works by the Sierra Leone Creoles Charles Marke, *Africa and the Africans* (Freetown, 1881), pp. 26–8, and A. B. C. Merriman-Labor, *An Epitome of a Series of Lectures on the Negro Race* (Freetown, 1900). It would be interesting to consider these late nineteenth-century efforts to establish the African roots of ancient Greece in light of Martin Bernal's fascinating investigation of this issue in his *Black Athena: The Afroasiatic Roots of Classical Civilization. Vol. I: The Fabrication of Ancient Greece, 1785–1985* (New Brunswick, N.J., 1987).

35. E. W. Blyden, *The Negro in Ancient History-Mohammedanism in Western Africa* (London, 1874), and *From West Africa to Palestine* (Freetown, 1873), pp. 104–10.

36. J. E. Casely-Hayford, *Ethiopia Unbound* (London, 1911); Cheikh Anta Diop, *Nations negres et culture: de l'antiquite negre egyptienne aux problemes culturels de l'Afrique Noire d'aujourd'hui* (Paris, 1954); Diop, "The Cultural Contributions and Prospects of Africa," *The First International Conference of Negro Writers and Artists*, vols. 18–19, *Presence Africaine* (Paris, 1956), pp. 349–54 (reprinted in Hans Kohn and Wallace Sokolsky, *African Nationalism in the Twentieth Century* (Princeton, 1965), pp. 140–8); Charles de Graft-Johnson, *African Glory: The Story of Vanished Civilizations* (London, 1954). Also see my *Creoles*, pp. 122–4. The conclusion of Diop's principal section of *Nations negres* argues that:

... the black man, far from being incapable of developing a technical civilization, is in fact the one who developed it first, in the person of the Negro, at a time when all the white races, wallowing in barbarism, were only just fit for civilization.

In saying that it was the ancestors of Negroes, who today inhabit principally Black Africa, who first invented mathematics, astronomy, the calendar, science in general, the arts, religion, social organisation, medicine, writing, engineering, architecture ... in saying all this, one is simply stating the modest and strict truth, which nobody at the present moment can refute with arguments worthy of the name (p. 253).

37. Léon Laleau, "Trahison," trans. Samuel Allen, in Jacob Drachler, ed., *African Heritage* (New York, 1963), p. 195.

38. Irele, "Négritude-Literature and Ideology," p. 499.

39. To be sure, as Stephen M. Poppel has indicated, "the hope for the messianic return of the Jews to Zion had been a main current in Jewish thought since the Exile, appearing as a central theme in the liturgy with which every Jew was familiar." But it was not until the end of the nineteenth century that the modern Zionist movement took real form. Poppel, *Zionism in Germany*, 1897–1933 (Philadelphia, 1977), p. 17. This point is also made

in Arthur Hertzberg, ed., *The Zionist Idea: A Historical Analysis and Reader* (New York, 1959, 1986); Bernard Avishai, *The Tragedy of Zionism: Revolution and Democracy in the Land of Israel* (New York, 1985); and Amnon Rubenstein, *The Zionist Dream Revisited: From Herzl to Gush Emunim and Back* (New York, 1984).

40. Hertzberg, ed., *The Zionist Idea*, p. 40.

41. On the tensions between political/cultural and religious/secular Zionism, see Hertzberg, ed., *The Zionist Idea*, pp. 51–72. Also see Rubenstein, *The Zionist Dream Revisited*, pp. 3–49; and Avishai, *The Tragedy of Zionism*, pp. 22–66.

42. Poppel, *Zionism in Germany*, p. 18; Hertzberg, ed., *The Zionist Idea*, p. 48.

43. Theodor Herzl, "The Jewish State (1896)," in Hertzberg, ed., *The Zionist Idea*, p. 209; Herzl, *Der Judenstaat: Versuch einer modernen Lösung der Judenfrage*, 1st ed. (Vienna, 1896), reprinted in Herzl, *Zionistische Schriften*, 3d ed. (Tel Aviv, 1934).

44. Herzl, "The Jewish State," in Hertzberg, ed., *The Zionist Idea*, p. 209.

45. Rubenstein, *The Zionist Dream Revisited*, p. 9; Poppel, *Zionism in Germany*, p. 18.

46. Herzl, "The Jewish State," in Hertzberg, ed., *The Zionist Idea*, pp. 209, 220.

47. Rubenstein, *The Zionist Dream Revisited*, pp. 20–34; Hertzberg, ed., *The Zionist Idea*, pp. 45–51.

48. Rubenstein, *The Zionist Dream Revisited*, p. 12; Hertzberg, *The Zionist Idea*, pp. 8–9.

49. Rubenstein, *The Zionist Dream Revisited*, pp. 4–5.

50. Quoted in Rubenstein, *The Zionist Dream Revisited*, pp. 3–4.

51. I am grateful to Dr. Jonathan Boyarin, of The YIVO Center for Advanced Jewish Studies, New York, for this insightful comparison.

52. Herzl, "The Jewish State," in Hertzberg, ed., *The Zionist Idea*, p. 213. Also see Theodor Herzl, *Old-New Land [Altneuland]*, trans. L. Levensohn (New York, 1960), pp. 80–81; Hertzberg, ed., *The Zionist Idea*, pp. 49–50; Rubenstein, *The Zionist Dream Revisited*, p. 11; and Avishai, *The Tragedy of Zionism*, pp. 40–41.

53. Herzl, "The Jewish State," in Hertzberg, ed., *The Zionist Idea*, p. 213.

54. Ibid. My italics.

55. Rubenstein, *The Zionist Dream Revisited*, p. 13.

56. "Ahad Ha'am" translates from Hebrew as "One of the People," and illustrates a widespread tendency among Zionists to drop their European names, changing them for real or invented Hebrew ones. Name-changing was, of course, also central to the "name reform" effort among Creoles in Sierra Leone in the 1880s, and among African Americans in the 1960s.

57. Ahad Ha'am, *Kol Kitvei* [Collected Writings] (Tel Aviv, 1947), p. 325. Quoted in Rubenstein, *The Zionist Dream Revisited*, p. 40.

58. These criteria derive from Rupert Emerson's definition of the nation in his *From Empire to Nation* (Cambridge, Mass. 1960), p. 104.

59. Otto Pflanze and Philip D. Curtin, "Varieties of Nationalism in Europe and Africa," *The Review of Politics* 28 (2) (Apr. 1966): 143–4.

60. As Leo Kuper has argued, mobilization and collective action on this basis in colonial nationalist movements was clearly a departure from classical Marxist theory, which postulated *class consciousness* and the conflict between classes as the determinants of social relations and political change. See his "Theories of Revolution and Race Relations," *Comparative Studies in Society and History*, 13 (1) (1971): 88–108; "Race, Class, and Power: Some Comments on Revolutionary Change," *Comparative Studies in Society and History*, 14 (4) (1972): 400–421; and "Race Structure in the Social Consciousness," *Civilizations* 20 (1) (1970): 88–102.

61. "Tribalism can be defined as the sentiments of loyalty to an ethnic or linguistic group, which seeks to improve its particular interest within the state.... This narrowed definition of tribalism is a useful tool for the analysis of competing nationalisms in tropical Africa. Before Ghana became an aspirant state-nation, Asante national sentiment was a nationalism, fully equivalent to nationalisms elsewhere. But the superimposition of a loyalty to Ghana changes the nature of loyalty to Asante. If the Asante are willing to accept Ghana and give up Asante, their national sentiment merely moves to a broader and more inclusive level. If, on the other hand, they insist on working in the interest of Asante within the state-nation of Ghana, they become a tribal force in the original sense." See Philip D. Curtin, "Nationalism in Africa, 1945–1965," in Pflantze and Curtin, "Varieties of Nationalism in Europe and Africa," pp. 147, 148.

62. The sharpest critique of this pattern of decolonization is still in Frantz Fanon, *The Wretched of the Earth*, trans. Constance Farrington (New York, 1964), pp. 148–205.

63. For a panoramic account of modern European revolutionary ideas and events, see James H. Billington, *Fire in the Minds of Men: Origins of the Revolutionary Faith* (New York, 1980).

64. See Fanon, *The Wretched of the Earth*, especially the chapter "Concerning Violence."

65. Fanon, *Wretched of the Earth*, p. 147.

66. Ibid., p. 94. Basing his theory on the experience of the Algerian Revolution, Fanon predicted that, for women, participation in violence would result in a literal unveiling leading to a transformation of traditional patriarchal family structures. Occasioned by their revolutionary activities, their emancipation would be accepted, and their integration into the new society on a basis of equality would be assured. "This woman," Fanon wrote in *A Dying Colonialism*, "who, in the avenues of Algiers or of Constantine, would carry the grenades or the submachine-gun chargers, this woman who tomorrow would be outraged, violated, tortured, could not put herself back into her former state of mind and relive her behavior of the past; this woman who was writing the heroic pages of Algerian history was, in so doing, bursting the bonds of the narrow world in which she had lived without responsibility, and was at the same time participating in the destruction

of colonialism and in the birth of a new woman." See Fanon, "Algeria Unveiled" and "The Algerian Family," in *A Dying Colonialism*, trans. Haakon Chevalier (New York, 1965), especially pp. 107–16.

67. Fanon, *A Dying Colonialism*, "The Algerian Family," pp. 99–120; Aristide R. Zolberg, "Frantz Fanon: A Gospel for the Damned," *Encounter* 27 (5) (Nov. 1966): 59.

68. Fanon, *Wretched of the Earth*, pp. 132–3.

69. The description of the "mesmerization" is Zolberg's. See his "A Gospel for the Damned," p. 58. For a stimulating and somewhat different reading of Fanon from mine, see Edward Burke III, "Frantz Fanon's *The Wretched of the Earth*," *Daedalus* (Winter 1976): 127–35.

70. See Renate Zahar, *Frantz Fanon: Colonialism and Alienation* (New York, 1974), pp. 93–9.

71. Ernesto Che Guevara, "Socialism and Man in Cuba," in *Che: Selected Works of Ernesto Guevara* (Cambridge, Mass., 1969), pp. 156, 159–60.

72. Fanon, *Wretched of the Earth*, pp. 313, 315, 316.

Index

"Act of Acclamation," 116, 118
Adler, Alfred, *Individual Psychology*, 129, 130, 131
Adler, Victor, 176
Adlerian psychology: and "fictional" goal, 129, 130, 131; notion of compensatory "striving," 130, 131; posits confrontation with racism as positive stimulant, 122; and assimilationist experience of May, Rebouças, Zweig and Brettauer families, 130–1, 132; providing partial explanation for range of responses to marginality, 132
Afonja, ruler of Ilorin province, 45, 47; *see also* Old Oyo Empire
African personality, concept, 192; *see also* Blyden, Edward Wilmot
Afro-Brazilians, 37, 109; freedmen and women, 12, 23
Alafin Abiodun, 45, 46; *see also* Old Oyo Empire
Alafin Awole, 46
Alagoas, 149
Althusser, Louis, 126, 129, 132, 133–4; *see also* ideology
Alvarez, Alfred, 174; *The Savage God*, 176
anti-Semitism: demographic factors in, 6; changing nature of, 99–100, 162, 165, 177; as perceived by Moritz and Ida Zweig, 137; as perceived by Stefan Zweig, 162, 165–7; and Zionism, 187–9
Anti-Slavery Squadron, 4, 50
acculturation: as a "level" of assimilation, 28
amalgamation: as a "level" of assimilation, 28
Anschluss, Austrian, 166, 167, 175
Arendt, Hannah, 165, 175; *The Jew as Pariah*, 174
Asante, 192
assimilation: during "Century of Emancipation," 6; as conformity, 28; "levels" of, as defined by Milton M. Gordon, 28–9; as process of adaptation on a continuum, 28; assimilating aspirants,
6; popular usage of term, 28; meaning of, for women, 172–3; reconsidered, 181–2; perceived failure of, 181, 187, 196; *see also* bourgeoisie
assimilationist process, 10, 41; adjustments involved, 29, 38; affect of individual perceptions and expectations, 38, 125; and bourgeois ideology, 134; and Adlerian "striving," 131; and age, 32–3; and class identification, 38, 181–2; and change over time, 38; and "cultural distance," 31–2; and gender, 33–7; and social climate, 29–30; generational differences in pattern of mobility, 70, 131; structural and psychological features of, 129–37; impediments to, 30–1; goals of, 37, 131; resistance to, 32; severs generational connections, 186
Aufbau (New York), 175
Austria, 6, 36
Austro-Marxism, 10

babaláwo of Ifá, 45, 47, 52
Badagry (Nigeria), 49, 51
Baechler, Jean, *Suicides*, 176
Banbury, G.A.L., 155
"barrier," concept of, 4, 6, 130, 135–6, 137; "escapist," individual, responses to, 176–81; "hurdling" over, 176; collective responses to, 181–97; *see also* blockage, "marginal situation"
Bahia, Brazil, 4, 108, 112, 115, 124; *see also* Salvador
Barbeton, Transvaal, South Africa, 152
Barzun, Jacques, 7
Baudelaire, Charles, 165
Beauvoir, Simone de, 173
"been to," concept of, 69
Benin, Nigeria, 192
Berlin, Germany, 139
"black is beautiful," concept, 183
"blockage," concept of, 38, 72; *see also* "barrier," "marginal situation"
Blyden, Edward Wilmot: view of differences among races, 157–8; *Christianity,*

243

7/